DATE DUE

Daniel

INTERPRETATION
A Bible Commentary for Teaching and Preaching

INTERPRETATION
A BIBLE COMMENTARY FOR TEACHING AND PREACHING

James Luther Mays, *Editor*
Patrick D. Miller, Jr., *Old Testament Editor*
Paul J. Achtemeier, *New Testament Editor*

W. SIBLEY TOWNER

Daniel

A Bible Commentary
for Teaching and Preaching

John Knox Press
ATLANTA

Library of Congress Cataloging in Publication Data

Towner, W. Sibley (Wayne Sibley), 1933–
  Daniel.

  (Interpretation, a Bible commentary for teaching and
preaching)
  Bibliography: p.
  1. Bible. O.T. Daniel—Commentaries. I. Title.
II. Series.
BS1555.2.T68 1984   224'.507   83–18791
ISBN 0–8042–3122–2

© copyright John Knox Press 1984
10 9 8 7 6
Printed in the United States of America
John Knox Press
Atlanta, Georgia 30365

SERIES PREFACE

This series of commentaries offers an interpretation of the books of the Bible. It is designed to meet the need of students, teachers, ministers, and priests for a contemporary expository commentary. These volumes will not replace the historical critical commentary of homiletical aids to preaching. The purpose of this series is rather to provide a third kind of resource, a commentary which presents the integrated result of historical and theological work with the biblical text.

An interpretation in the full sense of the term involves a text, an interpreter, and someone for whom the interpretation is made. Here, the text is what stands written in the Bible in its full identity as literature from the time of "the prophets and apostles," the literature which is read to inform, inspire, and guide the life of faith. The interpreters are scholars who seek to create an interpretation which is both faithful to the text and useful to the church. The series is written for those who teach, preach, and study the Bible in the community of faith.

The comment generally takes the form of expository essays. It is planned and written in the light of the needs and questions which arise in the use of the Bible as Holy Scripture. The insights and results of contemporary scholarly research are used for the sake of the exposition. The commentators write as exegetes and theologians. The task which they undertake is both to deal with what the texts say and to discern their meaning for faith and life. The exposition is the unified work of one interpreter.

The text on which the comment is based is the Revised Standard Version of the Bible. The general availability of this translation makes the printing of a translation unnecessary and saves the space for comment. The text is divided into sections appropriate to the particular book; comment deals with passages as a whole, rather than proceeding word by word, or verse by verse.

Writers have planned their volumes in light of the requirements set by the exposition of the book assigned to them. Biblical books differ in character, content, and arrangement. They also differ in the way they have been and are used in the liturgy, thought, and devotion of the church. The distinctiveness and use of particular books have been taken into account in decisions about the approach, emphasis, and use of space in the commentaries. The goal has been to allow writers to develop the format which provides for the best presentation of their interpretation.

The result, writers and editors hope, is a commentary which both explains and applies, an interpretation which deals with both the meaning and the significance of biblical texts. Each commentary reflects, of course, the writer's own approach and perception of the church and world. It could and should not be otherwise. Every interpretation of any kind is individual in that sense; it is one reading of the text. But all who work at the interpretation of Scripture in the church need the help and stimulation of a colleague's reading and understanding of the text. If these volumes serve and encourage interpretation in that way, their preparation and publication will realize their purpose.

Series Editors

CONTENTS

ABBREVIATIONS
used in this volume

AB	Anchor Bible
JB	Jerusalem Bible
LXX	The Septuagint, Greek version of the Old Testament
LXX-Dan	The Septuagint version of the Book of Daniel *circa* 100 B.C., Alexandria
LXX-Theod	The Greek version of the Book of Daniel identified with a second century A.D. convert to Judaism, Theodotion; probably as old as the first century B.C. Note that in the case of Daniel alone the Theodotion text supplanted the Septuagint.
RSV	Revised Standard Version of the Holy Bible
TEV	Today's English Version of the Holy Bible

To Jane, Ann, and Hope
for unfailing grace

Introduction

Why Read the Book of Daniel?

Between the modern reader of the Bible and the Old Testament Book of Daniel a formidable gap yawns. Although the tales about the wise Jew Daniel and his friends Shadrach, Meshach, and Abednego which make up Daniel 1—6 are familiar and beloved stories, they reflect a world about as congenial to our daily experience as the world of the *Arabian Nights*. Theirs is a world of kings and harems and eunuchs, of bawdy pagan rituals and drunken orgies, of bizarre methods of capital punishment involving fiery furnaces and pits full of lions, and of strange experiences with dreams and visions. Even those twentieth century readers who have passed through the furnace of fire or who live on the very same tormented segment of the earth's surface in which these stories are set or who have had their own strange experiences with dreams or visions do not really know their way around Daniel's world. It is simply too far away and too long ago.

Furthermore, the second half of the book, chapters 7—12, seems to have little to do with the first half. There the reader discovers a strange universe of symbolic beasts, of winged angels and rank upon rank of other heavenly beings, and of heavenly judgment scenes. Three distinct apocalypses and a lengthy prayer with angelic response, all presenting slightly different scenarios of the coming End, culminate in the terrifying prospect of divine intervention and the resurrection of the dead. This world is foreign to us, too, and, compared with the interesting court scenes of Daniel 1—6, is downright unattractive.

So why should we still attempt to read and understand the Book of Daniel? Why should teachers in the church still attempt to guide children and adults back across that formidable gap in time in search of the authentic experiences of faith which are said to be hidden in the book? Why should preachers risk taking

1

into their pulpits the time bombs that tick away in the Book of Daniel?

Some will say that we are duty-bound to read Daniel simply because it is Holy Writ. Fine. But why, then, have the mainline churches put off doing it for so long?

Some will say we should read it because it brings a word of hope to those who are perishing, encouragement to those who are crushed under the boot of the oppressor. It is a tract for hard times, and we are living in hard times. But are we? Are the circumstances in which the original circle of readers lived really comparable to those of our own church school classes and Bible study groups? Oh yes, the ominous shadow of the mushroom-shaped cloud perpetually falls across our consciousness, and in broad terms our world is in far more danger than theirs was in the second century B.C. But most of today's readers of the book are not members of a tiny persecuted minority struggling to survive in the face of an imperial policy committed to eliminating all non-conforming sects and to destroying the religion of Judaism itself. Most of us have not experienced the burning of our sacred books, the proscription of our regular worship customs; most of us have not had the food we most detest forced down our throats nor have we wept to see the corpses of our newly circumcised male infants hanging on the necks of their dead mothers. According to I Maccabees 1:41–64 and II Maccabees 6—7, such were the circumstances in which the people who wrote and first read the Book of Daniel lived. For people as oppressed as they were, the greatest source of hope lay not in God's mercy, but in his wrath—in his "righteous sentence writ in burnished rows of steel" or in the flames and screams of the Judgment Day. They could hear Daniel's message with keen appreciation. But can we?

Some have held not only that apocalyptic literature is generated by the oppressed of society, but that it can be fully responded to only by those of later generations who live in straits so dire that they perceive their only hope to lie in the destruction of the established order. Indeed, an impressive historical correlation can be developed between moments of national and cultural crisis on the one hand and the reawakening of the apocalyptic spirit on the other. Think of the Qumran community of the first century B.C.—first century A.D. responding to the oppressive power of Rome with "the War of the Sons of Light and the Sons of Darkness." Think of the Montanists of

2

the second-third centuries A.D., persecuted for their millennialism and their contention that their city of Pepuza in Asia Minor would be the new Jerusalem. Think of the left wing of the sixteenth century Reformation, especially the doomed Zwickau prophets led by Thomas Müntzer and the Anabaptist "Kingdom" in Münster. Think of the Adventist awakening in nineteenth century New York state, when William Miller and his adherents endured mockery as they waited in white robes for the End on October 22, 1842. Think of the deep faith in eschatological vindication expressed in their spirituals by the black slaves of white Americans.

Yet if one must have been in the pit of beasts with Daniel in order deeply and fully to receive his voice, then very frankly, few of us can hear it. Only the remaining survivors of Auschwitz, the living remnant of Hiroshima, the veterans of Biafra and the various tragedies of the contemporary Near East even have a chance to receive it as a living testimony. The ordinary reader of this book and the ordinary member of an American church or synagogue lives only with a vague sense of impending doom cast by that mushroom-shaped cloud. Otherwise life goes on, with summer vacations and sailboats, Christmas shopping and skiing, punctuating with pleasure our otherwise ordered lives. Even the most oppressed members of our society experience nothing like the political and economic disaster which faced the writers of the Book of Daniel day after day.

It is the contention of this commentary that the Book of Daniel is of theological significance to all contemporary Jews and Christians, even to those vast masses whose personal circumstances do not replicate the circumstances in which the Book of Daniel was written. This is not simply a tract for hard times! One does not have to be an underground freedom-fighter, a slave, or a survivor to understand the appeal of this book. This is a tract for relatively good times as well, though we take a risk in reading from our perspective of affluence—the message handed down to us may be our indictment!

Some modern readers of Daniel, particularly persons in the ranks of American Protestantism, agree that Daniel is a book of signal significance but do so on the completely different premise that the book is in fact a timetable for our future. For such persons, its value is related to its ability to help us pinpoint our location on that timetable and to say how close we are to history's destination, namely, God's triumphant final intervention

3

in the affairs of humankind. This is not the position taken in this volume. On the contrary, the view taken here is that the value of the Book of Daniel, fortunately, does not hinge upon its ability to function as a timetable, for it could never have succeeded in such an enterprise. No book written by human beings, not even a book of Scripture, has that capacity, because for better or for worse the flesh limits the human vision to events at hand or not too far around the corner. To say that the Book of Daniel breaks the bonds of human limitation at this point is to fail to take seriously the incarnate nature of the word of God to God's people. The Book of Daniel *does not* map the future. The Book of Daniel *does* render for us a picture of the agent of our coming redemption at work. In a narrative way, it makes certain profound religious truth claims about the future and thus evokes in us faith in God's success. And it is precisely that faith that makes this book so valuable to us.

This book glows with a deep conviction that God will not fail to achieve his redemptive purpose in the world. It glows with the trust that tyranny and oppression in all their forms are not the wave of the future but that the outcome of the human experience is finally the vindication of faithful obedience, goodness, and truth. God wins in the end, and all who seek to keep the faith with God are winners as well! That is a faith which can sustain the saints in good times and bad. It is a faith which the contemporary secular world longs to affirm, but mostly cannot, as evidenced by the secular eschatologies of our time—science fiction, apocalyptic novels, and the writings of scientific futurists. It is a faith which can lead us away from quietism and apathy and can energize us for the task of working for the good and safety of the creatures of the earth in the company of other persons of good will.

The Approach of This Commentary: Five Assumptions

The Book of Daniel confronts the interpreter with a set of critical problems as elaborate as any raised by a book of the Old Testament. Rather than enter in detail into these problems, however, the strategy of this volume is simply to acknowledge five assumptions which will be operative in the ensuing pages and to refer readers who wish to explore in more depth the background of the book to any of the modern critical commentaries which are recommended in the Bibliography. The real action of this commentary centers not in the task of answering

4

questions about the historical setting, literary unity, language, and authorship of the Book of Daniel but in the chapter-by-chapter discussion and theological assessment of the text itself. The former task is fascinating, technical, and indubitably fruitful; the latter task, however, is taken to be an absolutely essential support for the work of teachers and preachers in the church.

The five key assumptions about historical and literary problems in the Book of Daniel now follow.

The hero. Daniel is a non-historical personage modeled by the author(s) of the book after the ancient worthy who is linked in Ezekiel 14:14, 20 with righteous Noah and righteous Job, and who is described (Ezek. 28:3) as a wise man. As is the case with other Jewish apocalyptic writings, an ancient saint and sage has been selected to be the bearer of a message to an audience living in a totally different era.

Literary structure, date, and language. The Book of Daniel contains the writings of several authors working at different times. The radically divergent content of the two halves of the book requires this thesis, as does the fact that the book is written in two languages. In regard to content, Daniel 1—6 contain six hero stories told about Daniel and his friends in the novelette style favored by late Israelite wisdom circles. By their vocabulary and their knowledge of cultural *realia,* these stories betray considerable exposure to both Persian and Hellenistic influences. In their essentials these tales are assumed to have come down from the third century B.C. or even somewhat earlier. The three apocalypses and the prayer-vision of Daniel 7—12, on the other hand, can be dated rather more precisely to the first third of the second century B.C. (see the discussion of Dan. 11:2–39 and 12:5–13). They are visionary accounts narrated by Daniel himself, and they share the sectarian outlook of other apocalyptic writings of the last two centuries B.C. To account for the bilingual character of the book (Dan. 2:4b—7:28 is written in Aramaic; the balance is written in late biblical Hebrew), a definitive explanation has yet to be given. Most widely accepted is H. L. Ginsberg's view that the entire book (except for the "interpolated" prayer 9:4b–20) was originally written in the *lingua franca* of that age, Aramaic; and that 1:1—2:4a plus chapters 8—12 were later translated into Hebrew perhaps in the interest of rendering the book more acceptable to a community whose estimate of the sacredness of the Hebrew tongue waxed even as the vernacular use of it waned (*Studies in Daniel,* pp. 41–61). Though such a theory would not demand that the book be regarded as composite in authorship, it would surely imply continuing development of the Daniel tradition even after the text was essentially fixed.

The readers of Daniel whose goal it is to evaluate and appropriate its theological truth claims will find it quite possible to assume that the book grew over a period of time, even while they devote primary attention to the book as it now stands. The famed discrepancy between the two halves of the book may even turn out to be far less dramatic than has been supposed in the past. As will be shown at the appropriate points, the dream of King Nebuchadnezzar in Daniel 2 is in important ways recapitulated in the animal allegory of Daniel 7. The disaster which the empire of arrogance meets (2:34) is restated almost exactly at the climax of the apocalyptic vision of Daniel 8:25—"by no human hand" the tyrant will be broken. Further, the agent of the destruction of that last enemy kingdom, the stone cut out by no human hand, is identified as a "kingdom which shall never be destroyed" (2:44), a label thoroughly comparable to the ultimate and "everlasting kingdom" which is awarded to the "saints of the Most High" (7:18, 27). It is easy to extend to considerable length the evidence of this interpenetration of the two parts of Daniel. Suffice it to say that the Book of Daniel is a whole even if it is not a unity from the perspective of literary history. The decision taken in this commentary is to treat it as a whole.

The identity of the authors. The authors of the book were people who acted and thought like its heroes, Daniel and his three friends. In Daniel 1—6, these men incarnate the virtues of wisdom, piety, and trust. They are Torah-true Jews, noble illustrations of what unswerving loyalty to the covenant can mean. No matter how the cycle of stories in Daniel 1—6 may have originated and become attached to Daniel 7—12, the first block now serves to flesh out a strategy for living in the dangerous times before God intervenes in history to bring victory for his people over all oppressors. In short, they render for us a picture of the saints at work—those very saints who turn out to be the nameless but celebrated heroes of Daniel 7—12.

The saints of the Most High appear first of all in Daniel 7:18. There they are awarded the eschatological kingdom to rule in perpetuity. They reappear in each of the ensuing parts of Daniel 7—12. They are "mighty men and the people of the saints" (8:24); they are the "many" against whom the final oppressor acts with such terror (8:25). In the long prayer of chapter 9 they are simply those who entreat God's kindness; their claim upon him derives from his decision to call them and their city by his name (9:19). In the final chapter of the book the heroes are "the people who know their God" (11:32), "the people who are wise" (11:33, 35); above all, they are "those who are wise . . . those who turn many to righteousness" (12:3). On the strength of these titles, we should look in the context of sectarian Judaism of the second century B.C. for some group which could accept the sobriquets "righteous" and "wise," and whose covenant faithfulness and strict loyalty to the exclusive demands of a sovereign God would square with the pictures of Daniel and of the saints.

Among the various candidates the group which most easily matches these criteria and therefore seems most likely to have contained both authors and audience of the Book of Daniel is the observant party known in I Maccabees 2:42 and 7:13–17 as the "Hasideans." Not to be confused with medieval and modern Jewish hasidic sects, yet in many ways quite like them, these ancient *hasidim* swam against the stream of Hellenization. They were the observant school, not eager to rush to arms in the manner of the Maccabees or the Zealots of later ages (I Macc. 1:62–64), but urgent in their espousal of the "old time religion" and in their obedience to the Mosaic covenant as amplified by the ritual and cultic legislation of later ages. Although no contemporary sources fully describe these *hasidim* and their historical evolution, we may well believe that one branch of them only a half century later went out into the wilderness to found the community at Qumran on the Dead Sea. Others emerged later as the early Pharisees. Judging from the brief hints offered by First and Second Maccabees, the *hasidim* were scrupulous in their sabbatarianism (in I Macc. 2: 29–38 they or people like them prefer to die rather than fight on the Sabbath), in their dietary scruples and in their insistence on a priesthood that could demonstrate the legitimacy of its succession from the ancient Aaronic line (cf. I Macc. 7:13–17). In the second and first centuries B.C. they would have stood in opposition to the dominant ruling class of Hellenizing priests and new Hasmonean aristocracy in Jerusalem.

As a working hypothesis, then, consider the writer(s) of

Daniel *hasidim,* spiritual ancestors of the Qumran community on the one hand, and of the early Pharisees on the other. Consider them spiritual ancestors of Jesus, too, if you will—for to the degree that Jesus was sympathetic with the values and traditions of the Pharisees and drew for self-understanding upon their eschatological traditions, he, too, belonged in this lineage of the *hasidim.* He took the tradition in his own unique direction, however; his expectation of the Kingdom seemed to glow with the warm sense of its nearness—a nearness more spatial than temporal—and he identified the Kingdom with his own ministry.

Daniel and the wise. The *hasidim* who completed the Book of Daniel drew from the wisdom tradition of their people for the stories about Daniel and his fellow heroes. The wisdom circles of Israel carried on their didactic function by telling stories. In the canonical Book of Esther, and in the apocryphal novelettes of Judith and Tobit, in the tales of the three young courtiers of I Esdras 3—4, as well as in the beloved international tale of Ahiqar (cf. Pritchard, ANET, pp. 427–30), we experience the ancient sages and theologians at work teaching sound doctrine through the medium of hagiographa—tales about righteous women and men who through trust in God and unswerving allegiance to his sovereignty were able to survive in the face of overwhelming opposition and to glorify God by their piety. Clearly, the six stories in the canonical Daniel cycle belong to this narrative stream of the wisdom tradition. (That the cycle was even larger than the tales preserved in Daniel 1 —6 is confirmed by the presence in the Greek version of Daniel of the stories of Susanna and of Bel and the Dragon. Also, among the Dead Sea Scrolls of Qumran have been found fragments of hitherto unknown stories related to the Daniel cycle, including the "Prayer of Nabonidus"—a reflection of the same tradition of royal madness as that preserved in Daniel 4.) They tell the stories of young heroes who experience upward social mobility because of their extraordinary virtues. Daniel is, as we shall see, presented as a new Joseph. He and his friends are ideal courtiers and possess the skills of administration, dream interpretation, and all-purpose wisdom that suit them for high rank in the court of Babylon. The stories deal with the problem of theodicy, exhibit an inter-cultural and international perspective, and display human beings making decisions in mature and responsible

8

ways—all of which are themes at home in the wisdom tradition of Israel.

But all of these rather straightforward observations pose a problem for understanding the Book of Daniel. What has wisdom to do with apocalyptic? Does the combination of very dissimilar literatures in Daniel disclose some intrinsic literary and theological connections between them? Or is it simply the result of an arbitrary decision by some hasidic redactor who wanted to secure the authority of the ancient worthy Daniel, renowned for his wisdom, for the apocalypses of the sect?

A number of students of the Book of Daniel have taken the latter position. Gerhard von Rad, on the other hand, held to a view quite on the other side of the spectrum. He argued that the conjunction of wisdom and apocalyptic, far from being fortuitous, was illustrative of the very origins of the apocalyptic genre in Israel. Apocalyptic was an outgrowth of the wisdom tradition, according to him, and the wisdom element remained a fundamental one in Jewish apocalyptic (cf. "The Divine Determination of the Times," *Wisdom in Israel*, pp. 263–83; also *Old Testament Theology*, II, 301–15). The evidences of this relationship, according to G. von Rad, are many: Like wisdom, apocalyptic rejects history, reducing its flow to the mere playing out of predetermined orders; like wisdom, apocalyptic is therefore concerned with orders of all kinds, including the natural ones, and takes an interest in calendars, geography, and heavenly bodies. The skills of dream and vision interpretation are highly valued in both literatures, and wisdom itself is a virtue for both. For example, it is the "wise" who are raised to eternal life in Daniel 12:3. The meaning of the times and of the future, clearly the life blood of apocalyptic writings, can be nicely paralleled in Qoheleth's famous teaching, "for every thing there is a season, and a time for every matter under heaven" (Eccl. 3:1). Both literatures concern themselves with creation/new creation theology and employ the mystic imagery associated with cosmology. Finally, the two literatures share an interest in unlocking the secret of the destiny of the cosmos and develop an esoteric set of schemata for doing so—something which would have been quite foreign to prophetism.

This commentary finally does not agree with G. von Rad's argument that the apocalyptic movement rises out of the wisdom tradition. As the final working assumption will make clear,

9

the eschatological expectation which so profoundly marks Israelite prophetism and for which apocalyptic is the primary literary vehicle binds these two parts of the biblical canon together in an unbreakable tie. The apocalyptists stand above all in the lengthened shadow of the great anonymous prophet of the exile who wrote Isaiah 40—55. However, the manifold interpenetration of Old Testament wisdom and apocalyptic must still be affirmed. Nowhere is this interpenetration more visible than in the Book of Daniel. To those who ask the apocalyptists, "What shall we do while we wait for God's victory to take place?" Chapters 1—6 provide answers through the medium of hero tales. The apocalypses of Daniel 7—12 endorse the future of the saints who keep the faith in the way they do in Daniel 1—6. It is difficult to say how wisdom and apocalyptic came to be so closely related in Daniel, especially when narrative wisdom is so often associated with the internationally minded elite while apocalyptic is so often linked with the rural, xenophobic masses. Perhaps scribes and their tradition were to be found amid the embattled *hasidim* of the second century B.C. just as often as the heirs of prophetic eschatology were. Perhaps it is a mistake to draw overly sharp lines of demarcation between the various wings of a small ancient community. Finally, we must remember that all of this literature emerges at the end of the Old Testament period. The writers of Daniel had their Scripture, too, and it must have contained Ecclesiastes and Proverbs and Jonah as well as Deutero-Isaiah and Ezekiel. For whatever reason, then, wisdom tales and apocalyptic visions are firmly bound together within the canonical covers of the Book of Daniel, and it is the intention of this commentary to treat them just that way —together.

The prophetic roots and social setting of apocalyptic literature. Old Testament *apocalyptic* is a sub-type of the larger literary category of *eschatology.* The word "eschatology" means simply *a concern with the crisis of the End (eschaton).* All of the great Old Testament prophets, beginning with Amos, have an eschatology. For the most part, their vision of the decisive events at the End is expressed in the idiom of "realistic eschatology," so named because it understands the Day of Yahweh to lie within the historical experience of Israel. The writer of Isaiah 65:17-25 begins with a sweeping vision that initially appears to transcend this world altogether. Through the oracle, Yahweh says,

10

". . . I create new heavens and a new earth;
and the former things shall not be remembered
or come into mind" (v. 17).

And yet in due course the talk turns to the things of this world:

"They shall build houses and inhabit them;
  they shall plant vineyards and eat their fruit.
They shall not build and another inhabit;
  they shall not plant and another eat; . . ." (vv. 21–22).

Jeremiah also speaks of an age in which the fundamental alienation between Yahweh and his elect people is ended because "I will put my law within them, and I will write it upon their hearts; and I will be their God, and they shall be my people" (Jer. 31:33). That sounds other-worldly. Such a reconciliation never before existed, and cannot exist except in the best of all possible worlds. But the world is still this world, after all, and the talk is still of the elector, Yahweh, the elect people, Israel, and a covenant written upon human hearts. Such is the stuff of "realistic" or "prophetic" eschatology.

In distinction from "realistic" eschatology, apocalyptic is *a form of eschatology which has been dramatically amplified in a cosmic direction.* Under the influence of the mythic themes emanating from creation theology, the prophets' notion of the Day of Yahweh becomes a new world catastrophe. God's victory on that day is wrought out of cosmic as well as earthly struggle, and beyond that day lies a world that comes more and more to look like a new Eden, ruled by a new Adam. By this definition, the following Old Testament texts can properly be called apocalyptic writings (some prefer to consider all of them except Daniel "proto-apocalyptic" in character): Isaiah 24—27; Zechariah 9—14; Joel 2:28—3:21; Daniel 7—12. By comparison to the deutero-canonical apocalypse Fourth Ezra (II Esdras 3—14) and such pseudepigraphical Jewish writings as First Enoch, Second Baruch, the Sibylline Oracles, plus parts of Jubilees and the Testaments of the Twelve Patriarchs, even the Book of Daniel makes only a relatively restrained use of the apocalyptic idiom.

This way of distinguishing the two forms of eschatology is only one of many that have been proposed. Nevertheless, as a working definition of the broad literary genre "apocalyptic," it is helpful. The stress on the impact of myth upon prophetic eschatology, and in particular the mythic motifs of Conflict,

11

Judgment, the Golden Age, and the Savior (or King of the Golden Age) was proposed by Stanley Frost (*Old Testament Apocalyptic*, pp. 32–45). He offers an epigram, ultimately derived from Hermann Gunkel: "Apocalyptic is . . . mythologized eschatology" (p. 39). Though this sentence needs further explication in order to become very useful, it preserves the two basic features which seem most crucially important: the lineal descent of apocalyptic from earlier prophetic eschatology, and the cosmic and ontological aspects of the apocalyptic vision which we can only associate with creation theology and with myth.

The simple distinction between prophetic eschatology and apocalyptic literature is not, however, adequate in itself to explain how the former evolved into the latter. Of course, Scripture offers no explicit history of the development of apocalyptic, and any such picture has to be reconstructed from the meager evidence available. However, it is the assumption of this commentary that the lines of development sketched by Otto Plöger (*Theocracy and Eschatology*) and by Paul D. Hanson (*The Dawn of Apocalyptic*) are valid and helpful. Though these two writers do not present identical pictures, they begin at the same starting point—the juxtaposition of prophetic hope with priestly dominance in the postexilic restoration. During and after the reconstruction of the Temple in the years 520–515 B.C., a theocratic establishment emerged in Jerusalem. Its goal was a permanent polity, a stable order which in an ahistorical framework could guarantee a right relationship between God and the people Israel. With the resumption of the sacrificial cultus, a pleasing odor arose daily to Yahweh from the burnt offerings. The priestly redaction of the Pentateuch amplified the legal tradition so that people could know in concrete and detailed terms what the covenant required of them. (Their oath of allegiance to this new order is recounted in Nehemiah 8—10.) And yet in the midst of these postexilic scenes of theocratic bliss, disaffected persons were to be found. They were the heirs of prophetic eschatology, latter day disciples of Deutero-Isaiah, or at least persons who deeply believed in his vision of the restored community. They may even have stood in the spiritual lineage of the same non-establishment Levitical groups that in preexilic times had produced the reformist Book of Deuteronomy and the deuteronomistic history (Joshua—II Kings).

12

Plöger (*Theocracy*, pp. 47–50) makes no attempt to characterize these persons further except to suggest that they banded together in "conventicles" (not unlike what we might imagine the synagogue to have been in its early stages) for the purpose of worship and ideological training. They may deliberately have drawn upon non-indigenous ideas such as radical historical dualism (this age versus the coming age) so that their expression of hope for an absolutely distinctive elect community living in a truly transformed world of the future could be more sharply contrasted with the prevailing priestly consensus. They were an underground movement, not in the sense of an armed resistance to a vicious persecution, but in the sense of nonviolent and increasingly despairing resistance to the prevailing ethos of their community. These early hasidic groups—for so Plöger denominates them—began to pray and talk and write about the coming day when the great vision of the prophets for the total renovation of the world would come to pass. In this way the proto-apocalyptic texts came into being. At last, in the Maccabean era when the priestly order collapsed, and under the impetus of active persecution by the gentile authorities, the movement achieved focus in the circles of the *hasidim*. That maturity is reflected in the literary product of that last period, the Book of Daniel and in extracanonical apocalyptic literature.

Hanson employs a similar model to account for the appearance of apocalyptic literature. Increasingly antithetical wings of the postexilic Judean community developed increasingly antithetical descriptions of the ideal nature of that community. Hanson eschews a political analysis *per se,* warning that any "party theory" will not adequately account for shifting allegiances of priests and zealots alike for and against the apocalyptic vision (*Dawn of Apocalyptic,* p. 20). He prefers to adapt the sociological distinction employed by Max Weber, Carl Mannheim, and Ernst Troeltsch between the *realists* in society (affiliated with the dominant class, interested in maintaining order, and expressing themselves religiously in the institution of the "church" = temple), and the utopian *visionaries* (identified with the disaffected and disenfranchised, hopeful of altering the status quo, intending to express themselves institutionally in the "sect"). The great preexilic prophets had been able to hold these conflicting elements of faith—vision and reality, hope and order—in a necessary and creative dialectical tension. But in the postexilic restoration, "the spectre arose of a polarization in

13

which the pragmatic program of the hierocracy would become devoid of the visionary element of prophecy, while the vision of prophecy would cut its moorings with the real world and take flight into the realm of dreams" (*Dawn of Apocalyptic*, p. 210). In the century following the reestablishment of the cultus, the visionaries' disenchantment with the leadership of the sacerdotal or hierocratic community is graphically demonstrated in the growth of the Book of Zechariah toward an ever more radical apocalyptic vision. This culminates in the full-blown apocalypse of Zechariah 14 in which, in Hanson's view, the dialectic of vision and reality completely ceases and the "dreams" which he fears dominate the minds of the writers.

If this bipolar theory is correct, the essential lines of apocalyptic eschatology had already been developed long before the persecution of Antiochus ever began, or indeed, before life had even become very difficult for the majority of the Jewish community in Jerusalem. The movement out of prophetic eschatology into apocalyptic began as a protest by the observant and the dissident against the increasingly powerful, wealthy priestly establishment which had built Jerusalem this side of the eschaton. The traditional link between apocalyptic literature and an oppressed proletariat is maintained by this theory, but the approach does not require dreadful persecution at a particular moment in history to be the sole catalyst of the literature. This theory maintains the vital tie with prophetism without denying that the observant and scripturally literate groups which wrote apocalyptic literature may have had contacts with wisdom and the cult in Israel as well.

For Paul Hanson the trajectory of thought through Zechariah to chapter 14 and on into full-fledged apocalyptic is finally not a positive development. That trajectory represents an increasing loss of grip on reality by the visionaries. Like the sects and the utopian movements of our own age, that group becomes more and more detached from political realities of the age and more and more prone to rely on an impending divine solution. The theological evaluation of the movement out of prophetic eschatology toward apocalyptic taken in this volume differs somewhat from Hanson's assessment and can be summed up as follows. In postexilic times, in the period of dominance by an indigenous Judean priestly aristocracy, the apocalyptic movement begins to emerge out of prophetic eschatology. As it looks at the failure of the prophetic vision to be realized in the life of Judah, it becomes more radical. In the early proto-apocalyptic texts, the groundwork is laid for the full flowering of that literature which then occurs under the impact of the first real pogrom against observant Jews in the days of Antiochus IV Epiphanes. The literature is effective; it enhances the survival capabilities of those who read it and heed it. Judging by its reception and effect as well as by the structural and theological content of its canonical literary expression, the Book of Daniel, we can challenge the notion that apocalyptic was a "failure of nerve" theology or led to a visionary quietism which had no real grip upon reality. Without endorsing all of its theological presuppositions, the ensuing pages will affirm the validity and importance of the apocalyptic vision even for today. The basis of that affirmation is the call which rises from apocalyptic texts from the very beginning: "Do not settle for the status quo. Do not settle for the world as it is being presented to us. Do not settle for the inevitability of what is said to be inevitable. We can hope for more than this. God will triumph. Because we believe this to be true and certain, we can live courageously now, and move with courage into a better future."

Dates (B.C.)	Ancient Near East	References in Daniel
	The entire period covered by this chart is referred to in	Dan. 2:31–45; 7:2–8, 17

	NEO-BABYLONIAN EMPIRE	
605/4–562	Nebuchadnezzar	Dan. 1:1 2:1 Dan. 5:24–28?
562–560	Amel-marduk (Evil-Merodach)	
560–556	Neriglissar	
556	Labashi–Marduk	
556–539	Nabonidus	
	PERSIAN EMPIRE	
550–530	Cyrus, King of Persia	Dan. 6:28; 10:1
549–539	Belshazzar (co-regent in Babylon?)	Dan. 5:1, 24–28(?) 7:1; 8:1
539	Babylon falls to Cyrus	Dan. 5:30

	Events listed in remainder of chart may be referred to in	Dan. 8:3–26; 11:2–39
530–522	Cambyses	
522–486	Darius I Hystaspes ("Darius the Mede"?)	Dan. 5:31; 6:1; 9:1; 11:1
486–465	Xerxes I (Ahasuerus in Esther)	Dan. 9:1(?)
465–424	Artaxerxes I Longimanus	
423	Xerxes II	
423–404	Darius II Nothus	
404–358	Artaxerxes II Mnemon	
358–338	Artaxerxes III Ochus	
338–336	Arses	
336–331	Darius III Codomannus	

	MACEDONIAN EMPIRE	Dan. 7:7; 8:5–8, 21; 10:20; 11:3
336–323	Alexander the Great	
331	Alexander defeats Darius at Gaugamela	Dan. 11:3
323	Death of Alexander Wars of Succession begin	

CHRONOLOGICAL TABLE

Other Scripture References	Palestine	Dates (B.C.)
	END OF THE KINGDOM OF JUDAH	
	Jehoiakim	608–597
	Jehoiachin	597
II Kings 24:10–17	First deportation from Jerusalem	597
	BABYLONIAN EXILE	597–538
II Kings 25:1–21	Second deportation	
Jer. 39:1–10; 52:4–27	Destruction of temple and Jerusalem	587
	RESTORATION (PERSIAN CONTROL)	
Ezra 1:1–4	Edict of Restoration	538
Ezra 6:1–18	Temple rebuilt	520–515
	Mission of Ezra (?)	458
	MACEDONIAN CONTROL	332
	Alexander conquers Palestine	

(chart continues on next two pages)

Dates (B.C.)	Ancient Near East		References in Daniel
	EGYPT	SYRIA	
323–285	Ptolemy I Lagi		Dan. 11:5
312/11–280		Seleucus I Nicator	
301		Wars of succession end	
		Macedonian Empire divided	Dan. 8:8, 22;
		among the four Diadochi	11:4
285–246	Ptolemy II Philadelphus		
280–261		Antiochus I Soter	
261–246		Antiochus II Theos	
252		Antiochus married Berenice	Dan. 11:6 (2:43?)
		daughter of Ptolemy	
246–226		Seleucus II Callinicus	Dan. 11:7–9
246–221	Ptolemy III Euergetes I		
226–223		Seleucus III Ceraunus	Dan. 11:10
223–187		Antiochus III the Great	Dan. 11:11–19
221–203	Ptolemy IV Philopator		
203–181	Ptolemy V Epiphanes		
193		Ptolemy married Cleopatra	Dan. 11:17
		daughter of Antiochus III	
		End of Antiochus III	Dan. 11:18–19
187–175		Seleucus IV Philopator	Dan. 11:20
181–146	Ptolemy VI Philometor		
	(reigned jointly with		
	Ptolemy VII Euergetes II)		
175–163		Antiochus IV	Dan. 7:8,11,20–22,
		Epiphanes	24–25;
			8:9–11, 23–25;
			9:26–27;
			11:21–39;
			9:26; 11:22
169		Antiochus' first wars against Egypt	Dan. 11:25–27
			Dan. 11:28
168		Antiochus' second war with Egypt	Dan. 11:29–30a
			Dan. 7:21–25;
			8:24–25
			Dan. 8:11–13b;
			9:26–27;
			11:31; 12:7, 11
			Dan. 11:34a
			Dan. 11:38
163		Death of	
		Antiochus IV Epiphanes	

CHRONOLOGICAL TABLE

Other Scripture Reference	Palestine	Dates (B.C.)
	EGYPTIAN CONTROL Palestine controlled by Ptolemies	301–198
	SYRIAN CONTROL Antiochus III wins Battle of Banias	198
II Macc. 3:1—4:6		
	Antiochus IV	175
II Macc. 4:8–19	Polis founded in Jerusalem. Jason usurps High Priesthood and Onias deposed	174
II Macc. 4:23–26	Jason deposed. Menelaus is High Priest	172
II Macc. 4:33–35 I Macc. 1:16–19	Onias murdered	170
I Macc. 1:20–24 II Macc. 5:5–21	Antiochus loots temple with Menelaus	169
I Macc. 1:29–35 I Macc. 1:44–50 II Macc. 6:7—7:42	Citadel founded in Jerusalem by Apollonius Jerusalem persecution. Jewish revolt begins	168
I Macc. 1:54 II Macc. 6:3–6	15 Chislev "Abomination of Desolation" (desecration of temple)	167
I Macc. 2:15–28, 42–48; 3:10–26; 4:1–25 II Macc. 6:1–2; 8:1–36	Rising by Mattathias and sons Cult of Zeus Olympios	
I Macc. 4:36–59 II Macc. 10:1–19	25 Chislev Cleansing of the temple	164
I Macc. 6:1–16 II Macc. 9:1–28		

PART ONE

Six Diaspora Stories About Daniel

DANIEL 1—6

Daniel 1
The Story That Sets the Stage

The Tale of the Ideal Courtiers

Any initial direct reading of this first panel of scenes from the life of Daniel suggests that the subject is one of the hallowed themes of biblical religion: those who trust and obey God will be vindicated, and they will make it big, even in Babylon. This subject is summed up in verse 20 when, after they have survived the trial of a vegetarian diet and the rigors of a Babylonian court education, Daniel and his three friends from the land of Judah are personally examined by King Nebuchadnezzar and are found to be "ten times better than all the magicians and enchanters that were found in all his kingdom." Yet closer reading reveals that the story is dealing with themes more subtle than either works-righteousness or reward-and-punishment. Watch how it works!

As it is in all of the tales which comprise Daniel 1—6, the setting of chapter 1 is Babylon in the days when the flower of Jewish youth (note that they are already "skillful . . . endowed with knowledge . . . competent," v. 4) was brought into dramatic direct contact with the most important representatives of non-Jewish might and wisdom and there allowed to match their wits with the best of them. We cannot know if the person who wrote down this tale about Daniel and friends knew that this setting was, as we now believe, fictional and that the story was told by no contemporary or eye-witness of the sixth century but rather in circles of pious Jews three or four centuries later. Whether the narrator took the traditional setting at face value or embellished it in the playful spirit of a storyteller also cannot be known. It hardly matters very much now, because the story has become part of a collection of six court tales, all of which offer stories which typify the experience of trusting believers with a trustworthy and effective God. The setting is important to such a function primarily as a means of heightening the tension, enriching the danger, dramatizing the risk which faithful people will experience enroute to their vindication by the God who has supreme power even in the hanging gardens of Babylon.

Every detail of the story is essential to its proper understanding. And if the story presents itself to us as a bizarre and time-bound "oriental court tale . . . full of miracles and what to us are glaring improbabilities" (Jeffery, "Daniel," p. 359), so be it. That is the incarnate form in which the Word of God is witnessed to in Daniel 1. While we need to resist all interpretations which would bind the story in a needlessly rigid way to the alien world of third century B.C. Palestinian Judaism, thus rendering it hopelessly unavailable to twentieth century believers for their theological needs, we need at the same time to treasure the vivid and authentic cultural details of the medium for the necessary part which they play in setting forth the message of this chapter.

As the story begins, conditions are favorable to Daniel and the three other noble, unblemished youths who people chapter 1. True, they find themselves in exile, a fact which ought to be regarded as a terrible one. Here, however, it is glossed over lightly: The exile happened simply because the Lord gave the king and the temple treasure into Nebuchadnezzar's hands (v. 2). The writer is fuzzy on the details: Although Nebuchadnezzar's move against Jerusalem may have begun in the third year of the reign of Jehoiakim king of Judah, it was his son and successor, Jehoiachin who was taken into captivity (cf. II Kings 24:1–17, but note that II Chron. 36:5–7 supports Dan. 1:2). Clearly the writer's forte is narrative art, not historical detail! Nebuchadnezzar himself is presented as a powerful but benign tyrant and his officers, the chief eunuch Ashpenaz and the steward in charge of the youths' upbringing, as men of eminent kindness and common sense.

Like Pharaoh in the days of Joseph, the king needs dream interpreters and sages; and his search for them among the exiles of Judah seems perfectly legitimate to all parties. (A number of scholars have suggested that the "letters and language of the Chaldeans" [v. 4] is a technical phrase meaning the omen-reading lore of the Babylonian astrologers.) It is really Daniel who thickens the plot by saying No to the largess of rich food and wine—but not to the free higher education (v. 17)—that is gratuitously offered him (v. 8). This magnificent refusal sets the stage for the contest or ordeal which intensifies the action of the story up to its climax (v. 15). Of course, this decision by Daniel involved considerable risk. Had the diet of "pulse" (KJV) produced the wan pallor that vegetarians are popularly supposed to have, he and his friends might have forfeited the remainder of their lives. The chief eunuch refused to take responsibility for acceding to the exiles' request on this very ground (v. 10), though apparently he was willing to pass the buck—and the danger—on down the line to his appointee, the "steward." However, the observant Jew for whom the Book of Daniel was written, as well as devout readers through the centuries, would hardly have regarded the decision as a gamble. That the God of Israel was the true Lord of Babylon as well was a claim long established, so the outcome could hardly be in doubt. The decision not to "defile" himself was Daniel's, it is true (v. 8), and no particular legal or moral justification is given for it. "Defilement" in this instance must have had something to do with the food itself, though exactly what cannot be shown. However, God supports Daniel in the decision, as is made certain by his vital intervention in the heart of the chief eunuch. God proves to be an active if silent participant in the plot as well, and that precisely—but not surprisingly—in Babylon.

The trial by vegetables seems to have been a private affair, and the Jews' victory in that matter something known only in the household. However, further fruits of God's faithful support of "the people of Israel" (v. 3) are publicly displayed in the magnificent professional success of Daniel and his friends as wise men (vv. 17–21).

To the degree that the story is about God, its theme is the familiar one of his trustworthiness. But this story is Scripture,

23

and consequently it is about human beings as well. Daniel and his friends are meant to serve as paradigms, living illustrations of abiding truth claims. Readers need, therefore, to know exactly what the Jewish lads did, how their act of refusal was connected with God's favor, and thus what the subject of the story is, humanly speaking. We need to be careful at this point, for it is here that historical readings of Daniel 1 have run amok and close attention to the canonical setting of the story may prove to be most helpful.

The Food Fit for a King

It is difficult to know exactly what an observant Jew of the third or second century B.C., much less a contemporary of Nebuchadnezzar in the seventh or sixth, would have regarded as defiling in the king's rich food or in the wine which he drank. Was the problem that it was rich or that it was the king's? If the latter was the problem, was it because the king was a gentile or that a captive did well not to be indebted to the king and thus become corrupted? Especially because of Daniel's revulsion and fear of defilement (v. 8), nearly all modern commentators assume that the issue with Daniel's gastronomic scruples was directly related to that set of dietary practices characteristic of observant Judaism at least since the Maccabean period. Obviously any Israelite since at least the time of Deuteronomy and probably since the beginning of Israel would have pushed away a plate of the king's rich food were a pork chop lying in the middle of it. But our text makes no mention of pork. Nor is the appeal to several other narratives contemporary with this chapter particularly helpful. Although in Tobit 1:11; Judith 10:5; 12:1–4; I Maccabees 1:63 and Esther 14:17, we see evidence of revulsion and fear of defilement in other cases of righteous refusal to eat foreign and royal food, the comparisons are flawed for two reasons: (a) the texts are contemporary with Daniel and cannot serve as evidence for the prior law or scripture to which Daniel was being obedient; (b) they are also not specific about what was wrong with the food. At the most, they seem generally concerned about meat from which blood had not been drained (a fundamental concern of later kosher slaughter). Neither the biblical nor extrabiblical texts allow us to conclude that Daniel's refusal to eat the king's rich food is an act of obedience to known law, not even the laws of *kashrut* which had not yet come into existence as far as we know. Nor does the term "defile

24

himself" (v. 8, here used reflexively for the single time in the O.T.) really solve anything for us. The most that can be said is that a person is "defiled" by blood (Isa. 59:3; Lam. 4:14; in Isa. 63:3, Yahweh comes from Bozrah with his own garments "defiled" by blood).

In one sense, we can be grateful that close examination of Daniel's act reveals that it is not to be too tightly linked with any particular set of food laws, because to bind a story like this to its historical setting too rigidly renders it less, not more, available to us. By being left only indefinitely related to ancient taboos and prohibitions and by being made canonical Scripture, Daniel 1 is liberated from serving simply as a hasidic lesson on dietary discipline and the salutary effects of a vegetarian diet to serve as an abiding illustration, a permanent metaphor for the human experience of trusting in a trustworthy God.

What then is the reason for Daniel's refusal to eat if obedience to dietary law, respect for blood taboo, and prudential health considerations are all left unsecured by the evidence? Joyce Baldwin (*Daniel*, pp. 82–83) invokes a possibility which, while still speculative, comes closer to what the canonical evidence permits. After arguing that "it is not immediately apparent why [the royal food] should have defiled them" and at the same time pointing out "all food in Babylon or Assyria was ritually unclean (Ezk. 4:13; Hos. 9:3,4) and from that there was no escape" (and that presumably included vegetables), Baldwin takes her clue from Daniel 11:26, the only other text in which the rare word *pat-bag*, "rich food," occurs. As that text makes clear, those who shared the king's board also entered into a covenantal relationship with him; they became his courtiers, his shadow cabinet. Put another way, their freedom of action was preempted by the king. Baldwin concludes,

> It would seem that Daniel rejected this symbol of dependence on the king because he wished to be free to fulfill his primary obligations to the God he served. The defilement he feared was not so much a ritual as a moral defilement, arising from the subtle flattery of gifts and favours which entailed hidden implications of loyal support, however dubious the king's future policies might prove to be (p. 83).

This assessment of the problem of the king's food takes seriously the problem of the lack of legal background within the canon for alleged dietary scruples of Daniel and his friends and takes seriously the evidence of Daniel 11:26. Even though it

25

forces a slight reinterpretation onto the term "defile," ignoring its usual association with blood and bloody meat, it remains the reading of Daniels refusal which is most respectful of the canonical situation of Daniel 1.

In the last analysis, the text enables us to speak only about the function of Daniel's refusal (and its subsequent miraculous vindication), not about its motivation. Daniel's act—whether one of obedience, prudence, political sagacity, or simply symbol —had the effect of setting him and his companions apart from the common run of aliens and other students in the Babylonian academy of wisdom. The refusal set out their individual identity in sharp relief, and because of their victory in the trial by vegetables, they became a distinct and special group. The theological significance of this sharp identity is explored below.

Daniel and the Vision of Deutero-Isaiah

In a study of the intention and sources of Daniel 1—11, John Gammie concludes that the stories of Daniel 1—6, while not a commentary or midrash on Deutero-Isaiah, were probably told "to show how a number of the sentences of Deutero-Isaiah furnished examples of 'prophecies fulfilled' among Israel's sons who served in foreign courts," and how this service "included being a light to the nations (Isa. xlii 6; xlix 6) so that foreign monarchs might acknowledge Yahweh's sovereignty . . ." ("On the Intention and Sources of Daniel i—vi," p. 291). Such a conclusion bears on the story of Daniel 1 in several ways. Ostensibly written in the eighth-seventh centuries, in the time of Hezekiah, Isaiah 49:22–23 foresaw that kings would be "foster fathers" (Gammie, "tutors") to Israel's sons (and daughters); now in Daniel 1 (ostensibly written during the sixth century Babylonian exile), four noble Israelite youths enjoy the patronage and tutelage of Babylon's king. Is the writer indirectly saying to his actual late third-early second century B.C. generation, as Gammie believes, "In the success of Jews at living prominent and significant lives in diaspora settings while remaining uncompromised and undefiled is the prophecy of Isaiah fulfilled"? If so, the connection is applicable to all six of the narratives in Daniel 1—6.

26

Perhaps even more significantly, the assertion of Yahweh's sovereignty in Babylon, demonstrated in his ability to vindicate the discipline of Daniel and his friends even in the very innermost hearts of individual Babylonians (v. 9)—an exercise of divine power surely far more significant and demanding than mere earthquakes or fire storms would have been, yet one which is repeated time and again in Daniel 1—6—is a narrative representation of Deutero-Isaiah's sustained announcement of Yahweh's lordship over all parts of the earth (Isa. 43:3–7), all the nations (40:15–17), all other gods who are nothing (46:1–11), princes and rulers of the earth (40:23–24), and specifically Cyrus, king of Persia (44:24—45:13). Of course, other exilic and early postexilic prophetic works such as Ezekiel and Isaiah 56 —66 make the same claims for the universal sovereignty of the God of Israel; but given the other linguistic and theological affinities which obtain between Isaiah 40—55 and Daniel 1—6, we seem to be on safe ground in asserting that one function of the stories of Daniel 1—6 is to assure Jews that the visionary hopes and promises of Isaiah 40—55 were indeed capable of realization among the obedient and wise of Israel.

A THEOLOGICAL ASSESSMENT OF DANIEL 1

What is at issue in Daniel 1? What is the theological point of the narrative as it stands before us in its full canonical form? While various answers have been given to this question, one of the primary claims of the text is surely the general affirmation of the trustworthiness of God, even in the remote and difficult circumstances of exile, and the consequent basis for hope on his people's part. A Jew who is true to his heritage and his God can make it big in Babylon, but the credit lies not so much with his refusal of the fancy lunches and the fat expense accounts of the day as with God's ability to give "Daniel favor and compassion in the sight of the chief of the eunuchs" (v. 9). An exiled Jew can be a winner because the God of Israel is a winner!

However, even this theological truth claim, while significant and doubtlessly present in the text, ought not to be overly stressed if the story itself has more to say. After all, the theme of God's absolute trustworthiness can be misleading if the pattern of danger-obedience-divine intervention-safety is understood to be predictable and inevitable whenever God's people cry out to him in duress and exile. Jews were obedient and refused to defile themselves at Auschwitz, too, but they still went to the gas chambers, even though God was sovereign in that place as well. Christians, too, have been obedient in Nazi Germany and in the China of the cultural revolution and in the realms of Latin American dictators, but the goon

27

squads have not been prevented from coming to the door.

Therefore, while not denying the significance of the claim of universal divine sovereignty and trustworthiness for a world still emerging from the notion of tribal and national gods (or for our world, for that matter), we turn again to the behavior of Daniel and his friends as another substantive theological value of this passage. The text enables us to speak not about the motivation of Daniel's refusal but rather its function. The reader cannot finally say why Daniel did what he did. Perhaps the act was one of obedience to God-given law, and this had to do with the presence of too much blood in the king's rich morsels of meat; or perhaps it was prudential and thus pointed toward the need for an unencumbered, unco-opted, and clear mind. Perhaps it was an act of political sagacity or one of symbolic resistance. Perhaps; all we can know for certain, however, is that the lads of Judah said No to the menu at the high table. The food was fit for a king, but in Daniel's judgment it was not fit for a servant of the King of kings. The effect set the Jews apart in sharp relief from the common run of aliens and novices at the Babylonian academy of wisdom. In that sharp identity lay strength: the Jews were going to have to be reckoned with! A Yes at this point would have resulted in a significant loss of identity for a man undefiled and obedient to the God of Israel: he would simply have been another man with a price. In Daniel's No lay his own sharp focus, his own clear identity, and, as events proved, the key to Israel's identity as a special and divinely elect people.

The case can be made that chapter 1 and the other stories of Daniel 1—6 all provide components of an interim ethic, an answer to the question: Given our strong conviction that God will vindicate himself before the whole world at the end of this age and at the inauguration of his new era, how shall we who trust him live our lives in the meantime? That part of the answer which Daniel 1 provides says, Live vigorously, carry your trust into the very heartland of your oppressors, with God's help beat them at their own games of wisdom and understanding, contribute significantly to the safety of your people, and glorify God in your faithfulness. And above all, remember that in order to say Yes to this great challenge, you will have to say No to all the compromises that would blur your focus, co-opt you, and destroy a little bit of your true identity. Maintenance of sharp identity, uncompromised, unencumbered, and ramrod straight in the presence of the oppressive powers of the world, will prove to be a salient feature of the interim ethics to be practiced by the saints before the great day of vindication comes and the kingdoms of the world become that single kingdom in which integrity such as theirs prevails forever (2:44; 7:27).

Daniel 2
Daniel as Wise Man

The Court Tale of Contest

The second panel in the series of scenes from the life of Daniel continues to portray the idealized Jew of the diaspora who can successfully participate at the highest levels in the life of the gentile community. It presents Daniel as a man who, through the "wisdom and strength" given him by the "God of heaven," could do something which conventional wisdom asserted that no mortal could do (2:11). Chapter 2 thus functions as a miracle story, although W. Lee Humphreys ("A Life Style for the Diaspora") is undoubtedly also correct when he describes it as a "court tale of contest." Like Daniel 4 and 5, this court tale of contest emphasizes the superior wisdom or ability of a courtier; the crisis setting in which this wisdom is displayed and, for that matter, the burden of the courtier's message are of secondary importance in the story.

Since ancient times commentators have pointed out that the list of *dramatis personae* of chapter 2 could be a leaf taken from the Joseph cycle of Genesis 37—50. Try the equation for yourself! Let the Nebuchadnezzar of Daniel 2:1 equal the Pharaoh of Genesis 41:8; you will find that Nebuchadnezzar, like Pharaoh, is the mightiest foreign potentate of the time; like Pharaoh, he is subject to nightmares and his "spirit was troubled." Let the four general and roughly equivalent categories of wise men listed in Daniel 2:2 equal the two classes of seers and prognosticators mentioned in Genesis 41:8. Like their ancient Egyptian counterparts, these court functionaries are presented in a reasonably favorable light as persons who had specific tasks to do at the royal court which they were ordinarily capable of accomplishing. Let Arioch of Daniel 2:14, identified by an Aramaic title variously understood to mean "captain of

29

the guard" (RSV; cf. II Kings 25:8, 18), "chief cook" (LXX-Dan and Theod-Dan), "lord high executioner" or "chief of the royal police" (Hartman and DiLella), and "provost-marshal" (Montgomery) equal the Potiphar of Genesis 39:1, who bears the Hebrew equivalent of the same title. (Actually, though Potiphar is Joseph's master, it is the unnamed "chief butler" who performs the function of bringing to the king's attention the existence and the competency of the Jewish seer. These two figures merge into one in the Daniel story.) Of course, you must let Daniel himself equal Joseph; he, too, is a hero already renowned for his piety and loyalty to the command of the God of Israel. Both are skilled dream interpreters (as Joseph had already demonstrated in Gen. 40); both are becomingly modest in their success, for they attribute to God alone the power to know the truth through dreams (Gen. 41:16; Dan. 2:27–30). Finally, let the two plots themselves equal one another. In both, the miracle of truth-telling takes place (with Daniel outdoing Joseph by reporting the very dream itself, as well as its interpretation); in both, the life of the hero is spared and he is given power and authority over the servants of the king; both conclude with the extraordinary spectacle of a gentile king bearing witness to the power of the God of Israel (Gen. 41:38; Dan. 2:47).

It is surely not accidental that in the story of Daniel the dream-interpreter is drawn so closely to the outlines of the Joseph tale in Genesis 41. Joseph was already intended by the Pentateuchal writers to serve as the prototypical wise courtier, the model for all Jews of piety and wit who would aspire in years to come to serve in high places. The Jewish writers of the Hellenistic age understood this intention of the Joseph stories and, in such works as the pseudepigraphical "Testament of Joseph" and the romance "Joseph and Asenath," they used Joseph as an example of how a Jew could live successfully in the diaspora. Whoever composed Daniel 2 had good precedent for presenting Daniel as a new Joseph, indeed, as a super-Joseph with powers brought up to date to meet the demands of a situation even more dramatic than that which the first Joseph faced. But what difference does the discovery of this evidently intentional presentation of Daniel as a new Joseph make to us who revere this story as Scripture? It suggests at least this: The Daniel who comes to teach us religious truth is a fictional or at least fictionalized figure, shaped by the writers of the Book of Daniel in the mold of Joseph but set in a later and existentially far more

30

significant world, the world of their contemporary readers. The news that Daniel 2 is a work of fiction agrees, of course, with what common sense suggests and with internal evidence. It also comes as good news, for it means that we are set free from the problem of who the real Daniel was and from undue concern about evident chronological anachronisms and narrative flaws to ask the important questions: Whom does this Daniel represent? For whom does he speak? What claims about the character and purpose of the God of Israel are being made through his mouth?

Clearly the circles which gathered and edited Daniel 2 and the other "court tales" which make up Daniel 1—6 identified with Joseph and with the plight—and opportunities—of Jews living away from Palestine in the midst of the gentile community. The probability that such an outlook would arise in the diaspora rather than in the relatively parochial setting of Judea in the late Persian or early Hellenistic period has led scholars to conclude that those tales (and the contemporary novelettes such as Esther, Tobit, and the tales added to Daniel in the LXX) in fact originated outside the land of Israel, probably in the Babylonian Jewish community. In one sense, this theory merely takes seriously what the stories themselves say; after all, they are all set in the eastern diaspora. Even if this seems to be the most reasonable hypothesis about the geographical horizon of these stories, however, we shall have to acknowledge that it increases the difficulty of accounting for how the tales of Daniel 1—6 came to be conjoined with the manifestly Judean and even Jerusalemite apocalypse of Daniel 7—12.

The Miracle Story (vv. 1–30)

The plot of the story in chapter 2 develops in *five scenes,* as follows: *first scene*—the problem: the king's dream and the ordeal of the magicians (vv. 1–12); *second scene*—Daniel's intervention, disclosing the secret of Daniel's power (vv. 13–23); *third scene*—Daniel's proclamation to the king and the miracle of the recovery of the dream (vv. 24–30); *fourth scene*—the dream and its interpretation (vv. 31–45); *fifth scene*—the denouement, and the king's paean of praise (vv. 46–49).

The king has a problem with troubling dreams (v. 1), but his problem is far less dangerous than that facing the dream interpreters. The narrator skillfully develops this nuance through the *first scene* of the story by introducing the element

31

of dramatic irony. By the end of verse 6, the reader realizes that the interpreters are being asked not only to release the hidden meaning of the king's dream, but also to recollect the dream itself—a fact which really dawns upon the interpreters themselves only in verse 10. They twist and squirm and play for time, finally tacitly admitting (v. 11) what Jeremiah had already said about false prophets long before them (Jer. 23:18)—they cannot perceive and hear the word of God. They cannot gain access to the divine message vouchsafed to the king. Their remark correctly anticipates the point and denouement of the entire story: "none can show it to the king except the gods, whose dwelling is not with flesh." Exactly so! It is precisely the gods, or rather, the one true God, speaking through the one dream interpreter whose credentials are authenticated by that God, who ultimately solves the puzzle posed by the king.

The *second scene* of the story (vv. 13–23) shifts to Daniel, who, together with his three friends, is threatened with being caught up in the general purge of the "wise men of Babylon" which is now ordered by the disillusioned and enraged king. Faced with this crisis, Daniel prays for a boon and receives from the "God of Heaven" the solution of the "mystery."

The Aramaic term *raz* (mystery), a term borrowed from the Persian language, is found in the Old Testament only in Daniel—before (vv. 18–19, 27–30) and after (v. 47) the dream report in chapter 2, and once more in Daniel 4:9, again in connection with dream interpretation. Its exact sense is something of a mystery itself. Let it suffice to say that the kind of knowledge which is called a mystery in chapter 2 cannot be ascertained through reason or conventional wisdom, but only through divine revelation. God and God alone is the revealer of such mysteries: Daniel affirms this (2:28) and so does Nebuchadnezzar (2:47). And God will do this only through those whom he chooses to make his instruments of revelation.

The view is similar to that of Deutero-Isaiah, whose convictions on the matter of the universal rule of God are in so many ways parallel to the convictions of Daniel. As John Collins has pointed out (*Apocalyptic Vision*, p. 45), Second Isaiah scoffs at the claims of the wise men of the foreign nations to save by means of divining and foretelling the future (47:12–13; 44:25). This failure is due to the fact that the idols of the nations have no power or wisdom (Isa. 44:9–20); therefore, they cannot do what Yahweh can do (Isa. 40:12–15, 23–24). God reveals his

32

mysteries only to his servants, and the power which these servants exhibit is drawn from the same source as that which can throw down and set up kings, which is in fact the only source of true power. This affirmation brings us close to the doctrine of revelation held by the writer of Daniel 2: God makes known his purpose and plan through the medium of dreams and the instrumentality of his servants. A "vision of the night" (2:19; cf. Job 4:12–13) is just as surely a dream as is Nebuchadnezzar's. This notion fits very well with the doctrine of revelation of the apocalyptist responsible for Daniel 7—12, who, as we shall see, portrays God as one who uses the analogous device of visions interpreted by angelic guides to disclose his plan for the future. In short, "the understanding of revelation is the same in both halves of the book" (Collins). This coincidence suggests a line along which at least the internal ideological and editorial coherence of the Book of Daniel can be argued and opens the possibility that the circles of "the wise" (Dan. 12:3) who gave rise to the apocalypse in Daniel 7—12 were engaged in the same urgent quest for access to the secret thoughts of God as were those admirers of wisdom who wrote the court-tales in Daniel 1—6.

The doxology or hymn which Daniel offers to the "God of heaven" following the disclosure of the mystery (vv. 20–22; v. 23 assumes the related form of a brief psalm of individual thanksgiving) solves for the reader another mystery, namely, the secret of Daniel's power to perform the miracle of dream recall and interpretation. All credit for this power is ascribed by Daniel to God, and this position is maintained throughout Daniel 1—6 in similar doxological utterances (cf. 2:47 [a truncated version]; 4:1–3, 34–37; 6:25–27). In all of these poems (as in the hymnic literature of the Old Testament generally; cf. Psalms 29; 33; 104), God is addressed as creator, all-powerful Lord of the whole earth, and the one who has provided the specific boon or performed the specific miracle which is the subject of the story. No inexorable working out of fate here; God is personally in charge of events. In this instance, God is celebrated as, among other things, the one "who changes times and seasons." Further, God, who is himself surrounded by bright effulgence (cf. Job 37:22; Ps. 36:9; Wisd. Sol. 7:26; I Tim. 6:16), is the one whose gaze penetrates those realms of ignorance and mystery which to all others are "darkness" (v. 22; cf. Ps. 139:11–12; Job 12:22). Truly, God is the source of all wisdom, an affirmation repeated through the generations in Israel (cf. Job 12:13; 28:23;

33

Ecclus. 42:15–25); and those to whom God reveals wisdom are of the light, sent into the world to oppose the "sons" of darkness.

Necessary information in hand, Daniel now appears before the king. The *third scene* of the story is devoted to a proclamation by Daniel of God's capacity to give revelatory dreams (v. 28*b*) and their interpretation through his chosen functionaries (v. 30). Only a hint of the content of the dream is given: Daniel speaks of it as containing information of "what will be in the latter days" (v. 28) and "what would be hereafter" or "what is to be" (v. 29).

The Dream, Its Interpretation and the Denouement (vv. 31–49)

In the *fourth scene,* verses 31–35 narrate the dream itself; verses 36–45 contain its correct interpretation. Both parts have to do with the passage of world history, its end, and the coming of a kingdom that "shall stand forever" (v. 44): in short, they present a miniature apocalyptic scenario. Two features of this unit deserve mention: (a) its content is partially inconsistent with the very pro-monarchical, pro-Babylonian tone of the tale as a whole in that the head of gold which represents Babylon is finally crushed and destroyed like all the rest of the world empires; (b) in the denouement which follows, the king pays no attention to the rather threatening and unfavorable content of the interpretation, but rather rewards Daniel handsomely simply because he could "reveal this mystery" (v. 47). Because of these apparent rough places or seams in this otherwise smoothly constructed court tale, the usual practice is to regard the dream and interpretation as a unit having a separate tradition history, and possessing an intentionality quite different from that of the court tale in which it is now set. It must be noted here, however, that the incorporation into a wisdom tale of an apocalyptic vision of declining world ages culminating in the advent of an eternal kingdom provides another ground upon which the ultimate unity of the two very disparate and chronologically separable types of material found in the Book of Daniel can be argued. Consistent with the intention of this commentary to deal with the text of Daniel in the form in which ancient Israel gave it to us, we proceed to deal with the dream and its interpretation even while acknowledging its difference from the surrounding materials.

It would be a commonplace to say that dream interpreta-

34

tion stood high among the devices available for prognostication and long-range planning in the ancient Near East. Babylonian monarchs were particularly active consumers of the devices of dream interpreters who might be, as Leo Oppenheim has shown *(The Interpretation of Dreams in the Ancient Near East)*, intuitively qualified persons, or scholars trained in the arts of reading dream-omina, or priests or magicians who could invoke from the deity who had given the dream further clarification or verification. But the kings of the Old Testament tradition, too, dreamed important dreams and sometimes required interpretations: Abimelech (Gen. 20: 1–7); Pharaoh (Gen. 41); Solomon (I Kings 3:3–15); and, of course, Nebuchadnezzar. (For further discussion of the role of dreams in the Book of Daniel, see the commentary on chapter 7.)

The dream of Nebuchadnezzar in Daniel 2 involves a sequence. A gargantuan metallic statue is pictured in four parts, evidently arranged in descending order of excellence: its head is gold, its upper torso is silver, its lower torso is bronze, and its legs are iron with feet partly of clay. This statue is struck at its very weakest point, its terra cotta (?) feet, by a stone cut out by no human hand. The statue is smashed and carried away, and the stone which destroys it becomes a mountain which fills the whole earth.

The interpretation given by Daniel is that the four parts of the statue represent four sequential kingdoms, beginning with the golden head of the neo-Babylonian kingdom of Nebuchadnezzar himself. This head is followed by three unnamed and ever more inferior successor kingdoms down to and including a kingdom of iron mixed with clay. A great deal of ink has been spilled over the years concerning the true identity of the historical empires to which this allegory is intended to refer. All important in that discussion has always been the identity of the fourth kingdom of iron, since that world power is the one which immediately precedes the fall, and indeed, by virtue of its "feet of clay," prepares the way for it. Traditional interpreters inevitably located themselves within the chronological frame of that fourth kingdom and thus near to the time of the end; in this sense they were in general if not specific accord with the intention of the original writer who almost certainly was a near contemporary with the events described in verse 43 as mixing "with one another in marriage," and who must have believed that the culmination of history was at hand. In any event, most

35

modern interpreters agree that the historical epochs symbolized by the four parts of the statue are the Babylonian empire (the head of gold), the "Median empire" (although it hardly ever existed in actual historical fact but here equals the upper torso of silver), the Persian empire (the lower torso of bronze) and the Hellenistic kingdoms of the Ptolemies of Egypt and the Seleucids of Antioch in Syria (the legs of iron and the feet of clay). The fact that these four empires were not actually historically sequential does not invalidate the list given above, for in fact if one begins with the equation "the head of gold equals Babylon," as the text itself demands, and if one identifies the divided kingdoms contemporary with the writer with the Hellenistic regimes of the Seleucids and the Ptolemies after 323 B.C., no other list of four world empires is really possible. It is also generally acknowledged that the same four empires were in the view of the writer of Daniel 7, who indicated them by the alternative allegorical device of a series of beasts.

The allegory of history as four sequential kingdoms, followed by the catastrophic inbreaking of a fifth kingdom, can be separated from the conventional reference to world-epochs as ages of precious metals. Each of these metaphors has behind it a recoverable history of use outside of Israel and the Old Testament (cf. Collins, *Apocalyptic Vision*, pp. 37–43). Suffice it to say that the four-kingdom series can be found in Roman, Hellenistic-Jewish, and Persian sources, while the four-metal sequence, arranged in declining order of worth, appears in the same Persian sources and in that eighth century B.C. work called *Works and Days*, by the Greek philosopher Hesiod. The two familiar metaphors of kingdoms and metals have been combined in verses 31–45 with the additional motif of a colossus or gigantic statue. This element is unique to Daniel, and it gave to the Jewish reader an understandable and yet freshly awe-inspiring assessment of past history, present reality, and future destiny.

If one considers the combined four-kingdom, four-metal dream account of Daniel 2 for a few moments, a point of friction begins to make itself felt. The initial tone of the interpretation is pro-Babylonian, and favors the era of the golden head. Nebuchadnezzar is hailed as the "king of kings" (cf. Ezra 7:12—a title known in neo-Babylonian texts, but more commonly used in Persia, where even the modern Shahs affected it!), and the one to whom God "has given the kingdom, the power, the might, and the glory." He is veritably a new Adam, having power not only over his human subjects, but even over "the beasts of the field and the birds of the air" (v. 38), just as the first human being had in Genesis 1:26–28 (cf. Ps. 8:6–8). If the thought that the writer might have praised the Babylonian king as a new Adam seems a bit much, perhaps the source of the motif can be reckoned to be Jeremiah's oracles about the universal domination of Nebuchadnezzar (Jer. 27:6–7; 28:14). Collins even argues that this divinely ordained, exalted rule of Nebuchadnezzar suggests that the dream account, like the rest of the court tale, is of Babylonian origin: in its earliest form he sees "the prophecy as a Babylonian political oracle rather than a Jewish apocalypse" (*Apocalyptic Vision,* p. 37). However, this positive tone grows dissonant in verse 44 as the stone not cut by human hands rolls down upon the statue. This stone "shall break in pieces all these kingdoms and bring them to an end, and it shall stand forever," predicts Daniel; and this smashing conquest by the stone which represents "a kingdom which shall never be destroyed" is specifically made to include the head of gold (v. 43). No toadying prognosis this, but quite ominous, really. Even the golden head must go! However, King "Golden Head" Nebuchadnezzar hails Daniel's miraculous success at dream recovery and interpretation as though the future destiny of his house were not at stake. Why would the king behave in such a way?

Collins solves this problem by arguing that a Jewish redaction overlies the older pro-Babylonian oracle (*Apocalyptic Vision,* pp. 43–44). The redaction did not bring in the fifth kingdom (the stone) for the first time. Collins' own discussion of extra-biblical parallels shows that these, too, looked for a triumph and vindication at the end of the long four-part history of declining world empires. But this redaction might well have emphasized the degree to which this fifth kingdom is the antithesis of all that preceded it, even including the formerly gladly remembered "golden age." Collins attacks the position of H. L. Ginsberg, who solved the problem of why the stone cuts down and pulverizes even the golden head, by arguing that the writer had in view a moment in history, undoubtedly in his own time, when all four empires did in fact exist simultaneously if in an attenuated way (*Studies in Daniel,* p. 8). Not only does Collins deny that such a moment ever really existed, but he argues that the author or redactor is not even thinking of a chronological sequence of history but rather of a composite picture of the

37

Jewish experience with idolatry represented by the several metals. From this discussion as well as from the text of Daniel 3 and 5:23, it is clear that the heroes would rather die than worship a golden image, representing as it does mere fading earthly power. Here, too, the object is to show the transient nature of human power which, no matter how excellent and majestic it may be, falls before the overweening power of the God of heaven whose kingdom the stone is. No veneration is due to a power that is transient (although admittedly the text here in no way indicates that the image was to be worshiped).

In spite of the friction created by thus setting the traditional recollection of Babylon as a golden age in juxtaposition to a judgment that all human empires as such are transitory creations destined to be crushed by the "stone not cut by human hands," the writer pushes on. Never mind this narrative flaw—let Nebuchadnezzar praise and celebrate at the news of his own ultimate demise! The writer has something more urgent to say. The kingdom that is promised and which is certainly coming can and will supplant the aggregate of human power. Like the stone, it will fill the whole earth (v. 35). Ringing with echoes of many earlier prophetic descriptions of a coming eschatological kingdom (cf. Ezek. 17:22–24; Isa. 2:2 ‖ Micah 4:1; and above all Isa. 11:9, ". . . for the earth shall be full of the knowledge of the Lord as the waters cover the sea"), the promise is of an *earthly* dominion which is *eternal,* and the sovereignty of which is placed in the hands of God's own chosen people. Who are these people? The people to whom sovereignty is finally given in chapter 7 are the "saints of the Most High." These are undoubtedly that very sectarian group within Israel with which the writer of Daniel is identified and who are also known as "those who are wise" (Dan. 12:3). Here no clear identification is made, and interpreters through all the ages have joyfully seized upon this open-endedness to identify the fifth monarchy with themselves!

With the coming of the fifth kingdom, what had been a depressing history of decreasingly brilliant human regimes becomes an eschatological scenario for the intersection of human and divine history. If we put the dream interpretation in more contemporary terms, it might go like this: The decline which has dogged history for many generations and which we have experienced acutely in our own time cannot go on forever. The end-point is not entropy—some undifferentiated age of

38

dull mediocrity or relentless tyranny. Nor is it some kind of omega point, at which all things work themselves around to the full realization of their potential. Rather, the end of this decline is the in-breaking of a destroying, purging power of God and the establishment in the place of what is palpably fading and insufficient—namely, human power and autonomy—of a power and autonomy granted by God!

The implications of this dream and interpretation for the question of the authorship of Daniel 1—6 are three. First, the concerns of these chapters are, by this dream, tilted toward the concerns of the apocalypses of Daniel 7—12. Chapter 7 will once again take up the series of world kingdoms in an allegorical presentation and will show them destroyed simultaneously by the in-breaking Kingdom of God. So the same final editor or author of the Book of Daniel must have found both types of literature—the tales and the apocalyptic visions—usable and congenial. Second, the writer of chapter 2 and the redactor of the Book of Daniel alike, together with the circles which they represented, presumably identified with that "kingdom which shall never be destroyed" and considered themselves allied with if not already participants in it. Third, the approach of the end events is signaled by the mixing of the iron and the clay, since that mixing not only immediately precedes the sudden appearance of the stone, but even provides for the fatal weakness—the literal "feet of clay"—in the statue which the stone can exploit. Whatever marriage between royal houses may have been involved here, to the writer of the dream-account of Daniel 2 it was a "sign of the times" and evidence of the weakness and swift decline of the empire of the day.

The court tale of the wise dream interpreter Daniel concludes with a *fifth scene* (vv. 46–49) in which Daniel and his friends are rewarded and, most importantly, in which the Babylonian king Nebuchadnezzar praises Daniel's God in an abbreviated but richly ornamented paean (v. 47): "Truly, your God is God of gods and Lord of kings, and a revealer of mysteries, for you have been able to reveal this mystery."

Daniel 2 is a court tale by virtue of its setting and its characters. But it must also be remembered that it is also a miracle story. Miracle stories in the Bible often conclude with praise of God offered either by one or more witnesses or by a beneficiary of the miracle. The expression of praise often comes from a non-Israelite who has no *prima facie* obligation to express faith

39

in the God of Israel. Indeed, if one takes as examples stories such as Elijah and the raising of the son of the widow of Zarephath (I Kings 17:17–24; parallels in II Kings 4:18–37; Luke 7:11–17), or many of the miracle stories in the Synoptic Gospels (e.g., Mark 2:1–12; 7:31–37; Luke 9:37–43), it appears that this confession of faith by the bystander is the real point of the story. The same thing seems to be true here: the climax and essential burden of the miracle story of dream interpretation is Nebuchadnezzar's change of heart and his testimony to the power of Daniel's God. James Montgomery saw this years ago: "The king's confession of Daniel's God as God of gods and Lord of kings is the real climax of the story" (*Daniel*, p. 181). Note, too, how carefully the king's utterance has been phrased. Although he acknowledges Daniel's role in the miracle of revelation which has taken place, and though he does homage to Daniel and orders offerings made to him as if Daniel were a demi-god (which obeisance Daniel apparently accepts!), he nevertheless confesses the source of the miraculous knowledge to be God, the God of gods, just as Daniel had suggested (v. 28). Nebuchadnezzar is presented as a veritable convert to the worship of the God of Israel.

A THEOLOGICAL ASSESSMENT OF DANIEL 2

Modern commentators commonly argue that three religious truth claims predominate in this chapter: (a) the God of Israel is sovereign; (b) the wisdom of his servants is manifestly superior to the wisdom of the gentiles and their deities; (c) and therefore, his faithful servants, that is, those who have access to his wisdom, can take hope amid otherwise hopeless circumstances. No doubt these teachings are indeed part of the plain meaning of the text. Yet can we not also see a broader framework of thought behind these ideas? If we cannot, we are in trouble, for frankly, the latter two propositions are neither very true nor very interesting as they stand. Take the second claim, for example. No matter how strictly the author may have intended it or how sincerely we may believe it, of what real significance to the daily conduct of the lives of Jewish and Christian believers today is it to say that the wisdom of the God of the Jews is superior to all other wisdom? After all, we neither have access to that wisdom in the immediate manner illustrated by Daniel, nor do we find that other important wisdoms, including the

40

modern "wisdom" of scientific and technological knowledge which God has graciously granted to the people of our era, are in any way restricted to Jews or Christians or unbelievers or any other particular group.

Or take the third claim. Of what practical significance is it to the lives of believers at least in the affluent Western world today to lift up an undoubtedly correct historical observation, namely, that a text like Daniel 2 was written to buck up the hopes of the oppressed and frightened Jews of long ago, to the status of a religious truth claim? Is Daniel best understood as a "theology for hard times"? Granted that it may bring special comfort even in modern times to black slaves and imprisoned dissidents and persecuted sects, has it not also something to say to those many believers who are not at the moment frightened and oppressed and who even enjoy a considerable measure of political and economic power? Inasmuch as we can and must share its basic conviction that God will prevail in his contest with the powers of this age, can we not discover in it as well a guide to our own plan of action?

Three theological motifs appear to provide a somewhat broader framework in which to view the religious truth claims of the author and from which to build bridges from the text to our own situation. They are legitimate because they really are present in the text; they provide the broader base because they push behind the ostensible and understandable chauvinism of an embattled ancient people to the broader human concerns with which they ultimately had to deal.

One truth claim being made by the story is indeed the strong assertion that the God of Israel is sovereign. But the claim has depth and nuance. God is in no way the victim of circumstances, impinged upon by other powers, or obliged simply to react. Power and wisdom, those excellences of kings and wise men, are derived from him alone; and he mediates them through his chosen servants. This theological conviction is, of course, in full accord with the convictions of Old Testament writers of all generations; it remains a valid component of Jewish and Christian thought about God to this day, though in our theological reflection on the matter of the relation of human authority and kingship to the sovereignty of God we will allow more play for human freedom, historical causality, and mere chance than verse 21*b* might seem to suggest. The validity of

41

the doctrine of the sovereignty of God abides, even though we may find foreign to our experience the narrative expression of revelation found in Daniel 2, namely, that God in the exercise of his sovereign power sends revelatory dreams and visions to those whom he selects for the purpose and empowers others of his servants to interpret them.

A corollary claim of the story is that successful, effective ministry to human needs—service which may indeed result in preference and recognition—is predicated upon prayer and devotion to the purposes of God. This conviction, not unrelated to the third claim frequently discerned by the commentators, certainly retains validity in our time as well. However, this teaching of the tale has shadows falling across it—for Christians the shadow of the cross above all. We have learned from painful experience that no piety, no interim ethic, no obedience however exquisitely sensitive to the purposes of God, is guaranteed to deliver the believer from adversity and to result in reward and success. If Daniel's piety, loyalty, and wit are intended to be offered as a sure-fire formula for successful living in an alien land, then we must part company with the naïve hope of the ancient writer. It is doubtful, however, that at least the final editor of the Book of Daniel cherished any idea as wistful and simplistic as that. After all, the latter half of the book is very much aware that even the saints "shall fall by sword and flame, by captivity and plunder" (Dan. 11:33–35). No, surely the writer intends to make the case that only those human efforts at heroic service which place their ultimate reliance in the wisdom and power of the "God of gods and Lord of kings" can hope to stand the test of authenticity and so ultimately to be judged just and good. That is a teaching with which we can stay. The notion need not be expressed pietistically or sentimentally, as Neale's hymnic response to II Corinthians 4:17 would have it:

The trials that beset you,
    The sorrows ye endure,
The manifold temptations
    That death alone can cure,
What are they but His jewels
    Of right celestial worth?
What are they but the ladder
    Set up to heaven on earth?
O happy band of pilgrims,
    Look upward to the skies.

Where such a light affliction
Shall win you such a prize!

(John Mason Neale, 1818–1866,
"O Happy Band of Pilgrims")

It can, in fact, be articulated in Bonhoeffer's realistic and hard-headed manner, when he wrote,

> in the cross of Christ God confronts the successful man with the sanctification of pain, sorrow, humility, failure, poverty, loneliness, and despair. That does not mean that all this has a value in itself, but it receives its sanctification from the love of God, the love which takes all this upon itself as its just reward. God's acceptance of the cross is His judgement upon the successful man (*Ethics*, pp. 58–59).

The life style appropriate for living in between the times, the interim ethic which anticipates the new age that is coming and which is illustrated in several ways by the six court tales of Daniel 1—6, can affirm that lives given certainty by the perceived power of God to effectuate the divine purposes may not only respond fruitfully to harsh adversity, but may even be given a measure of heroic triumph.

The most challenging of the theological values of Daniel 2 remains yet to be explored, however. God loves Nebuchadnezzar, too, and has a role for him to play in the fabric of his history! Considering the antipathy with which the sacred writings of ancient Israel usually viewed Babylon and its kings—particularly those writings which were contemporary with the direct impact of Babylon's power on the Judean populace (Jer. 25: 12–14; 50–51; Isa. 47; Ps. 137)—the fact that Nebuchadnezzar can here be made to testify to the power and graciousness of God is all the more remarkable. In fact, it boggles the mind! The case for the primary importance of this third motif rests upon the position of the words of praise within the story. As shown earlier, 2:47 is really the goal of the story as a whole, and its point is the main point.

This theological tendency can only be called universalistic. The idealized picture of the mightiest of all foreign monarchs humbling himself before the true God, though set in the distant past by the literary medium of the court tale, really expresses an anticipation of the future on the part of the "wise" who gave Daniel 1—6 to us and who speak through their hero's life. In days to come, even the most unlikely foreigners, yes, all foreigners, will come to know and trust the God of Israel; and the love

43

and protection which that God wishes to extend to all will be plain to see. Montgomery does not take this text seriously enough when he dismisses Nebuchadnezzar's words by saying, "There is no reason for cavil at the pagan king's confession, for a polytheist can always take on new gods, the monotheist never" (*Daniel*, p. 181). No, the story is not recounting the theological dalliances of the Babylonian king but is in fact giving expression to Israel's eschatological faith. This faith in the coming universal acknowledgment of the rule of Israel's God is expressed in very different terms (in such texts as Isa. 43:8–9; Zech. 8:23; and 14:16–19), but it is the same faith. It is the faith which Paul exhibits in his own expression of future hope, using the words borrowed from Isaiah 45:23, ". . . at the name of Jesus every knee should bow, in heaven and on earth and under the earth, and every tongue confess that Jesus Christ is Lord, to the glory of God the Father" (Phil. 2:10–11). It is the faith which gleams in the brief but extraordinary glimpse of the inimical "kings of the earth," the very enemies of the gospel, coming at last to share in the triumph of the one true God (Rev. 21:24–26).

How, you may well ask, does a wisdom tale come to express an eschatological faith at its very climactic moment? It may be that Nebuchadnezzar did not speak this way in the earliest versions of the story and that his paean of praise (v. 47) is the work of the final editor. Be that as it may, the important affirmation of the universal and universally recognized lordship of God which now animates Daniel 2 provides another commonality between the wisdom materials of Daniel 1—6 and the apocalyptic vision of Israel which comes to expression in Daniel 7—12.

It remains necessary to make a theological assessment of the dream itself and its interpretation. Let us begin by being very candid. As some kind of prediction of the future, this dream interpretation offered by Daniel to Nebuchadnezzar is of no value to us. Even though the writer of this dream interpretation may well have intended it to be predictive at least of the onset of the End, the suggested time-line proved to be all wrong! The "everlasting kingdom" did not appear at the collapse of the Hellenistic dynasty of the Seleucids, as the dream apparently suggests it would do, any more than it came with the appearance of the archangel Michael at the demise of Antiochus IV Epiphanes (Dan. 12:1). Still, the dream has theological values for us, and this is true whether it was originally part of

44

the court tale of chapter 2 or was secondarily combined with that story.

First of all, the dream interpretation reaffirms the claim that Daniel's God is absolutely sovereign. That conviction, already made clear in the miracle story by the words of Daniel and the ascription of Nebuchadnezzar, is enhanced by the assertion of verse 44 that the God of heaven can throw down all the kings of the earth and set up his own "kingdom which shall never be destroyed, nor shall its sovereignty be left to another people." In the dream itself, the kingdoms seem to succeed one another in an organic, almost historical, way (vv. 39–40). Certainly no stress is placed on absolute divine determination, God throwing down each king in his turn. Kingdoms do wax and wane, though of course the entire sequence takes place within the realm of God's sovereignty and ends when God ends it. In the dream interpretation a new dimension is added to this basic theological conviction. Here there is absolute confidence that the purposes of God will be completed. In the fullness of God's time, at the end of the sequence of world kingdoms, powerful and dramatic as they may be, God can and will displace corrupt and fading human power with his own abiding and certain power, expressed through the kingdom which shall abide forever. That kingdom is not a heavenly one. Rather, it fills the whole earth (Dan. 2:35). In other words, it is the culmination of the good purpose of the Creator for the creation. It is peopled by real people—in the first instance, undoubtedly, the people with whom the writer of the book identifies. But indefinite numbers of other saints can hope to be there as well.

That confidence in God's ability to complete and perfect the divine purpose in history enhances in turn the other two theological claims of the court tale in which the dream interpretation is now embedded. The first of those claims was that those who persevere in obedience can hope to succeed. In the interpretation that hope is projected even into the future and to the end. The implication of the dream surely must be that those who rely upon God's power and serve him can hope to participate in some way in that ultimately successful human community, the "kingdom which shall never be destroyed." Furthermore, the second claim of the lordship and hegemony of the God of Israel, affirmed by Nebuchadnezzar himself in the court tale, has all the more poignancy when reinforced by the

45

dream interpretation. For now, he who proclaims the God of Israel as Lord of kings is one of those whose very downfall in the fullness of time is evidence of the truth of the assertion which he makes. Nebuchadnezzar hails Yahweh's universal rule partly —so the story seems to say—because Yahweh will show his power even over Nebuchadnezzar himself and will best him in the demonstration of that power.

Daniel 3
"It's Cool in the Furnace, Lord!"

The Court Tale of Conflict

An initial reading of the subject matter of chapter 3 of the Book of Daniel reveals a story of a conflict in the court of Nebuchadnezzar between the king and the Jews. Not only is Jewish faithfulness on the line, but the ability of the God of Israel to deliver those who trust in him is also being tested. The essential drama of the story is set up by the king himself when, after having commanded all of his subjects to worship a golden image, and having threatened Shadrach, Meshach, and Abednego with death in a fiery furnace for refusing to do so, he hurls down the gauntlet directly to God: "Who is the god that will deliver you out of my hands?" (v. 15). That God proves, of course, to be the God of these Jews, and his ability to deliver his servants who trust in him even from so great a danger leads to the denouement of the story.

The setting of the story follows upon the conclusion of chapter 2. At the end of that "court tale of contest," the three young men, Shadrach, Meshach, and Abednego, were made officials in the province of Babylon at the request of their leader, Daniel. That is the position which they occupy in chapter 3, as is acknowledged by certain Chaldeans who maliciously accuse them (vv. 8–12). The setting is the court of Babylon during the period of the exile (597–538 B.C.) Again, however, internal evidence in the form of Persian and Greek loan words suggests that the story actually came into existence at a much later time, probably after the rise of strong Hellenistic influence in the Middle East had begun, perhaps even after Alexander's conquest in 332 B.C.

46

The lead characters of this story carry on from the previous two chapters, with the puzzling exception that Daniel is now absent. (Most commentators take this fact as evidence that the story originated and circulated independently of the Daniel cycle.) Even more difficult is the appearance (vv. 24–25) of a mysterious fourth figure who walks with the three young men in the fiery furnace. Who is this individual? Nebuchadnezzar wants to know the answer to that as well!

In this chapter, Nebuchadnezzar moves toward the model of a persecuting tyrant. Up to this point he has been presented in a much more benign light; and even here, when all is said and done, he is a man of reason who can rescind the royal orders in the face of determined fidelity. Perhaps it is essential that he be a persecuting tyrant here in order that the absolute steadfastness and loyalty of the Jews be proven to all. The question of whether Nebuchadnezzar is the type of a persecuting *divinized* tyrant hinges on whether one assumes that the statue of gold which he set up in the plain of Dura was a statue of himself. Is he now being presented as the Nebuchadnezzar of Judith 3:8, who sends his officers to destroy all local sanctuaries, "so that all nations should worship Nebuchadnezzar only, and all their tongues and tribes should call on him as god"? Was he a prototype of Gaius Caligula who, as Philo reports in his account of his mission to see the emperor in A.D. 40 *(On the Embassy to Gaius)*, placed an image of himself in the temple in Jerusalem, thus touching off resistance and resulting in persecution of the Jews? Is it correct to say, with Desmond Ford *(Daniel*, p. 106), that because of his idolatry and his desolating persecution, "Nebuchadnezzar, as well as Belshazzar and Darius, posed for the portrait of antichrist"? Our source does not tell us, nor is there any way of determining from extra-biblical sources whether or not Nebuchadnezzar posed for the portrait of a god. In favor of saying that the issue is idolatry rather than the worship of a divinized tyrant is the fact that Nebuchadnezzar backs away so quickly from his command once the miracle of the fiery furnace has been accomplished and speaks so warmly of the sovereignty of the God of Israel. However, it is worth remembering that the young lads seem to make some distinction in their resistance to the king's command between his gods and the golden image which he set up (v. 18).

Before proceeding with a detailed discussion of the plot of this story, a comment is in order about the amazing redundancy

47

of this chapter. Why the constant return to the list of "satraps, prefects, governors, counselors, treasurers, justices, magistrates, and all the officials of the provinces," the constant repetition of the king's command, and the formula so often repeated, "a burning, fiery furnace"? What does the "concatenating style" (Lacocque) of the chapter signify? That it is of inferior literary quality, the work of a hack writer? Or is this perhaps part of its folkloristic way of heightening tension and of introducing into a very serious situation a certain delightful quality? After all, this story has an almost humorous tone, in that the little orchestra becomes the signal for a mass obeisance by all the toadies of the kingdom. (Once one reads the list of instruments contained in it [vv. 5, 7, 15], one can imagine that the orchestra squeaked and piped in a very non-euphonious way.) The highly exaggerated heat of the fire (v. 22) is obviously raised to the nth power in order to make all the more marvelous the fact that the Jews emerged from the furnace not only without any burned spots in their clothing or singed hair, but with "no smell of fire . . . upon them" (v. 27). While not exactly funny (!), such a motif has the playful feel of a storyteller's elaboration on the basic plot.

The genre of this story has been termed by Humphreys a "court tale of conflict" ("A Life-Style for the Diaspora"). Along with chapter 6, it is one of only two stories of this genre in Daniel. Here the focus is not on the superior wisdom of the Jewish heroes—the issue of wisdom is not raised at all—but on the power of their God to deliver them. In general sequence this tale follows the pattern displayed in the Joseph story, in Esther, and in the story of Ahikar. As Collins, following Nickelsburg, shows, the sequence is as follows: the heroes move from a state of prosperity to one of danger, usually because of a conspiracy; then, in their moment of direst straits, the heroes are released, their greatness is recognized, and they are given even higher standing than before (*The Apocalyptic Vision*, p. 50). The miracle component typically embedded in the stories is not peculiar to the court tale of conflict—we have already seen it in both Daniel 1 and 2, each of which is a different type of story. The case of verses 24–27 is typical in that it is the miracle which leads to the testimony of the foreign king to the greatness of the God of Israel.

The story can be broken rather easily into four distinctive

48

parts, and this brief structural analysis will form the outline for the ensuing paragraphs: the crisis (vv. 1–7); the conflict (vv. 8–18); the punishment (vv. 19–23, followed by the rather awkwardly placed interlude of the mysterious fourth figure in vv. 24–25); and the miracle and the royal testimony (vv. 26–30).

The Crisis and the Conflict (vv. 1–18)

The plot begins to unfold with the crisis described in verses 1–7. Nebuchadnezzar sets up a great golden image in the plain of Dura in the province of Babylon and commands all of the officials of the kingdom (listed in order of rank) to attend its dedication and to worship it. How likely was such an event? The ancient writer Herodotus (i, 183) speaks of a great golden statue of Zeus in Babylon. Much earlier, the Assyrian king Ashurnasirapal (*Annals,* ii, 133) brags of the great stone and gold image to Ninib which he had erected. It seems quite possible that either Nebuchadnezzar or Antiochus IV Epiphanes might have had giant idols erected and even have had them plated with gold. The statue in our story has credibility, then, even if the proportions of sixty cubits by six cubits would haᵛ e made the figure uncommonly tall and skinny! Further, much evidence from antiquity shows that a great festival would be held on the occasion of the dedication of some sacred statue or building, replete with liturgical offerings. In fact, we need only look at I Kings 8 for a comparable moment in Israel's history, when "Solomon assembled the elders of Israel and all the heads of the tribes, the leaders . . ." (I Kings 8:1) to dedicate the newly built Temple.

Not only literature but archaeology lends credence to our statue, for it has uncovered gigantic images from ancient Mesopotamia, bas-reliefs and free-standing sculptures which guarded the entrance to the hanging gardens of Babylon. The poetic imagination has always responded to these gigantic monoliths, silent witnesses to the vanity and pomp of ancient times. In his sonnet "Ozymandias" (1817), Shelley spoke for all when he had the inscription on the pedestal of the broken, half-buried remnant of a gigantic statue read, "My name is Ozymandias, king of kings. Look on my works, ye Mighty, and despair!" The reality of that ancient power was there and yet, in retrospect, its boasts and threats were utterly foolish. Shelley's sonnet concludes,

49

> . . . Round the decay
> Of that colossal wreck, boundless and bare,
> The lone and level sands stretch far away.

And yet there is little reason to suppose that kings of old risked political disaster and stirred up trouble deliberately by simply commanding people to worship images against their will. Although there is evidence that Hellenistic and later Roman regimes frequently attempted to install a unifying imperial religion in all corners of their provinces, as far as we know this practice did not touch the Jews until the time of Antiochus IV Epiphanes (cf. I Macc. 1:41–42). Therefore, the time of Antiochus rather than that of Nebuchadnezzar fits best the literal terms of this story. It is believed that Antiochus erected in the temple in Jerusalem a statue of Zeus Olympios and that an altar was consecrated to his worship with the sacrifice of swine—the "abomination of desolation" spoken of in Daniel 11:31 and elsewhere. Is the statue on the plain of Dura a cipher for this idol, understandable to those who have ears to hear?

These historical questions can be answered only in a speculative manner. But if we ask about analogies in contemporary experience which might bind the story to our time, all speculation ceases forthwith. The demand placed upon all of his subordinates by Nebuchadnezzar is surely analogous to the contemporary experience of the loyalty oath. The notion that a king might delight in testing the willingness of the toadies and sycophants who surround him to lick his boots and do his will is by no means unknown in our own time. Eugene Ionesco's memorable drama *Rhinoceros,* in which under the influence of small bands of rhinoceros-like storm troopers the rest of the herd of humans become rhinoceri one by one and viciously persecute all who resist the trend is a literary formulation of our profound contemporary experience with the phenomenon.

As always, the Jews tend to resist the rhinoceros-like rush to lick the king's boots and bow down before the false image on the plain of Dura. We are not told the form which their resistance took at first; presumably an initial obeisance had taken place in which they alone remained standing. However, the Chaldean informers who "maliciously accused the Jews" (v. 8— the Aramaic phrase could literally be translated "ate pieces of the Jews") were surely not wrong when they said that Shadrach, Meshach, and Abednego refused to acknowledge the validity of the king's order and so did not worship the golden image. Their maliciousness appears not in the truth of what they say but rather in their desire to embarrass and destroy these "foreign" officers who have been placed over them. Their accusation galvanizes Nebuchadnezzar into furious rage, and he takes action. Not only does he examine the three young men (v. 14), but threatens them with the sanction, and in a rather offhand way sets up the climactic clash of the story with his supposedly rhetorical question, "Who is the god that will deliver you out of my hands?" (v. 15).

The following verses (16–18) contain one of the great dramatic scenes of Old Testament literature. Since time immemorial this scene has served as a paradigm for every tiny group of resisters standing before tyrannical authority. In the three Jews standing before Nebuchadnezzar one can see the forebears of Peter and the apostles before the High Priest in council, saying, "We must obey God rather than men" (Acts 5:29); Paul, before Felix and Agrippa (Acts 24—26); and above all, Jesus before Pilate (Matt. 27:11–14). In the calm solidarity of the young men who have an absolutely firm grip upon their identity and who know clearly what they are commanded to do, standing before the towering, wrathful authority, one sees the spiritual ancestry of the Quakers making their hat testimony before the magistrates, or the covenanters refusing to acknowledge any sovereignty but God's. Calvin himself loved the scene: "When, therefore, . . . death was placed straight before their eyes, they did not turn aside from the straightforward course, but treated God's glory of greater value than their own life, nay, than a hundred lives, if they had so many to prove faith . . ." (*Daniel*, I, 219).

From the testimony of these young men, we learn that unswerving faith in God's power to deliver is not really the issue here as it was in chapter 1. If one misreads the first sentence of the young men's answer to the charge brought against them (v. 16) as the supercilious response of persons already clued into God's upcoming act of deliverance, one misses the point. Nor is verse 16 an arrogant answer to the king (in effect, "We do not deign to answer you"). Rather, it is a plea of *nollo contendere* to the charges, a sense well captured by the TEV: "Your majesty, we will not try to defend ourselves."

Although verses 17–18 are difficult to translate, and the

51

RSV solution seems unclear, the general intention seems to be that if God can deliver us, he will; but even if he cannot, we will not worship the gods and the golden image of Babylon. It is interesting to note the degree to which more recent translations have read the straightforward Aramaic text in such a way as to emphasize the uncertainty and ambiguity of the lads' reply. Following the ancient versions, the King James Version obfuscated the answer by translating "If it be so, our God, whom we serve, is able to deliver us . . . but if not. . . ." The Revised Standard Version maintains this translation in the text —never clarifying to what the inserted word "so" is referring —but offers a clearer but theologically more daring alternative in the margin. Today's English Version (like JB and Lacocque) goes all the way with the daring alternative and offers, "If the God whom we serve is able to save us . . . then he will. But even if he doesn't. . . ." (This is exactly what the Aramaic says.) Perhaps this willingness to embrace the terrible possibility of divine inaction or even divine failure reveals the ambiguity of our age which has known absurd, excessive, inexplicable evil and suffering at Auschwitz, at Hiroshima, in Biafra, Cambodia, and elsewhere.

The dominating motivation in the hearts of Shadrach, Meshach, and Abednego is their utter loyalty to the first and second commandments, their utter refusal to participate in idolatry. Now they are not so sure that God can save them from such a hopeless situation, but they know what he demands in any case. They are clear on what they must do, and it is that clarity and not their impending deaths that makes them immortal figures. As Augustine put it, "The martyr is made by his cause, not by his punishment" (cited by Calvin; cf. *Daniel*, I, 224.) In a sense, here is where the plot becomes thickest. In their statement of loyalty even in the worst-case scenario, the martyrs have already defeated the oppressor—now no consideration can shake their resolve.

The realism of this scene exceeds the otherwise naïve optimism of the miracle story, and its application to contemporary discipleship whether Jewish or Christian is obvious. André Lacocque makes this point by the simple expedient of the translation of these verses: "Shadrach, Meshach, and Abednego answered the king in these terms: 'Nebuchadnezzar, we do not need to answer you in this matter. If our God, whom we serve, can deliver us, he will deliver us from the crematory oven and

52

from your hands, O king! If not, be it known unto you, O king, that we do not serve your gods, and we will not worship the gold statue which you have set up' " (*Daniel,* p. 62).

The Punishment, the Song of the Three Young Men, and the Stranger in the Flames (vv. 19–25)

Verses 19–23 prepare for the actual event of the miracle. That the punishment for mutiny of officers against the king's command should be death by burning need come as no surprise. Death by burning was prescribed early on for certain crimes, as we know from Genesis 38:24 and Joshua 7:15, 25 (cf. Lev. 21:9). In his letter to the Judean exiles in Babylon, Jeremiah had already prophesied such a fate at the hands of Nebuchadnezzar for the two false prophets Ahab and Zedekiah, "whom the King of Babylon roasted in the fire" (Jer. 29:22). Contemporaries of Antiochus IV Epiphanes experienced it, too, if the legend in II Maccabees 7 is accurate in reporting the martyrdom of a Torah-true mother and her seven sons by frying in a giant pan. The only surprise in Daniel 3 is the hellish heat of the fire, so hot that the very men who threw the three Jewish lads into it were killed themselves by the flames. (A. Jeffery, "The Book of Daniel," p. 402, points out that "it is characteristic of martyr legends that the tormentors of the righteous suffer the very penalty they proposed for their victims." In Dan. 6:24 the lions eat Daniel's accusers; in Esther 7:10 Haman is hanged on the gallows prepared for Mordechai; in Susanna 62 the wicked elders are put to death as they had planned to do to Susanna.)

The executioners' deaths were meaningless ones. But the deaths of Shadrach, Meshach, and Abednego would have been meaningful, for they would have been deaths consequent upon a stand on principle. In a sense, for those who have subsequently died in faith and for their faith, whether in the Roman persecutions of the early Christians or in the Inquisition or at Auschwitz, at least this possibility is open, that death is meaningful. To be cast to no purpose into a holocaust or to be carried off in the process of perpetrating a holocaust are both events essentially absurd in their character. It is only when death is made meaningful by the great refusal which has led up to it, the unwillingness to violate conviction or divine command, the unwillingness to be perjured or pre-empted, that death becomes meaningful. As they plunged into the furnace the three young

53

men had at least this satisfaction: their deaths subverted the power of the authorities to crush integrity and to silence truth.

Between verses 23 and 24 of chapter 3, the Greek version of Daniel contains two lengthy psalms that are known as the "Prayer of Azariah" (Azariah = Abednego) and "The Song of the Three Young Men." We can now be confident that these materials were never present in the Aramaic text from which the Greek translators worked because they are missing in the most ancient examples of the former, the Qumran Daniel text 1QD^b. Nevertheless, these two psalms have played an important part in Christian theological and liturgical tradition. The first opens with a standard Jewish benediction, "Blessed art thou, O Lord, God of our fathers, and worthy of praise; and thy name is glorified forever. For thou art just in all that thou hast done to us, and all thy works are true and all thy ways right, and all thy judgments are truth." It then proceeds in the form of a collective psalm of lament, in which the right of God to punish his people is acknowledged, the present unhappy state of Israel is declared ("at this time there is no prince, or prophet, or leader, no burnt offering, or sacrifice, or oblation, or incense, no place to make an offering before thee or to find mercy") and an appeal for deliverance is issued. The prayer closes with the call for a theodicy: "Let them know that thou art the Lord, the only God, glorious over the whole world." Following this prayer, the miracle takes place, and the angel of the Lord comes into the furnace to be with Azariah and his companions. It is recounted that he "drove the fiery flame out of the furnace, and made the midst of the furnace like a moist, whistling wind, so that the fire did not touch them at all, or hurt or trouble them." In the aftermath of this miracle, the three young men sing a psalm that is known in Anglican and Roman Catholic liturgical tradition as *Benedictus es Domine,* a psalm very much in the form of the four hymns which close our canonical Psalter, Psalms 147—150. (Actually, this prayer is divided into two parts, that portion just mentioned, which blesses God directly, and the longer portion, known as *Benedicite, omnia opera Domini,* in which all creatures are exhorted to bless Yahweh. In the *Book of Common Prayer,* the two portions of the Song of the Three Young Men are two alternatives to the *Te Deum Laudamus;* one of these three canticles is sung during any morning prayer.) After a lengthy benediction of Yahweh, the song exhorts all creatures and all the aspects of creation to bless the Lord, culminating

54

with the self-address: "Bless the Lord, Hananiah, Azariah, and Mishael, sing praise to him and highly exalt him forever, for he has rescued us from Hades and saved us from the hand of death, and delivered us from the midst of the burning fiery furnace; from the midst of the fire he has delivered us." Although it is only in this addition to Daniel that the identification of the fiery furnace with Hades is made, that identification becomes a standard part of Jewish and Christian interpretation of this text and is an assumption in the artistic representation of this story throughout the ages.

The Song of the Three Young Men assumes that the fourth person in the fiery furnace is an angel sent from the Lord. That same assumption apparently is made by Nebuchadnezzar himself (as v. 28 suggests). Its correctness is reinforced for the reader of the Book of Daniel by the ministering presence of an angel with Daniel in the lions' den (6:22). However, verses 23–25 themselves give us no clue as to who this mysterious person "like a son of the gods" is. Lacocque, who emphasizes the angelology of the Book of Daniel, sees this figure as a heavenly person (*Daniel,* p. 66). It is God with his children as he was in the burning bush (Exod. 3:4). The term "one like a son of the gods" is reminiscent of the language of the prologue of the Book of Job, where before the trial of Job begins, we hear of an assembly of "the sons of God" (Job 1:6; 2:1) who are obviously angelic figures. At the same time, Lacocque stresses that the distinction between angels and human beings is generally not a very sharp one in the Book of Daniel. For example, although Daniel himself is a "son of man" (8:17), and the people of the saints as a whole are "like a son of man" (7:13), angels also "look like men" (8:15; 10:5; 12:5). Is the converse also true in Daniel, that a human being could be called "one like a son of the gods"? After all, Nebuchadnezzar looks at Daniel as one "in whom is the spirit of the holy gods" (4:8). Is it possible that the fourth figure is Daniel, or a kind of heavenly counterpart of Daniel?

No definitive answer can be given. The only certainty is that the figure is a miraculous God-given presence, whether it be an angel or the divine *persona* himself, or perhaps Daniel in a kind of ideal form. The history of Christian treatment of this passage has, of course, been animated by the conviction that the figure is that of Jesus Christ; some have even listed Nebuchadnezzar among the witnesses to the Incarnation. No longer do many of us imagine that such an idea was present in the

55

mind of the writer of Daniel 3, for surely had the intention been to give a preview of the coming Messiah, the writer of the chapter would have told us. In one sense, however, the figure can serve as a kind of functional prototype of the coming savior, for whoever he may be, he is present as Immanuel. In him God is with his people in the time of their deepest need and effects salvation for them from the direst threat to their existence. In that functional sense, then, a typological analogy between this mysterious fourth figure and the incarnate Lord of New Testament faith does not seem illegitimate!

The Miracle and the Royal Testimony (vv. 26–30)

The preceding discussion anticipates the claim made by generations of preachers and artists, the actual miracle account itself (vv. 26–30). They traditionally understood the emergence of the young men from the fiery furnace as a paradigm of the resurrection of Jesus Christ from the grave. If by paradigm one means some kind of secret message about that coming event intrinsic to the text which can be made available by the use of allegory, we shall perforce have to part company with them. However, the reappearance of the three young men from the vale of death once again does provide quite an adequate functional analogue to the experience of Jesus and of those who were witnesses to his resurrection on the third day. If, however, we can understand the resurrection of Jesus as the anti-type of this prototype, then we must recognize that the anti-type or counterpart exceeds the prototype. Unlike the three young men, Jesus was dead, buried, and—as the creed understands it —descended into Hades. The three young men, while experiencing fire like hell, never died and thus never achieved the full experience of human suffering and tragedy which would have identified them with the human tragedy in its ultimate forms of death and destruction.

At the conclusion of this panel Nebuchadnezzar straightforwardly and instantly leaps to an acknowledgment of God's power. The God of the Jews can *deliver;* this thematic word resonates to its first use in the king's sarcastic question (v. 15), and to the tentative but faithful use of it in the testimony of the Jews (v. 17). It will resonate again in Daniel's own trial by lions in chapter 6 and finally at the moment of universal divine deliverance (12:1). His use of the epithet "Most High God" (v. 26) is not necessarily a statement of faith, but rather is a respectful

56

acknowledgment known in extra-biblical literature and even in the mouths of pagan seers: Melchizedek (Gen. 14:18–20) and Balaam (Num. 24:16), of a demon-possessed person (Mark 5:7), and a pagan slave girl (Acts 16:17). In his benediction (v. 28), however, the king assumes that the virtue in the piece is God's and he responds to that virtue in a way which, while a bit bellicose to our taste (his threat to anyone who speaks against the God of Shadrach, Meshach, and Abednego with being "torn limb from limb, and their houses laid in ruins" [v. 29], tends toward overkill!) is nonetheless thoroughly sincere. He does not identify the God of the Jews as his god, but at least he acknowledges God's reality and undoubtedly in so doing declares Judaism a legal religion to be tolerated in his realm. What more could Jews have asked from Nebuchadnezzar or—above all— Antiochus IV Epiphanes (cf. I Macc. 1:41–50)?

A THEOLOGICAL ASSESSMENT OF DANIEL 3

King Nebuchadnezzar himself assesses the work of God in this story (v. 28): "Blessed be the God of Shadrach, Meshach, and Abednego, who has sent his angel and delivered his servants." It is the work of God which leads Nebuchadnezzar in the subsequent verses to acknowledge the transcendent power and dominion of the God of Israel. But what about the work of God's servants, the "interim ethics" which they practiced? The work of God is not connected by any subordinating conjunction to the activity of the three young men. God did not act because of their trust. Rather the work which the three young men did is merely the predicate which describes them more fully. They are the servants, "who trusted in him, and set at nought the king's command, and yielded up their bodies rather than serve and worship any god except their own God" (v. 28). This threefold assessment by Nebuchadnezzar of the discipline of these three young men refers to the events earlier in the story. They trusted in God even though they had to hope against hope that God would deliver them (v. 17). They set at nought the king's command in their categorical refusal to serve the golden image or the gods of Nebuchadnezzar (v. 18). They yielded up their bodies rather than worship any other god (v. 21).

We can understand and honor the work of the three young men. But what about God's work of deliverance? Is this story too facile in its optimistic expectation that God will deliver the saints from the furnace? Is the victorious outcome too predeter-

57

mined to seem credible to a generation which has known the failure of both God and humankind to deliver the saints from the ovens of the crematoria? The answer to both of these questions surely must be No, for the stand of the three young men on principle was taken without hope of deliverance but for the sake of fidelity to the will of God as they understood it. That is why verses 16–18 are such a crucial element in this passage. Furthermore, the deliverance which God effects for these saints is not presented as a direct reward for their faithfulness; rather, as Nebuchadnezzar puts it so carefully (v. 28), it is an act of faithfulness on God's part which is parallel to but not triggered by the faithfulness on the part of the three young men. From the human point of view, therefore, this chapter is a story about faithfulness carried out for its own sake, about martyrdom by those willing to make sacrifice for principle, confident that in some way this sacrifice will be vindicated, even though how that way might come to pass is left entirely in God's hands. From the side of God's nature, this story tells about a God who has, in fact, that which Nebuchadnezzar doubts (v. 15), namely, the ability to deliver the servants from the fire in Babylon. We cannot insist that the deliverance come precisely in this miraculous and happy manner, but neither did the three young men (though the prophets and singers who went before had spoken of the deliverance of God's people from the fire; cf. Isa. 43:2; Ps. 66:12). Nevertheless, the faith that God can deliver and can be trusted and will be vindicated is a faith which is appropriate for living in between the times; and if, in the terrible circumstances in which we now live, threatened with extinction not at God's hands but our own, we have yet to wait a while to see the full vindication of God's power to deliver his world from the hands of demonic forces that dwell within the collective human heart, then wait we shall. This story encourages us to be about our tasks of faithfulness and our great refusals, so that we do as little as possible to participate in the destructive tendency of human against human and so that we do as much as we can to demonstrate that those who are clear about their own identity as disciples can stand up against the glowering powers which require our allegiance to false and demonic claims. In the end, God's way will be vindicated—that is the faith of this chapter. Indeed, it is the faith of the Book of Daniel, for, as Austin Farrer puts it, "the ultimate vindication and enthronement of the Saints over the whole world [cf. Dan. 7:27] is prefigured in the

58

miraculous deliverance of the three children from the furnace, in the king's recognition of their God, and in his promotion of them over the affairs of Babylon (*A Study in Saint Mark*, p. 253; cited by Ford, *Daniel*, p. 210)." And though we may go to the wall before the firing squad or into the heart of a fire storm, we can make such events meaningful, not absurd, by facing them squarely and denying on principle the right of the powers of this world to deflect us from the ways of justice and peace.

Daniel 4
The King Goes Mad and Then Recovers

The Court Tale of Contest

The story told in Daniel 4 does not recount a conflict between the king and his Jewish subjects, as chapter 3 did, but begins—like chapters 2 and 5—with a contest between rival courtiers; it is, nevertheless, a court tale. The setting is the court in Babylon, the two characters are Nebuchadnezzar and his chief magician, Daniel, and the issue is dream interpretation. Obviously, the formal affinities of this story with the dream interpretation account of chapter 2 are many, yet here no one's head is at stake. Daniel's role is well established; the king has no doubt that he can give a correct interpretation of the dream. When thoughts of dismay and alarm momentarily cross Daniel's mind (v. 19), because he can see that he will have to play the dangerous role of the bearer of bad news, the king reassures him. The real focus and center of this story is Nebuchadnezzar himself; here even Daniel lacks personality and character and functions merely as a conduit for the message of the Most High. In this sense, it can be said that the real protagonists of this narrative are two sovereigns, one in heaven and one in Babylon.

Once this fact is clear, it becomes possible to offer an initial assessment of the subject of this panel of Daniel 1—6. Chapter 4 is a story about two sovereignties. It comes to juxtapose the strength or power of the greatest of all human sovereigns (making the Aramaic term *t-q-f*, "grow strong, mighty," a kind of pivot—cf. vv. 11, 20, 22, 30 as applied to Nebuchadnezzar, and v. 3 as applied to the Most High God) with the strength and power of the Most High. Needless to say, the human sovereignty comes off second best in this comparison. In fact, as the refrain of verses 17, 25, and 32 drives home, the human rule proves to be utterly derivative, utterly contingent, and totally dependent upon the divine will: "the Most High rules the kingdom of men, and gives it to whom he will. . . ." The punch line of the story has to be Nebuchadnezzar's own acknowledgment of this truth, expressed at the end of his hymn of praise (vs. 34–35):

> ". . . none can stay his hand
> or say to him, 'What doest thou?' "

A close reading will add further nuances to this initial assessment of the subject of this story. Let us begin that task by tracing the course of the development of this theme in more detail. The account quite naturally falls into five parts: the prefatory hymn of praise (vv. 1–3); Nebuchadnezzar's dream report to Daniel (a first-person account) (vv. 4–18); Daniel's interpretation of the dream (a third person account) (vv. 19–27); the fulfillment of the dream (third person) (vv. 28–33); the king's restoration and concluding hymn of praise (first person) (vv. 34–37). The shifting point of view represented by the change of narrator surely has to do with the history of transmission of this story. Some traditions had Nebuchadnezzar tell the tale, while others—perhaps because they found it narratively unconvincing to report a direct account by a foreign king in a Jewish text—elected to tell *about* the king's experience. The shift might also reflect uncertainties regarding the genre of the story, which presents itself at the outset as an "encyclical epistle" (Montgomery), though in a very informal style (compare the more formal Ezra 1:1–4), but settles eventually into a simple court tale.

The prefatory hymn of praise (vv. 1–3), seems to fit rather unsteadily in the story. It feels out of place; it is in many ways a doublet of the king's hymn (vv. 34–35), and the tradition is unsure even with which chapter it belongs. (LXX-Dan moved it to the end of chapter 4, and placed it alongside vv. 34–35; Theod-Dan reinstated it to its position in the Aramaic text.) Is it an insertion by another hand, then? Perhaps so. Shall we cut it out and set it aside, then? Certainly not. Surely the writer of Daniel 1—6 intends to teach something very important by placing a paean of praise in the mouth of a foreign pagan king. Something of this significance has already been discussed in

60

connection with similar hymns in two of the previous panels of this book, that is, in connection with 2:47 and 3:28–29. The proposal here is that these little benedictions uttered by foreign kings can best be understood when taken together as a group: Daniel's prayer (2:20–23); Nebuchadnezzar's prayers (2:47; 3:28–29; 4:1–3, 34–35); and the prayer of King Darius (6:25–27). When one looks at these texts all together one is struck that the great hymnic tradition of Israel, particularly as it is expressed in the so-called wisdom psalms such as Psalms 1 and 112, has been placed in the mouths of non-traditional speakers. (In the case of Daniel 2:20–33, the prayer is uttered in the hope that a foreign king might experience God's power.)

> The prayers focus the point of the narratives roughly as follows: God's decision to allow evil its hour of ascendancy will be vindicated before the eyes of all the nations when good ultimately triumphs; this vindication will come about because of God's own transcendent power and endurance; to this fact the evil powers of the world will themselves be obliged at last to testify (Towner, "The Poetic Passages of Daniel 1—6," pp. 322–23).

Far from being additions to the text which deserve to be excised, these little prayers would appear therefore to contribute an important component to the theological direction of the texts. They show in a way perhaps more convincing than any other the power of Yahweh to vindicate his way with suffering and evil in the world and to demonstrate his hegemony over even the most powerful forces of humankind.

The similarity of the initial impact of his dream upon Nebuchadnezzar to the account in 2:1–2 has already been noted. In the dream report section of chapter 4 (vv. 4–18), however, the failure of the indigenous magicians, enchanters, Chaldeans, and astrologers to give the king a satisfactory interpretation is not at issue, nor is the success of Daniel/Belteshazzar. King and reader alike expect Daniel to be able to solve the problem; not only is he now the "chief of the magicians" (v. 9), but he also is recognized three times by the king as the one "in whom is the spirit of the holy gods" (vv. 8, 9, 18). Indeed, the wonder is that the king did not save himself time and anxiety by bringing such a staff member into the scene right from the beginning!

This strong, tall tree which the king saw in his dream was like the national tree of Israel in Ezekiel's parable (Ezek. 17: 22–24), or even the cedar of Eden to which Ezekiel compared Pharaoh in 31:1–9. Like these trees of folk-lore and legend (see

61

Eliade, *Patterns in Comparative Religion,* pp. 265–326), this tree provides food for all flesh, as well as shelter for birds and beasts (v. 12). It is a world tree, rooted in the center and visible all over the earth; in the Greek version, it becomes cosmic, for even the sun and moon dwell in its branches! But this marvelous, beneficent tree is not to survive. In the dream vision, "a watcher, a holy one, came down from heaven" to order the tree cut down and to scatter its fruit. In verse 16, the imagery shifts; the fallen victim is a man now, a man whose mind has become that of a beast, and who must remain that way until "seven times" (LXX: "seven years") pass over him (v. 17). And a reason is given for this tragic fall and this unusual punishment: "to the end that the living may know that the Most High rules the kingdom of men, and gives it to whom he will, and sets over it the lowliest of men" (v. 17—a similar lesson is drawn in Ezekiel's parable of the cedar, 17:24; cf. 31:14).

Mysteries abound! How can a tree have the mind of a man, only to find it transmuted into the non-mind of a beast? Furthermore, who is this watcher, this holy one? In the entire Old Testament, the term *watcher* is used only in these verses, though the word is used frequently in the pseudepigraphical books of Enoch, Jubilees, and the Testament of the Twelve Patriarchs as a euphemism for an angel. So it must be here, for not only is the watcher "a holy one," a term used in Daniel 8:13; Zechariah 14:5; Job 5:1; 15:15 for an angel, but it must participate in the heavenly council (cf. Ps. 89:6–7) because the word which it brings is revelatory of the intention of the Most High (v. 17). Montgomery points out that the Talmudic sages used this verse to support their notion that God is surrounded by a supportive, heavenly family (*Daniel,* p. 236): "the Holy One does nothing without first consulting the family above, as it is said (Dan. 4:17, English): 'by the decree of the watchers,' etc." (Babylonian Talmud, Tractate Sanhedrin 38*b*).

Daniel is the man of the hour because no mystery *(raz)* is too difficult for him (v. 9). As we saw in connection with Daniel 2:18, a mystery of this sort is one which has been created and therefore can only be solved by God. However, he does use human intermediaries to do so, those in whom God's spirit does in fact dwell, those to whom he chooses to give the power of interpretation. Perhaps such persons enjoy a peculiarly close relationship with the heavenly court, almost to the point of participation in it. Such seems to be the case with Daniel, who, though a man, a Jewish exile, knows what the "watchers" mean when they speak.

In verses 19–27, Daniel tells the king what the mystery of the watcher means. As the reader suspected all along, the tree-man is Nebuchadnezzar himself, already tall and strong (v. 22). But the time of reckoning is coming; God (not the watcher) has decreed that this great king is to be cut down to size, until he comes to "know that the Most High rules the kingdom of men, and gives it to whom he will" (v. 25). Although the bound-up stump promises ultimate restoration, only a faint glimmer of hope of total escape from this humiliation and reduction to a bestial state is offered. The king may gain some time of tranquility if he breaks off his sins by practicing righteousness, and his iniquities by showing mercy to the oppressed (v. 27).

This judgment seems unfair in the context of the story. Far from a stand-in for the hated Antiochus, Nebuchadnezzar has played the part of a good guy in this chapter. We have not been told about his unrighteousness, or his oppressive injustice. In fact, he has spoken with tender sensitivity to his Jewish slave and courtier. Nor has he set himself up in pride against the Most High. The dreamer does not challenge the right of the Most High to be kingmaker; in fact, he began his entire narrative with a psalm of praise to the God of Daniel. Questions press in on us. How can the king learn of God's power anyway if his mind is gone and he is like an animal? If he has to learn a lesson about God's sovereignty, surely he has to learn it in the mode and depth appropriate to a human experience. And finally, is not the antidote which Daniel rather gratuitously offers nothing but an invitation to a piety which would appease God and head off disaster through good works? Traditional Protestant commentators often have struggled with this point in verse 27, especially when it was recognized that the word "righteousness" may already have come to mean simply "almsgiving" (cf. Ps. 37:21; Tobit 12:9; and especially Ecclus. 3:29—4:10). But more recent writers, like Montgomery and Porteous, have made the simple point, "So what is wrong with good works?" Indeed, earlier writers made the point as well (see Matt. 6:1–4 and Acts 9:36)!

No character in the tale addresses any of these questions. In the spare style of late Old Testament narrative, the story simply moves on. Not unexpectedly, as verses 28–33 disclose, the dream is fulfilled. Nebuchadnezzar slips up, finally utters a

63

rather mild boast about his "mighty power" and "the glory of [his] majesty" (v. 30) which could be understood as an arrogant assertion of his sovereignty, and a heavenly voice immediately pronounces and implements the sentence. The king suffers the fate which humans fear the most, exclusion from the human family, abandonment, alienation, and becomes a veritable were-wolf, long-haired and with talons, but herbivorous like an ox.

Verses 34–37 report the restoration of the king "at the end of days." The phrase has no eschatological content, but simply indicates the passage of a previously determined period of time, in this instance, the "seven times" of verses 16 and 25. One cannot determine whether Nebuchadnezzar's gesture of submission and worship toward heaven, the lifting of his eyes, triggers the restoration of his reason, or whether the entire sequence is simply running along its predetermined course. The former seems more likely in the light of the reason given for the entire traumatic event, that God wishes to teach the sovereign who is sovereign. At the sign that the lesson has been learned, the pressure is relaxed, and Nebuchadnezzar is able not only to acknowledge the universal and absolute sovereignty of the Most High God, but, in verse 37, to repeat with great accuracy the lesson that has been learned: in every respect God is right and just, and "those who walk in pride" (presumably pitting their power against his) are without a doubt going to experience the exertion of his hegemony over theirs. Lacocque rightly calls attention to the most famous slogan of the Old Testament wisdom tradition at this moment of conjunction of faith and reason: "The fear of the Lord is the beginning of wisdom" (Prov. 1:7; Job 28:8; Ps. 111:10). With his gesture of repentance or obeisance, and his two paeans of praise of God, the king—in a transaction reminiscent of Job 42—recovers his reason (even though he had already recovered it enough in v. 34 to take the steps necessary for his restoration), his majesty and splendor return to him, his abandonment and rejection are overcome by the return of his court, and he ends up with a net gain over his earlier position.

Has this story line demonstrated the point which animates the narrative, namely, that "the Most High rules the kingdom of men, and gives it to whom he will" (vv. 17, 25)? Certainly the first clause is richly illustrated by the events of chapter 4. In the persons of the watchers and Daniel, God has servants who can give prior warning of his intentions; furthermore, with perfect effortlessness as well as with perfect justification, he can break the most powerful monarch on earth in the twinkling of an eye, with the word of the heavenly voice, and make him grovel on all fours until he releases him again. Truly, no human power can even approach the power of the "king of heaven." The king or commoner who thinks to become superman becomes instead a beast—Lacocque sees in this the Genesis creation story run backward (*Daniel,* p. 80)! The theme of God's absolute sovereignty will be taken up again in chapter 5, where Nebuchadnezzar's success at learning the truth about this matter will be contrasted to the failure of his "son," Belshazzar, to acknowledge God's superior right. Indeed, the theme is a scarlet thread which runs through all of the stories of Daniel 1—6 and ties them with the same theme which is put forward in the strongest possible form in the apocalyptic narratives of Daniel 7—12.

For the second claim, that God can give the kingdom "to whom he will," the support of the story is more ambiguous. Nebuchadnezzar is king in the human world at the beginning and at the end. Evidently God willed that Nebuchadnezzar be king and wished only to give him a good lesson about the derivative and contingent nature of human kingship. In the full context of the canon such a positive evaluation of Babylonian monarchy is hardly to be found elsewhere, even though the prophetic writers can speak of Assyria as the rod of God's anger against Jerusalem (Isa. 10:5), of the Medes as God's instruments against Babylon (Isa. 13:5), and of Cyrus, as God's anointed (Isa. 45:1). All the nations are of course held to be subject to Yahweh's punitive judgment, but here Nebuchadnezzar is presented as sovereign by divine right and decree as long as he acknowledges his subjection to the King of heaven.

The most likely rejoinder to this line of thinking seems to be that Nebuchadnezzar is being treated here not as a representative of Babylon or foreign powers generally but as an individual, a type specimen of a human being of power and influence. It is not the case that a judgment is being made about the acceptability of the Babylonian dynasty to the God of Israel, nor is a kind of covenant relationship being proposed which would assure the continuance of that line, analogous to the covenant ideology which runs through the history of the Davidic monarchy in the deuteronomic corpus. All that is being

65

said here is this: Any human power or glory wherever it may be does not exist outside the sphere of Yahweh's authority. A wise ruler or mover or shaker will acknowledge that superior authority and seek to conform his or her own exercise of power to the just demands of God. It is a lesson which, according to the prophets, other kings failed to learn, to their great dismay: the king of Assyria (Isa. 10:12–19), the king of Babylon (Isa. 14: 12–20), the king of Tyre (Ezek. 28:1–10).

Yet one more thing must be said about the claim that God gives the "kingdom of men" to whom he wills. The first time this refrain is used (v. 17), an additional clause is added: "and sets over it the lowliest of men." Now that makes it even more difficult to understand how the story illustrates the point! Nebuchadnezzar can hardly be called the lowliest of men, either before or after his seven times of trial, although during the actual period of the fulfillment of his nightmare he was so lowly that he ate grass like an ox and went around without any glint of rationality in his eyes. Is this temporary lowliness enough to illustrate the point and drive it home? Perhaps so—in the storyteller's art a mere foretaste of what might take place is often adequate to effect great changes in the protagonist. Think of Scrooge after the night spent with the three Christmas ghosts! But perhaps the narrator is looking beyond Nebuchadnezzar here, toward the people of his own day. Perhaps the address is directed to that later audience, those truly lowly and oppressed saints who will be addressed again with words glowing with promises of power and future sovereignty in the apocalyptic scenario of chapter 7: "but the saints of the Most High shall receive the kingdom, and possess the kingdom for ever, for ever and ever" (v. 18). Perhaps the writer is offering something more like a claim of abiding truth, illustrated momentarily in the case of Nebuchadnezzar's madness, but yet to be illustrated most grandly in the coming age in the exaltation of the lowly saints to a position of universal hegemony under the aegis of the Most High: God's choices are surprising; God exalts those of low degree and places them over the whole kingdom of humankind. It is a truth affirmed long before by the scorned woman Hannah as she stood before Eli in Shiloh (I Sam. 2:2–8). In the full context of the Christian canon it is a point reaffirmed in a most eloquent way by the lowliest and most unlikely of persons, a pregnant peasant girl. Standing in a dusty place beside her kinswoman Elizabeth, a newly disclosed destiny fraught with terrors and wonders lying ahead of her, she announces as an abiding religious truth the principle that Nebuchadnezzar once learned:

> He has shown strength with his arm,
> he has scattered the proud in the imagination of their hearts,
> he has put down the mighty from their thrones,
> and exalted those of low degree;
> he has filled the hungry with good things,
> and the rich he has sent empty away (Luke 1:51–53).

A THEOLOGICAL ASSESSMENT OF DANIEL 4

To some persons, God's absolute sovereignty can appear to be a threat. These are the persons who possess power in the human domain and who cherish it as a thing to be used autonomously and in the interest of the self. To be told that no human sovereignty is autonomous, that it is always subject and accountable to a greater power, is not, for such persons (perhaps we should admit, for any persons of affluence and standing in the human community) welcome news.

To other persons, God's absolute sovereignty appears to be a promise. To Jews languishing in Babylonian exile it is a long-term basis for hope. To *hasidim* trying to keep the faith in an era of Torah-burning and child murder, it warrants confidence in the coming of an age in which the world will be turned upside down and the just and the righteous will at last bear rule in the world on behalf of their sovereign Lord, the Just One. To Mary it means the fulfillment of the long-awaited hope of the coming of the Messiah, even through the lowly medium of her peasant body. To Jesus it means trust that his ministry of healing and peacemaking would be vindicated against the exertion of the double sovereignties of Caiaphas and Pilate. To obedient and loyal persons in every generation it is a promise that though the arc of justice bends slowly it bends down at last, and that the stake and the gas chamber, obloquy and redundancy are not the last words.

A fortunate few can possess the worldly crown and yet maintain a prior and more basic allegiance to the King of Heaven. Daniel 4 tells about one who comes to that fortunate knowledge, and there have been others—David, Josiah, Charlemagne in his way and time, Catherine the Great in hers, Elizabeth I, King Christian IV, Cromwell, William Bradford, Lincoln. Scandalous to mention such names in one breath, is it not, even if they are in the same series that begins with Nebu-

chadnezzar! Yet if the canon intends to present Nebuchadnezzar in some way as a type, a shining example of one who learned
to subordinate his fading and derivative sovereignty to the King
of Kings and thus was at last able to exercise power and exhibit
glory in a way that played an appropriate role within the divine
economy, then we ought to expect to be able to see some answering lights, or at least flickers, all down the way.

When we take a parting look at the theological significance
of this subtle, unheralded chapter of Daniel, we are amazed. To
a beleaguered and oppressed community of the age of Antiochus IV Epiphanes, victims of one of the truly sick sovereignties
of the world, the writer offers as the basis of hope and even as
an interim ethic these convictions: God is the overlord of kings,
he will bring those who wager their sovereignty against his to
their knees, and he can and will do this in such a way that good
sovereigns will emerge. It is not power that is bad—you will
have it, too. Glory is not bad, either. There is a place for it
among people, even among the lowliest of people. Think of
that! Think how that sounded to people who reeled before the
royal might and had no glory of their own! But power and glory
have their legitimate place only within the framework of righteousness and justice which God has established and of which
he is the head and chief cornerstone.

Daniel 5
God's Graffiti

The Court Tale of Contest

An initial reading of the subject of Daniel 5 reveals it to be
another tale illustrative of the sovereign power of the God of
Israel, even outside the land of Israel. In theological content it
thus resembles chapter 4 in many ways, though the role of the
prophet as a mediator of God's indictment and judgment is
greatly heightened in this narrative. The narrative itself is also
reminiscent of chapter 2, for it makes Daniel the man of the
hour, the only person in the kingdom able to "interpret dreams,
explain riddles, and solve problems . . ." (v. 12).

The genre of the story must once again be termed a "court
tale of contest" (Humphreys, "Life-Style," p. 220). Like chapter

2, and to a very minor degree, chapter 4 (cf. 4:7), Daniel's skill as one who can solve a mystery *(raz)* or give an interpretation *(pesher)* of a conundrum is pitted against the magic of the court. Once again the regular staff prove hopelessly incompetent. In chapter 2 they could not tell the king his dream; and here they cannot even read the writing on the wall, much less interpret it! One wonders why the royal family of Babylon simply did not get rid of the lot of them and rely exclusively upon the wisdom of the seers of the Jewish diaspora. Ah well, perhaps the indigenous enchanters had job security arrangements, tenure or the like! This designation of a genre is, perhaps, not very significant for the theological appropriation of the passage, but it can help provide a nuance. In chapter 2, outwardly the contest was between Daniel and the other courtier-sages; inwardly it was between the respective sources of power to interpret events. Daniel's opponents despair of telling the king his dream, saying ". . . none can show it to the king except the gods, whose dwelling is not with flesh" (2:11). In contrast, Daniel receives the meaning of the king's dream directly from the King of Heaven "in a vision of the night" (2:19). Similarly, in chapter 5, the contest between Daniel and the courtiers is a non-contest, because all the power to give an interpretation is derived from God alone. Here Daniel does not identify the source of his interpretative power, but the king does, using the language of chapter 4, "the spirit of the holy gods is in you" (v. 14). In short, the contest is between the figments of the vain and foolish imaginations of human imposters on the one side, and, on the other, the one true source of knowledge, the Most High God. Surely in that refinement of the genre designation "court tale of contest" there is theological significance!

The cast of characters in this story includes, in order of appearance, King Belshazzar, presented as the "son" of the Nebuchadnezzar who has been the protagonist in all of the narratives of Daniel up to this point; a large crowd of banqueters, including one thousand lords, numerous wives and concubines of the king (their exact relationship to him and relative standing in the harem is difficult to determine due to the obscurity of the Aramaic terms employed), plus the usual bumbling staff of enchanters, Chaldeans, and astrologers; and the queen (vv. 10–12). The commentators universally take the latter to be the queen-mother because (a) she talks to Belshazzar about "your father"; (b) she has intimate knowledge of events of the

69

previous generation; (c) Herodotus (i 185–88) tells us the story of the wise and powerful queen named Nitocris, who fortified Babylon with a canal system (he thinks she was the *wife* of Nebuchadnezzar and the *mother* of Nabonidus); (d) the term *malketa* given as her title (v. 10) differs from the term used for Belshazzar's wives (v. 2) and perhaps is intended to suggest an analogy to the queen-mothers whom we know elsewhere in Scripture (cf. I Kings 15:13; II Kings 10:13; 24:12); (e) unlike Esther, who dared not enter the presence of her husband, Ahasuerus, king of Persia and Media, even though she was his favorite wife (Esther 4:11), this queen bursts right in on the revelry in the "banqueting hall" (Aramaic: "house of drinking"). Finally, there is Daniel, who is by now presumably nearing the end of his ministry-in-exile at about the age of seventy-five.

The place is the royal court in Babylon on the eve of its seizure and destruction by the "Medes" and Persians (i.e., October 11, 539 B.C. [Lacocque]). All of this seems precise and history-like, but it proves to be the stuff of brilliant, colorful storytelling more than the date of actual history for the simple reason that Nebuchadnezzar had no son named Belshazzar and his actual successor to the throne was Amel-marduk, the Evilmerodach of II Kings 25:27. Nor was Babylon captured and its king slain by anyone named "Darius the Mede." This person never existed; as the notably cautious and judicious scholar H. H. Rowley put it, "he is a fictitious creation" (*Darius the Mede*, p. 59). In fact, the Median dynasty (which led an obscure existence during the period of the Neo-Babylonian empire) had ceased to exist prior to the fall of Babylon. The conqueror of Babylon and successor to the last of its kings, according to contemporary secular sources and later historians, was Cyrus, king of Persia!

Belshazzar and Darius the Mede

Montgomery, Hartman and Di Lella, and others have assembled the evidences for and against the historical existence of the two kings whose names bracket the account of chapter 5; and readers who wish to pursue that issue in more detail are referred to them. Suffice it here to say that it can now be shown that the last monarch of the neo-Babylonian dynasty, Nabonidus, did in fact have a son named Bel-shar-uṣur, who ruled in Babylon during the king's absences, and who may, therefore, have been in Babylon on the night of October 11, 539 B.C., when Gobryas (Ugbaru), the general and advance man of Cyrus, entered the city. He may even have been killed on that very night.

As to the historicity of Darius the Mede, there is none. However, commentators and historians point out that the reference to the division of the empire into a hundred and twenty satrapies (Dan. 6:1) suggests that the king in mind is Darius I Hystaspes (522–486 B.C.), the second successor to Cyrus as head of the Persian empire. This Darius was noted for his organizational gifts. It seems, therefore, that some authentic historical reminiscences do in fact inform the muddled setting given the story of Daniel 5. The fact remains, however, that no Median empire succeeded Babylon and no Darius "received the kingdom" from Belshazzar.

In our own reflection and exposition of Daniel 5 as a text of sacred Scripture, how shall we handle the fact that a story which has the appearance of history is in fact encased in a fictional setting? The discovery should come as no surprise, for after all the story itself contains the fabulous account of a disembodied hand writing on the wall—an element which clearly belongs to the literary realm of folklore, not history. In fact, this discovery is a liberating one, for it frees us from undue concern with historical detail or miracle story to ask after the kerygmatic thrust of the account as it now appears in its canonical setting. That the story has authentic memories of the eastern Jewish diaspora can gladly be acknowledged; it may even have originated in the Persian period, prior to 331 B.C. Yet now it is one of a block of six tales which have been attached to an apocalypse clearly addressing events of the reign of Antiochus IV Epiphanes, 175–163 B.C. This story in itself contains no veiled allusions to Antiochus. But it is one of several stories which drive home the assurances that no tyranny can forever withstand the power of the true sovereign of the world, that those who make light of the sacred gifts of the Most High will themselves prove to be lightest of all, and that the saints who side with the Sovereign can endure suffering and humiliation for his sake because he is also the winner in the struggle!

The structure of the story may be analyzed as follows: the problem (vv. 1–9); the queen introduces Daniel and the king invites him to solve the problem (vv. 10–16); Daniel indicts the king (vv. 17–23); Daniel interprets God's sentence to the king by solving the riddle on the wall (vv. 24–28); Daniel receives his

71

reward and the king receives his (vv. 29–31). Under these headings we may now proceed to a detailed reading of the text.

The Problem (vs. 1–9)

The scene opens on what evidently is intended to be a
revolting picture. The great king of Babylon, Belshazzar, after
drinking wine "in front of" a thousand of his lords, commands
that the gold and silver vessels which Nebuchadnezzar "his
father" had taken from the temple in Jerusalem (Dan. 1:2; cf.
II Kings 25:13–17) be brought into the banqueting hall. As soon
as this is accomplished, he distributes them to the assembled
multitude and all begin to drink wine and to praise "the gods
of gold and silver, bronze, iron, wood, and stone" (v. 4). The
combination of drinking and praising sounds like a cultic act or
libation. Why did the king elect to toast his gods with the sacred
vessels taken from the temple in Jerusalem? Perhaps it was
merely the wild whim of a mad monarch, comparable to the
surprising behavior reported of Antiochus IV Epiphanes who
"used to drink in the company of the meanest foreign visitors
to Antioch," and once, when bathing in the public bath with the
common people, had a huge jar of precious ointment poured on
his head, "so that all the bathers jumped up and rolled themselves in it, and by slipping in it created great amusement, as
did the king himself" (Polybius xxvi 1). Or was it the naked use
of power for its own sake, a deliberate challenge to the God
whose vessels these were? Is Lacocque correct in saying that
the king "makes" the hand that writes upon the wall, that is, he
allows his dark side to do acts which dare his divine opponent
to unleash swift and certain retribution? If so, why would he do
it? Perhaps Belshazzar sought to unmask the God of Israel as a
phony; or, like the iconoclasts of old, who scratched out the eyes
of religious paintings on the walls of their churches in order
to destroy their sacred power, perhaps he was trying to
bring Yahweh under his control and thus win the battle of
sovereignties.

Whatever the reason, the "gods of gold and silver, bronze,
iron, wood, and stone" remained mute, but the fingers of a
man's hand "immediately ... appeared and wrote on the plaster
of the wall of the king's palace ..." (v. 5). The Aramaic says that
the king saw "the palm of the hand which wrote," suggesting
to some commentators that the hand was disembodied and
consisted only of a wrist, palm, and fingers, and to some that he

was sitting directly beneath the hand and could see its palm by looking straight up! The description of the king's reaction to this sight is a marvelous example of the psychological insight of the biblical writer. His "color changed . . . his thoughts alarmed him; his limbs gave way, and his knees knocked together" (v. 6). One can hardly imagine a more comprehensive description of the physiological manifestations of terror, even though it is hard to know what each of these terms means precisely. The Anchor Bible translates the phrase "the king's color changed" three different ways: his "face blanched" (v. 6), he "turned ashen" (v. 9), and he looked "pale" (v. 10).

Today we might have assumed that the king was hallucinating, especially had he been the only person in the hall who could see the handwriting on the wall. However, verse 8 suggests that when the wise men came to meet the emergency that had arisen, they also could see the writing but could neither read it nor interpret it. We are clear that they tried their best, too, for the king promised to give the winner the purple of royalty, the golden ornament that was in Persian circles a symbol of high status, and the rank of number three ruler in the kingdom.

One of the most marvelous illustrations in Western art of a scene from the Book of Daniel is Rembrandt's 1639 depiction of Belshazzar's feast. This painting, done when Rembrandt was thirty-three years old, shows a splendid feast in which the vessels stolen from the temple in Jerusalem—looking rather more baroque than Persian—are being used. The morbid hand is writing on the wall, and Belshazzar has jumped up from his seat, upsetting a beaker of wine. Terror is written on his face. For our purposes, however, the matter of keenest interest is the solution which Rembrandt offers for the exegetical problem of why no one could read the inscription. The hand has written a cryptogram, with the Aramaic inscribed from top to bottom beginning in the right hand column, rather than from right to left. The notion that the inscription was written in some kind of puzzle form was known already in rabbinic tradition and had been given to Rembrandt by his friend in the Amsterdam Jewish community, Manasseh ben Israel.

The Queen Introduces Daniel (vv. 10–16)

The queen-mother, whose identity was explored in the first section of this panel, has unusual memory and authority. She recites the language of chapter 4 in which Daniel is said to possess the "spirit of the holy gods." Now linked to that attribution are three new elements: light (perhaps better understood illumination or even brilliance), understanding, and wisdom. Furthermore, Daniel has the ability "to interpret dreams, explain riddles, and solve problems"—skills which refer to the training which he enjoyed in the king's palace (1:17), to the record which he established (2:47), and to the reputation which he enjoyed (4:18). Daniel has the ability to give an interpretation which exceeds even the skill of a riddle-solver and dream-interpreter, because it is a skill which can come only from God. The king summons Daniel, politely invites him to make the interpretation, and promises him, one of the exiles from Judah, rewards equal to the ones promised his own wise men: the purple of royalty (which Mordechai, too, received from a Persian king in Esther 8:15) and a gold emblem (certainly comparable to the golden chain which Pharaoh presented to Joseph in Gen. 41:42).

Daniel Indicts the King (vv. 17–23)

Both formally and in terms of the content, Daniel's response to the king's kindly invitation to interpret the meaning of the handwriting on the wall amounts to a prophetic indictment comparable to that of any of the other great prophets of Israel. It is followed (vv. 24–28) by a threat. One is reminded of Jeremiah before Zedekiah (Jer. 38:17–23), or even at a much earlier period, Nathan before David (II Sam. 12:1–15). Daniel begins with a review of the history of his "father" whose sovereignty over the kingdoms of the earth is presented in dramatic terms: "Whom he would he slew, and whom he would he kept alive; whom he would he raised up, and whom he would he put down" (v. 19). Normally, such power is reserved for God alone, but Nebuchadnezzar learned the lesson that his sovereignty, grand as it was and a matter of life and death for many, was nevertheless a derived sovereignty. All of this, says Daniel to Belshazzar, "you knew" (v. 22). But Belshazzar did not act according to his knowledge. In the list of particulars in the indictment which Daniel brings against the king, we find the following elements: he did not humble his heart (v. 22); he lifted himself up against the Lord of heaven (v. 23a); he drank from the sacred vessels while praising the gods of gold and silver, bronze, iron, wood, and stone; and he did not honor God (v. 23b). It is a dramatic and devastating indictment. One is hard pressed to know what the heart and core of it is. Is it the hybris which fails to recognize Yahweh's sovereignty over kings and gods? Is it the stupidity of praying to gods who cannot answer? Or is it the blasphemy of using cultic vessels sacred to the God of Israel? It is difficult to factor out all of these elements, and perhaps they are intended to stand all together under the general over-arching charge of Belshazzar's failure to acknowledge the pre-eminence of "the God in whose hand is your breath, and whose are all your ways, . . ." (v. 23).

Daniel Interprets God's Sentence upon the King by Solving the Riddle on the Wall (vv. 24–28)

Added to the previous prophetic indictment, the threat or the divine sentence comes now. All the verbs are in the perfect tense. What God has decreed and announced through the handwriting on the wall is as good as done.

But what did God decree through the mysterious words, MENE, MENE, TEKEL and PARSIN (v. 25)? Many theories have been advanced to explain the original sense of these mysterious words, all acknowledging that they have been given a secondary meaning in the interpretation which Daniel offers (vv. 26–28). What did the three words mean before they were interpreted in a paranomastic (punning) way by Daniel? Some have actually contended that they meant nothing at all, but since late nineteenth century, a great number of scholars have accepted the theory that the three words are weights of coinage: MENE signifying a mena, TEKEL simply an Aramaic spelling of shekel, and PERES a reference to a half mena. Even though such a series is peculiar in the sense that the ratio between the three coins is something like sixty to one and thirty (the middle term, shekel, being the least valuable of the three or four coins), a great many scholars nonetheless have agreed that this riddle is based upon such a series and that Belshazzar is presented a mysterious inscription which in modern terms might read, "(A half dollar), a half dollar, a penny, and two bits." (Two bits would be more appropriate than "a quarter" since the word *parsin* is apparently a dual form of the word *peres*, "half.")

So Belshazzar saw on the wall a cryptic reference to three or four coins. Even had he understood what the words meant, he could hardly have understood what was going on. After all, what would weights of coinage have had to do with anything significant to an oriental despot?

75

The solution contained in the text is based upon folk etymologies of the three words, each turning on a pun. The three nouns listed in verse 25 are treated as three passive verbs by Daniel in verses 26–28: MENE is related to the verb m-n-h, "numbered"; TEKEL is related to the verb t-q-l, "weighed"; and PERES is construed as the verb p-r-s, "divided." Belshazzar's days are numbered; his rule has been weighed and found wanting and his kingdom will be divided two ways, half to the Medes and half to the Persians (the word *peres*, Persia, is itself another pun on the word p-r-s). The divine decree has been revealed and it is inexorable. The element of numbering, which is an apocalyptic notion, suggests a destiny which cannot be changed. Lacocque very rightly points out that the weighing of the Babylonian kingdom reveals its intrinsic lightness: "The importance of a kingdom is not measured by its size or by the weight of centuries, but by its reason for being. Here is the whole argument of the Book of Daniel: History is the bearer of God's judgment. History is both theophany and verdict" (*Daniel*, p. 105).

Daniel Receives His Reward and the King Receives His (vv. 29–31)

Our panel concludes with the expected denouement. The king follows through with his promise. Daniel receives his reward by becoming the number three man in the kingdom, complete with the insignia of office: purple garments and a golden chain. He has made it as far as a Jew can go in the kingdom of the East and his prosperity will continue through the reign of "Darius the Mede" and into the time of Cyrus, King of Persia (6:28). For his part, the king swiftly receives the retribution that was promised: "That very night, Belshazzar the Chaldean king was slain" (v. 30).

A THEOLOGICAL ASSESSMENT OF DANIEL 5

Our detailed review has confirmed the initial direct reading of the subject of this tale. Like chapter 4, this is indeed a story about the sovereignty of the God of Israel and his power to act even outside the land of Israel. However, in contrast to chapter 4, the role of the prophet is emphasized here. It is through his mediation that God's power to effect his sovereign purposes over the earthly sovereignty of Belshazzar is demonstrated.

The prophet can make an accurate indictment and through the solution of a riddle can forecast the king's sentence.

Still in all, one can surely find a more substantive theological truth claim in this chapter than simply the acknowledgment of human limitations and the observation that "leadership was lacking and a change of government was overdue. There can be little doubt that in this case it was a change for the better" (Baldwin, *Daniel* p. 126). The element of "sacrilegious insolence" (Hartman and Di Lella) adds a special nuance to this story. In chapter 4, Nebuchadnezzar repented of his insolence and pride; in chapter 5 Belshazzar does not. As far as we are told, he persists to the end in believing that the gods of gold and silver, bronze, iron, wood, and stone are somehow efficacious and that the profane and idolatrous use of sacred things is of some significance before them. As far as Belshazzar is concerned, that is where matters are left, relatively speaking; all that remain are his indictment and destruction. One can hardly follow Lacocque in terming Belshazzar's death his liberation, his "ultimate way to self-realization." Nor can one see any evidence that Belshazzar is joyous at being allowed to die and so to move from the ethos of unsatisfying idolatry to the realm of chaste Yahwism. No, Belshazzar's destruction is itself the message. One can perhaps see this as a sermon to a Jewish community which confronts a similarly insolently sacrilegious monarch in the person of Antiochus IV Epiphanes—a sermon which contains within it the glad news that such insolence will ultimately be brought down by the sovereign power of the God of Israel. Note that there is no notion here that insolence brings about its own automatic reward and that inevitably it will be brought down by the weight of its own sinfulness. It is God who destroys Belshazzar, not some automatic principle. Furthermore, he is brought down in a direct encounter with God following his challenge to God in the sacrilegious use of the devoted things. This suggests that God's decree was not written from the beginning of the ages but was rather issued in response to Belshazzar's immediate activity. Things could have gone another way for him, as they did for his "father" Nebuchadnezzar. The determinism of the apocalyptic ideology is not as all-pervasive within the Book of Daniel as might at first appear to be the case.

77

God will not fail to exercise his sovereignty over a sovereign who scoffs at God's power and makes light of the sacred things. God sends his agents to make known the truth of his sovereignty and to reveal the lifeless gods for what they are. This is the faith of the writer. It may be the only hope of those mocked and oppressed by the king. But is it true?

We do not have exact contemporary analogies to the pagan idols, but we certainly make profane use of dedicated things. The arrogance of nuclear warfare, which takes the good and holy material of the God-created world and uses that material to blind every sighted creature through the depletion of the ozone layer; that arrogance which is willing to risk the entire human community for the sake of mere ideology must surely be a contemporary and indeed hugely amplified form of the arrogance of Belshazzar. God's good gifts, our analogies to the dedicated things, are taken to the place of power and used profanely. That we can see, and the inevitable earthly and human result we can identify. But dare we proclaim divine judgment? Can we proclaim it in a way that is appropriate for our time and not simply a direct carry-over from the biblical story? Can we get beyond saying that the arrogant people who play with nuclear things will die? The text invites us to hear and to say, in a manner that is meaningful and credible to the twentieth century, that God will maintain his sovereignty over all human sovereignties and will effect the redemption of this world, preserve its beauty and goodness, release it from its bondage to sin and decay and death in spite of the arrogant users of power who revel in their debauchery and challenge God to do his worst.

Daniel 6
Man of God Against Lions

The Court Tale of Conflict

It requires no very elaborate reading to discern the subject of Daniel 6. It is a story of conflict between the exemplary and successful Jewish courtier to the Persian king Darius, Daniel, and his detractors and rivals in the court. By further extension, it is a story of a contest between immutable laws: "the law of the Medes and the Persians, which cannot be revoked" (v. 8), and the law of Daniel's God. God wins in the struggle by stopping the mouths of the lions, to whom Daniel had been thrown

78

as food for them and punishment for him, and so vindicates both himself, his law, and his servant. It is a story that could have been told in any age, but here it is placed at the culmination of Daniel's ministry in Babylon/Persia. Its location in this canonical environment, as a final example of God's wondrous working through his chosen servants against insuperable odds and as a preface to an account of God's coming great and final victory against all of his foes, even death itself, suggests that the ancient and traditional consensus that the story of Daniel's safe emergence from the lions' den is in some way illustrative of resurrection and emergence of the just from the tomb is not entirely foreign to the purpose of this story.

A more detailed reading of the narrative will enlarge this preliminary sense of its subject matter and development. But before proceeding to that reading, a word about its structure and the chief figures in the narrative will prove to be helpful. The elements typical of a "court tale of conflict" (Humphreys, "Life-Style," pp. 217–21, followed by Collins, *Apocalyptic Vision,* pp. 49–51) are present in this tale as in some of the preceding chapters: Beginning in a state of prosperity, the protagonist is victimized by jealous rivals and condemned by the king or other authority, being saved in the nick of time from some life-threatening peril, released, and publicly honored for displaying piety and merit. The same kind of story in this same form is told of Joseph in Genesis 39—41, of Esther and the Jews in the court of Ahasuerus, and of course of the three men in the fiery furnace of Daniel 3. Although writers have seen this chapter variously as a miracle story, a martyr story, and the like, the contest dimension seems to predominate. Perhaps this can be illustrated by diagramming the architecture of the tale as follows, showing its balanced structure and identifying the moment at which Daniel is determined to have triumphed in the conflict as the high point of the story.

> Daniel emerges as best satrap
> His enemies plot
> The king makes a fatal decree
> Devout Daniel is arrested and sentenced to death
> DANIEL DELIVERED—GOD WINS!
> Daniel released
> The king makes a saving decree
> The enemies are destroyed
> Daniel confirmed as best satrap

79

The protagonists in this story are the hundred and twenty satraps, the three "presidents," of whom Daniel is one, and the king, Darius "the Mede." We have already canvassed the historical problems associated with the latter figure in connection with the first mention of this king (5:31). Whether the other chief protagonist, Daniel, "is really a figure of the Jewish people" (Hartman and Di Lella, *Daniel,* p. 198) depends upon how much consciousness of metaphorical writing one wishes to attribute to the editor of the Book of Daniel. In its own terms, the story is uplifting moral fiction, illustrative of the fruits of pious obedience and the power of God and featuring a beloved Jewish hero of olden times. Those intrinsic aspects of the story should never be lost sight of lest the tale become mere allegory and lose its vivid human virtues. Yet because it is a narrative of the Old Testament canon, it remains open to the future as an example of the experience of God's faithfulness, which faithful people and saints have had time and again over many generations. It is a narrative which has a remarkable parallel in the account of the passion, death, and resurrection of Jesus of Nazareth. That parallel will emerge as we now examine the story in more detail under three broad headings: the conspiracy (vv. 1–9); Daniel's passion (vv. 10–18); Daniel's deliverance and the denouement (vv. 19–28).

The Conspiracy (vv. 1–9)

The first portion of the narrative of chapter 6 picks up the hero, Daniel, at the high level at which he was left by Belshazzar in 5:29. Daniel is preeminent and has been made one of the three "presidents" placed over the satraps (120). In verse 3, the king is of a mind to bring him to an even higher status, perhaps that of "grand vizier" because "an excellent spirit was in him." Simply in the style of their translation, Hartman and Di Lella (*Daniel,* p. 192) underscore the problem with the superb performance of Daniel: "But Daniel, because of the extraordinary spirit that was in him, so outshone the other chief ministers and the satraps, that the king was inclined to set him over the whole kingdom" (v. 4). Whatever this spirit may have been, it brought forth the inevitable jealousy from the other two presidents and the one hundred twenty satraps, who evidently did not have an excellent spirit within them. As Lacocque points out, "one may be his majesty's Chancellor even though one only has a very ordinary spirit" (*Daniel,* p. 110), a fact which hardly comes as

80

news to any one in the twentieth century. When these ordinary rivals see that they cannot blackmail Daniel or pin anything on him which might reflect upon his virtue, they decide to trap him in a conflict between two immutable laws.

Some have asked whether the attitude of the courtiers might not reflect more than mere jealousy. Lacocque even has an interesting discussion of the tension between centripetal and centrifugal forces in an empire. With the triumvirate of presidents and the many satraps, a kind of decentralized system is in operation; therefore, the possibility that Daniel might be made *number one* behind the king would also undermine local prerogatives and the rights of officers within the realm. This might be especially threatening when the man of distinction is also a foreigner and a Jew. In any case, the courtiers—though ordinary from a moral point of view—were perspicuous in their conspiracy. They saw a way to establish an inevitable clash between two immutable laws. They are confident that Daniel would not side with the law of the Medes and Persians were the law of God threatened with violation. Just as Caiaphas and the chief priests and the council sought to bring Jesus' fidelity to his own mission into conflict with the laws and customs which they represented (Matt. 26:57–68), thus preparing the way for his trial and execution, so here the satraps have rigged a trap which will certainly catch Daniel in its toils.

The presidents and satraps then "came by agreement" or "came in collusion" (an Aramaic word which has some sense of "swarming") to the king and said, "All the presidents of the kingdom, the prefects and the satraps . . . have agreed that the king should establish an ordinance and enforce an edict that whoever makes petition to any god or man for thirty days except to you, O king, shall be cast into the den of lions" (v. 7). In this they lied, because not all the presidents had agreed—Daniel had not and had not even been consulted!

Conspiracy comes as no surprise to the reader, but the gullibility of Darius might. Astonishingly, he agrees to "establish the interdict and sign the document." Why would such a naked appeal to the ego, such an invitation to a raw display of power, have appealed to the king? Could he not have foreseen the conflict of interest into which this would throw his dear friend and faithful courtier, Daniel? Could he not have sensed that his acquiescence in the courtiers' plans would also place him in their power? Nor would such a claim of despotic divinity

81

have been religiously appropriate if in fact Darius and his successors had sworn fealty to the high god and overlord, Ahura Mazda. If Darius is really a metaphor for a king closer to the time of the appearance of the Book of Daniel, Antiochus IV Epiphanes (his title means, after all, "God Manifest"), the ego trip might be somewhat more understandable. But even Antiochus demanded no worship of himself as far as we know. Perhaps we have simply to attribute this detail to the storyteller's art and understand that the odds of Daniel's survival through this last court contest are being made infinitesimal!

The storyteller is a true artist, and keeps the reader thoroughly engaged. As the king's pen or stylus nears the dotted line of the edict, the reader wants to cry out "Stop! This is a mistake and not one that can be corrected—for the law of the Medes and the Persians cannot be revoked!" This idea, which has become proverbial in our language for any utterly fixed and unchangeable fact, is obscure in origin. Very little secular evidence from Persian times suggests that Persian law was regarded as more or less immutable than any other. Within the Bible itself Esther 1:19 knows also about the "laws of the Medes and the Persians" and Esther 8:8 throws helpful light on the notion when it says ". . . an edict written in the name of the king and sealed with the king's ring cannot be revoked." In these late texts, law and decree are seen to be as definitive as the vow or oath was in earlier times. Ancient Israel had always regarded a vow as unalterable once pronounced. Jephthah had to sacrifice his daughter in order to fulfill his promise made in oath (Judg. 11:29–40); Hannah had to give her son to the Lord all the days of his life because she had vowed it before the Lord in the sanctuary (I Sam. 1:11). Though no written text nor signet was involved, oral promises were binding and could not be taken back. King Darius' word is regarded in the same light by the storyteller and the characters of the story, whether ancient Medes and Persians felt the same way or not.

Daniel's Passion (vv. 10–18)

Now the unalterable law of the Medes and the Persians comes into direct and fatal conflict with the eternal law of the God of Israel. The confrontation is not public and violent; it takes place quietly, non-violently, in the private realm. Still, Daniel's act is one of civil disobedience. He dissents, with his body, on his knees three times a day, praying through the win-

82

dows toward Jerusalem. His is not the dissent of a religious fanatic, for he merely continues his usual practice—he prays and gives thanks. He does not court martyrdom, but when disaster threatens he remains steady; and it is his sharp profile as an observant and obedient Jew that is both his downfall and his salvation.

Jerusalem, the object of every exile's hopes and desires, comes under the interdict. One now must no longer turn the face toward the holy city but only toward the fading and corrupt splendor of a mere king of flesh and blood. But in the tradition of Old Testament eschatology with which this story is now affiliated, Jerusalem is no ordinary city. Jerusalem is the summation of all the redemption that is to come. Jerusalem is the *future.* To prohibit a person from turning the body and the mind toward Jerusalem is to quench that person's vision and to deprive that person of a reason for being. "What the Babylonian wise men—representing the nations caught up in their static world view—hold against Daniel-Israel is his hope" (Lacocque, *Daniel,* p. 114). Of course Daniel disobeys the edict! To live without hope in God's victory in the restoration of the world and the completion of his redemptive work is to become a slave to Big Brother, a rhinoceros bellowing through the streets in blind allegiance to an ugly and fatally flawed leader. Daniel disobeys and remains free!

The entrapment works, of course. The plotters swarm in and find Daniel at prayer (or see him through his open windows). But the king is trapped, too, in the toils of his own decree; verse 14 has him struggling to free himself and Daniel, but to no avail. An ill-advised stab at divinization by decree, combined with the carefully fostered myth of the immutability of law, render the king unable to act except to carry out the sentence of death by lions. His last remark to Daniel, before the entrance of the lion pit is closed, is enigmatic: "May your God, whom you serve continually, deliver you!" Perhaps this is a benediction. Perhaps it is a challenge to God, uttered in hope against hope by one who has nonetheless arrogated to himself the right to put him to the test (Lacocque). Perhaps it should be translated as Hartman and Di Lella translate, as a statement of faith (but based on good philological grounds): "Your God whom you serve so constantly will come to rescue you." Whatever the case may be, the king's parting word springs from his own disquiet, and he repairs to his house to fast and mourn (v. 18).

83

Before proceeding to the last section of this chapter, it remains necessary to explore a parallel between the account of Daniel in the lions' den and the passion of Jesus. This section of the discussion of Daniel 6 is sub-titled "Daniel's passion" because of certain striking affinities between the two accounts. The chapter begins with an account of a conspiracy and betrayal by fellow satraps; in Matthew 26 Jesus' passion begins with his announcement of his own betrayal (26:2), word of the conspiracy of the chief priests, scribes, and elders to catch Jesus (vv. 3–5), and finally Judas' decision to betray him (vv. 14–16). The satraps despair of catching Daniel in any compromising situation and so seek to force a confrontation between his rock-like integrity and the law of the state; similarly, the accusers of Jesus can trap him only by reporting to Roman authority his messianic title, "King of the Jews" (Matt. 27:11). On the eve of his arrest Daniel "prayed and gave thanks before his God, as he had done previously" (Dan. 6:10); Jesus, too, is taken by the soldiers as he maintained his accustomed dialogue in prayer with God (Matt. 26:36–55). In the actual confrontation with the authority, the king sympathizes with the accused and works for his release until at last—with deep misgiving—he is forced by his own law to bind the prisoner Daniel over for execution; in Matthew 26:19 Pilate's wife warns her husband of Jesus' innocence; Pilate himself protests his innocence to the crowd (v. 23). In the end he honors the law that allows him to release to the crowd the one condemned man whom they demand. He then washes his hands of Jesus' innocent blood (v. 24). The parallel continues from this point, though without the ongoing participation of the authority; Daniel is executed and his torture chamber/tomb is closed with a stone and sealed (Dan. 6:17); Jesus is executed and his tomb is closed with a stone (Matt. 27:60) and sealed (v. 66). And of course the denouement of both accounts is the same: the person presumed dead reappears from the tomb, vindicated by God's saving power. The fundamental difference in the two accounts emerges just here, of course; Jesus really did die and was raised, whereas for Daniel an angel shut the lions' mouths and when he emerged from the den "no kind of hurt was found upon him, because he had trusted in his God" (Dan. 6:23). Jesus trusted God, too, but grievous—indeed, fatal—wounds were found upon him—and God's victory over them and death was therefore all the more overwhelming. Still the parallelism in the two accounts is strik-

84

ing and throws light upon the persistent tendency through all the ages of Christian interpretation of Daniel to see his descent into the pit as a type of Christ's crucifixion and descent into hell; and to understand his emergence as a type of Christ's resurrection—even though no metaphorical intention on the author's part can be detected. Further, to the degree that the experiences of Daniel in chapters 1—6 are to be seen in the light of their canonical juxtaposition to the eschatological hope of Daniel 7—12, the lions' den event can be understood as an anticipation (prolepsis) of the experience of the faithful in the face of ultimate testing. Even though the danger is extreme and the injustice is outrageous, God will prevail and will vindicate those who trust him. Daniel's courage and trust thus prove to be components of an interim ethic—just as Jesus' style and behavior are understood by the church to be dynamic guidelines on how to wait while the vision tarries (cf. Hab. 2:3). As is often the case in analogies, the antitype exceeds the prototype in this instance, for Jesus' story is understood not simply to be a foreshadowing of the new eschatological age, but as its actual first event (I Cor. 15:20). But the dynamic relation of faithful obedience and eschatological victory is already present even in the Old Testament prototype, the passion of Daniel!

The Deliverance (vv. 19–24)

The king, hastening to the scene of Daniel's supposed death, continues to recognize that deliverance from these severe straits could be accomplished only by the living God. But in fact deliverance has taken place! The Septuagint version of Daniel reports that God closed the lions' mouths directly; but with a delicacy that befits the late Old Testament notion of a somewhat more transcendent and remote God, the Aramaic text trusts such a direct miraculous intervention to an angel. More significant for our purposes are the two reasons given for the deliverance. Daniel says, "And they have not hurt me because I was found blameless before him"; . . . (v. 22). The narrator testifies that it happened "because he had trusted in his God" (v. 23). There is great strength in this dual testimony: blamelessness and trust are the keys to successful survival in the face of overwhelming odds. It is even a welcome note that there is a dependable order at work in the world. Human faithfulness is matched by divine faithfulness, and Daniel's certainty of that enabled the writer of Hebrews to list him among those faithful

85

ones of old who "died in faith, not having received what was promised, but having seen it and greeted it from afar" (Heb. 11:13). For many faithful people whose steadiness in trust ought to have earned them their safety, no angel stopped the lions' mouths or knocked down the cross or turned off the gas; and yet they too—in the power of their faith—have overcome the ultimate fear that their deaths were meaningless and their lives failures. We should also think of the eschatological dimension of this. Viewed from the perspective of God's coming victory, all faithfulness whatever, and all the good that has ever been wrought, are vindicated. In this light, the salvation of good and trusting Daniel from the lions' den is an anticipation of the rescue from destruction by God's own transcendent power of God's people. This way of understanding the eschatological context canonically provided for Daniel 6 is more helpful than the proposal of Baldwin, who finds in prophetic literature (and in Heb. 11:33, as well, where it is actually the prophet himself who closes the lions' mouths) the notion that in the age to come human beings will again enjoy dominion over the beasts (*Daniel*, p. 131; cf. Isa. 11:6; 65:25; Hos. 2:18). Daniel is not being pictured as a man of the age to come, marvelously able to exercise dominion over the beasts; instead, we have depicted here a man of the present age, like ourselves, who by trust and steadfastness gives a hint of the way in which believers can deport themselves now even as they draw strength from the certainty of God's coming great victory.

The folkloristic touch with which the story of Daniel's deliverance is rounded out can give an interpreter considerable pause. After Daniel's release, "those men who had accused Daniel were brought and cast into the den of lions—they, their children, and their wives" (v. 24). We learn that the lions "broke all their bones in pieces" before they even hit the bottom of the pit. Montgomery points out that if taken literally this would mean the deaths of one hundred twenty-two men plus wives and children (*Daniel*, p. 278). Such a case of overkill, hardly befitting the work of a just God, has led some commentators to explain the matter away as a mere narrative detail. Others simply have moralized. After pointing out that such treatment would agree with the rule about the false witness ("You shall do to him as he had meant to do to his brother," Deut. 19:19), Porteous remarks, "The author of our book had not learnt everything that God had to teach about the nature of justice" (*Daniel,* p. 91). The scandal of this passage had already impressed interpreters (LXX-Dan) long ago, leading to a rendition in the Septuagint which reduces the punitive scope to the two co-presidents only. On the basis of this variant and others like it, Nathaniel Schmidt argued that it (LXX-Dan) is the earlier Greek version of Daniel 6 because it has not yet undergone the process of elaboration and exaggeration typical of a longer tradition and which typifies Theod-Dan (see "Daniel and Androcles"). However, Porteous used the same data to argue in just the opposite direction: "By confining the plot to Daniel's two co-presidents, [LXX-Dan] makes the story more plausible and, for that very reason, is not to be regarded as presenting the original text" (*Daniel,* p. 89). In other words, we are faced with a decision between two laws of the tradition process: the law of elaboration, which requires that stories get better and better as they are retold over the years, and the law of rectification, which requires that stories be corrected, problems solved, and scandals quietly eliminated. Either one can be used to explain the discrepancy before us.

As to the faith that the righteous will finally be delivered from their severe straits and that the wicked will receive the recompense which is their due, we can only acknowledge that this still mirrors our own inner hopes and aspirations. In the large eschatological sense we believe it to be the right order of things, though our experience with God's judging and saving activity in the person of Jesus Christ leads us to believe that God will achieve his redemptive purpose without "breaking in pieces" the bones of all those who sin against him. On the contrary, he will achieve his purpose while bringing those very same bones to bow in repentance and adoration before him.

This last theme of the universal significance of God's power to deliver in fact permeates the decree of Darius which follows in verses 25–27. In this liturgical precis of the entire story, the new decree that now offsets the royal decree that thickened the plot in the first place, we see another example of the "universalist theodicy" pattern which we have already observed in 3:28–29; 4:1–3, 34–35. Into his call for the acknowledgment of the universal hegemony of the God of Daniel, Darius also injects an eschatological dimension, the only explicit note of its kind in the entire story:

87

for he is the living God, *enduring forever;*
his kingdom shall *never* be destroyed,
and his dominion shall be *to the end* (v. 25, author's emphasis).

The phrase "to the end" requires us to think of the earthly chapter of God's kingdom which does end along with the earth itself. But the full formula seems to blend earthly finitude with heavenly timelessness as though the earthly kingdom will meld directly into the eternal kingdom of the God who endures forever, whenever the border between the two is reached. In other words, there is no real end of God's kingdom except in its fading historical aspects.

The panel closes with a chronological note that brings the work of Daniel down into the reign of Cyrus the Persian. Daniel's life and work are understood to have spanned the entire period of the exile and to have continued even after 538 B.C. If Daniel went to Babylon as a young man sometime shortly after the first dispersion in 597 B.C., he is a very old man by ancient standards by the time he ceased his work sometime early in the reign of Cyrus. This last verse of Daniel 1—6 provides a framework for the six stories; however, it also provides a chronological overlap with Daniel 7—12, for chapters 10—12, the final lengthy dream vision report, are set in the third year of Cyrus king of Persia. Although the inner history of Daniel the seer and dreamer does not begin until the first year of Belshazzar, king of Babylon (7:1), it at least goes down to the end of the period spanned by these six stories which constitute the outer history of Daniel's ministry in exile.

A THEOLOGICAL ASSESSMENT OF DANIEL 6

The closer reading of Daniel 6 has confirmed the initial direct reading with which this discussion began. The story is indeed about a conflict between the powers that be and a righteous man, supported by God. God prevails and vindicates his servant Daniel against insuperable odds. The story offers a foretaste of the coming victory of God over all foes, even death itself.

To say that escape from the jaws of death is the point of the story is hardly to say enough even when that point is understood to have been capable of giving comfort even to the generation which suffered under Antiochus IV Epiphanes. The miraculous deliverance is only an illustration of the inevitability with which all human claims to immutability have always had to yield before the abiding law and will of God. It is really no contest

88

between the law of the Medes and the Persians and the law of God.

Immutable human law also always threatens to trap its own makers. In verse 14 we saw the king struggling desperately to free himself from the consequences of his hasty decree. Daniel is the free man in this story, and the king—preeminent in the realm though his position was—is trapped in the myth of the immutability of his own law; he is thus in bondage. Had he been free to drop the notion that his law and decree could not be changed, he might have gotten out of the bind he was in, but he chose to live out the lie partly out of fear of the courtiers (who already knew it was a lie, or at least knew how to manipulate the fiction to serve their own ends). Were he to make public admission of the mutability of the law, his own boys could destroy him! We should never believe people who say that human decisions cannot be changed! That is more than a mere moral to this story; that is a vital truth for our times. It is a lie when they say that the troop train which is rolling toward the border to launch the First World War cannot be stopped; or that nuclear stockpiling cannot be stopped; or that Jim Crow or apartheid are the law of the land and cannot be changed. When unjust or wrong, human law and human praxis can always be changed, though it may seem more dangerous to admit that fact than to risk the consequences of refusing to change.

The corollary question is whether God is trapped by the immutability of his law. One is sometimes stunned at the intensity with which the psalmist reminds God of his own commitments to crush the wicked and to slay the psalmist's own opponents (e.g., Psalms 28; 35; 55; 59). When expressed in its hard-lining forms, the retributional theology of the Old Testament suggests that God is triggered by human sin to act in violently punitive ways (cf. Deut. 28:15–57; Job 20:1–29). However, we also have words to Israel that God is capable of transcending his own law. God's law is immutable, and yet God himself can suspend it if compassion so demands:

How can I give you up, O Ephraim!
    How can I hand you over, O Israel! . . .
My heart recoils within me,
    my compassion grows warm and tender.
I will not execute my fierce anger,
    I will not again destroy Ephraim;
for I am God and not man,

the Holy One in your midst,
and I will not come to destroy (Hos. 11:8–9).

God's law is immutable and binding on human beings, but God is greater than his own law. This truth should also be remembered in connection with verse 24 where the weavers of the tale caught the death of Daniel's opponents up into the fabric of the miracle of the chapter. It should also be borne in mind in connection with the blamelessness to which Daniel attributes his escape. It is right to speak of blamelessness, but God is not simply programmed by human blamelessness. God acts in larger dimensions as well, and this sets the stage for the coming vindication of all of God's children.

Finally, what shall we denominate the true act of God in this chapter? The stopping of the lions' mouths is a powerful, Godly act, it is true; but even more fundamental is that human response which God elicited from King Darius. Surely it is nothing short of miraculous that the king of the mightiest empire of the day and a follower of a god other than Yahweh should be presented as singing a hymn of faith and praise to the God who saved Daniel from the power of the lions. Darius' confession is an act of God of profound significance. The same can be said of the confession of the widow of Zarephath. After Elijah raises her son, that Canaanite woman cries: "Now I know that you are a man of God, and that the word of the Lord in your mouth is truth" (I Kings 17:24). Even the New Testament transformation of the latter account in the story of the raising of the widow's son at Nain (Luke 7:11–17) concludes not with the miracle itself but with the people's confession. Their very words, "God has visited his people!" are in themselves a veritable act of God. It is with such an act that the cycle of stories in Daniel 1—6 comes to a close.

PART TWO

Three Apocalyptic Visions and the Prayer of Daniel

DANIEL 7–12

Daniel 7

The Vision of the Son of Man

The Dream Vision

Modern commentators are generally agreed that chapter 7 is the single most important chapter of the Book of Daniel. Its position is pivotal, both in terms of the architecture of the book as a whole and in terms of the brilliance of the vision which it contains. A noticeable shift in point of view now takes place. Daniel 1—6 consisted of tales about the hero, his external history, so to speak. This same Daniel turns now from public demonstrations of the power of the God of Israel in a strange land to the private reception of visions of the future destiny of God's chosen ones. From "Daniel said" (7:2) forward, the account is always in the first person—as it were, the internal and hidden experience of the saint, to be stored up for disclosure at the time of the end.

Daniel 7 is a dream-vision report which can be further subdivided. After the setting is given (7:1), the dream-vision itself follows. It consists of an animal allegory on history (vv. 1–8), a heavenly scene featuring the judgment of the earthly kingdoms by the Ancient of Days (vv. 9–12), and the vesting of all earthly dominion in "one like a son of man" (vv. 13–14). Then follow a report of the visionary's fear and the introduction of a heavenly interpreter, together with a prose interpretation of

91

the judgment scene (vv. 15–22), and a detailed poetic interpretation of the fourth beast and the judgment scene which looks almost like an expansion or midrash upon the preceding prose interpretation (vv. 23–27). Verse 28 is simply a concluding formula or "aftermath." In the discussion which follows, the second part of Daniel 7 will be treated in connection with the first section rather than separately, thus dealing simultaneously with the vision and its interpretation.

That the first pericope in Daniel 7–12 should be a narrative of a dream vision need not surprise the reader, for dreams and visions are media of revelation favored by biblical writers. Take the Book of Daniel itself. Chapter 8 falls into exactly the same outline as does this chapter, except that it is a vision account only, without the dream. Chapter 2 exhibits the same formal structure as well, though of course the interpreter is the Judean sage Daniel and not an angel. (As has already been shown in the commentary on chapter 2, the stories of Joseph as dream interpreter in Gen. 40—41 are formally parallel to Dan. 2.) The same is true in chapter 4, Nebuchadnezzar's dream of the felled tree, although the heavenly watchers do play a role in signifying that vision. In no other biblical dream accounts do we have extended narratives of visionary experience, designed to provide an interpretation of events available to the entire community. The rest appear to be simply individual instructions or disclosures of destiny unaccompanied by the full apparatus of fear manifestations and angelic interpreters, as for example, Genesis 20: 1–7, wherein Abimelech is given Sarah's true identity in a dream, and Genesis 28:10–22, in which Jacob gets a covenant message while dreaming of the ladder used by angels.

Of course, we hear of messages brought directly to human beings by angels without the dream element appearing. This phenomenon is particularly associated with call narratives, as with Moses at the burning bush (Exod. 3:1–6), Gideon (Judg. 6:11–24), and the annunciation to Mary (Luke 1:26–38). Finally, much of the Book of Revelation is one extended vision account involving angelic interpreters. However, like Daniel 8, it lacks the dream component (cf. Rev. 1:10–20, which serves as an introduction to the rest of the entire book). On the other hand, in the apocalyptic portion of the deutero-canonical book of II Esdras, the fifth and sixth visions of Ezra (chaps. 11—12 and chap. 13 respectively) make lengthy use of the same form as that of Daniel 7, with all the elements present save one: the interpretation of the dream is done by the Most High directly rather than through the mediation of an angel. Inasmuch as angels speak for God and often, in Hebrew and Jewish literature, seem indistinguishable from God (cf. Moses' experience at the bush; the angel of Exod. 3:2 turns out in 3:4 to be Yahweh), we can assert that these two visions provide the closest parallels to the dream vision of Daniel 7. In IV Ezra 10:59, Uriel, Ezra's angel-interlocutor, even uses the technical term which has been employed here: "the Most High will show you in those *dream visions* what the Most High will do to those who dwell on earth in the last days."

The question of the role of dreams, visions, and the like in the understanding of revelation in apocalyptic literature—or in any biblical literature, for that matter—is a difficult and disturbing one. It will require some further discussion in the theological assessment of Daniel 7 below.

The Animal Allegory and the Meaning of Myth

That the animal allegory dream of 7:1–8 is parallel to the dream of the colossus in chapter 2 is self-evident. Like the metals of chapter 2, the four beasts represent four kings or kingdoms (7:17). Relative intrinsic worth plays a less important role here than in chapter 2—all four of the beasts are strong and fearsome—but the historical order remains the same. The lion (7:4) equals the golden head which equals the neo-Babylonian empire (2:32, 34–38). Some commentators point out the appropriateness of the lion-eagle symbol for Babylon, since the lion was beloved of the Babylonians and can be seen to this day gracing the walls of the famed "Procession Street" in the remains of their city. However, too much emphasis should not be given to this kind of animal/history correlation, for one is hard pressed to find any corresponding link for the three remaining beasts.

Again with reference to chapter 2, the bear (7:5) must be equated with the statue's silver chest and arms (2:32, 39); it should be the Median kingdom. If the leopard (7:6) equals the bronze belly of the statue (2:32, 39) and stands for Persia, as is commonly if not universally held, then the fourth, terrible beast with the iron teeth and the ten horns (7:7) must equal the legs and feet of iron and clay (2:33, 40) which stood for the Greek empire introduced into the Middle East, 332–331 B.C. Like

93

chapter 2, with its discussion of the weakness of the feet (2:41–43), the dream also acknowledges divergency and strife within the fourth beast, represented by conflict among the ten horns (7:8) and the ultimate superiority of an eleventh one equipped with "a mouth which uttered enormities" (Lacocque). By means of this animal allegory the historical framework is established with which the apocalyptic visions of Daniel 7—12 will take place (see Introduction, Comparative Chronological Table).

The beasts of this allegory may have had their origin in the myths of the ancient Near East. Here, however, they no longer possess mythic character but have become more arbitrary symbols for a succession of historical kingdoms. The discussion raises a larger issue which confronts anyone who wishes to engage in the serious business of interpreting Daniel in the midst of the community of believers. Commentators may agree among themselves on the presence of myth or at least of mythic images in Daniel 7:1–8 and other passages. How should such agreement affect the way in which such texts are heard in the synagogue and the church?

The answer, though not simple, has got to be clear. People do not want to play games when the burning question is, Does the Scripture which we believe to possess God-given authority contain mythic elements? The answer is Yes, but. . . .

"Myth" must be defined properly as a narrative about primeval events centering on the activity of the gods in their own realm and which helps to account for the present realities of the world around the narrator. (That definition is a literary one and eliminates the popular misuse of the term "myth" as a synonym for "lie.") When defined in this way, myth clearly emerges as an identifying characteristic of the apocalyptic writings of the Old Testament, including the Book of Daniel (see the Introduction). It is no surprise, then, that apocalyptic literature will have recourse to the language of myth, for it is precisely the essence of this literature that it must speak about God as creator and re-creator. When the cosmic activity of God was the subject under discussion, no language except that of myth was available to ancient theologians. The precise images used to set forth the motifs of divine struggle and the cosmic enemies of God varied from time to time; to be sure, the enemies were not always depicted as a series of beasts rising up out of the sea. New cultural environments might provide new mythic decor, but the stage upon which the drama of creation/re-creation was played remained basically the same.

The Historical Environment of Daniel 7

The animal allegory (vv. 1–8) concludes in verse 8 with the figure of "another horn, a little one, before which three of the first horns were plucked up by the roots; and behold, in this horn were eyes like the eyes of a man, and a mouth speaking great things." If the four beasts represent four kingdoms and the one of which this horn is an outgrowth is intended to represent the Hellenistic kingdom established in the Middle East between 331 and 323 B.C. by Alexander the Great, then presumably the various horns are monarchs who arose in the historical sequence after Alexander. (The identification of the 10 + 1 = 11 horns with monarchs is confirmed by v. 24: "As for the ten horns, out of this kingdom ten kings shall arise, and another shall arise after them;. . . .") This verse obviously is a crucial one, then, for identifying the actual historical setting in which the Book of Daniel was written, because it is given to Daniel to witness the demise of this particular eleventh post-Alexandrian king and no other. Whether Antiochus IV Epiphanes was actually the eleventh king in this sequence of monarchs from Alexander to the time of the writer is open to considerable question, though one way of counting produces just such a number (cf. Hartman and Di Lella, *Daniel*, p. 214). However, if one makes the correlation between the *hasidim* of I Maccabees 2:42; 7:13–17 and the community which wrote the Book of Daniel, then the chronological horizon created demands that Antiochus be the king referred to here. For at least two reasons, this seems to be the identification intended by the writer. First, in order to accede to the throne, Antiochus resorted to the murder of the Heliodorus who once failed to seize the treasures of the Temple in Jerusalem (II Macc. 3), as well as the son of his brother and predecessor, Seleucus IV. In other words, Antiochus came to the throne by murder and violence, though we know of only two "horns" which he uprooted, and neither "horn" was actually a predecessor king, as stipulated by verse 24. (This problem, taken together with the fact that Dan. 7:20 refers to the horns as "fellows" of one another, has led some commentators to suggest that the eleven horns were meant to be understood not as a series of Hellenistic rulers of Syria beginning with Alexander the Great but rather as eleven contempo-

95

rary rulers of states known to the writer.) Second, from the perspective of Israel, Antiochus, the instigator of the first anti-Jewish pogrom in all of recorded history, could preeminently qualify as one who wore out the saints and prevailed over them (vv. 21, 25), who thought to change the times and the law (v. 25), and whose mouth arrogated to itself the right to speak "great things" (v. 8). After all, it was he who in the name of the holy mission of Hellenistic culture to unify all of humanity around the ideals of common language, common kingship, and common religion executed those who possessed the Torah (I Macc. 1:57), sacrificed swine upon the altar of the temple (I Macc. 1:47,54), and hung the bodies of infants who had been circumcised from the necks of their mothers' corpses (I Macc. 1:60–61).

Assuming the correctness of this identification (vv. 1–8), then, we have been given a historical environment in which the great events which are about to follow will take place. We know from a variety of ancient sources that Antiochus IV Epiphanes ruled the Seleucid kingdom of Syria from his capital at Antioch from 175–163 B.C. From I Maccabees 1:54 we learn that the temple was desecrated by order of this same Antiochus in December, 167 B.C. Surely this act and the accompanying general persecution of the Jews lies behind the invective of Daniel 7 against the "little horn" with its "mouth speaking great things." Since chapter 7 understands the punishment and destruction of the little horn to be a coming event, part of the judgment scene which has yet to be played out in history (cf. v. 11), we can assume that the writer does not know of the death of Antiochus —which must have taken place in 163 B.C. (cf. I Macc. 6:16). Daniel 7 must have been written, then, some time between 167–163 B.C. If the cryptic reference in 7:25 to the period of the persecution of the saints as "a time, two times, and half a time" is translated simply into years and if we assume (under our well-used principle of "prophecy after the fact") that the writer has already seen most of this period and is living near the end of it, we can even argue that the chapter was written late in 164 when the fever of persecution and the pressure on Antiochus alike were at their very zenith.

The Dream Account (vv. 9–14)

96

The stage of history thus having been set by means of the device of the great animal allegory (vv. 1–8), the writer then unfolds the second dramatic scene of the dream-vision account

(vv. 9–14). Now a total change of scene takes place. Instead of the horrible series of beasts, which represented the ongoing tragedy and trauma of Israelite history, the author now gives us a placid heavenly prospect. The oracle is a highly visual one in which we immediately observe God taking a seat upon the throne. Throughout the earlier writings of the Old Testament, events themselves were occasions for evidence of God's power over his enemies. In Exodus 14:25 the Egyptians cried out, "Let us flee from before Israel; for the LORD fights for them against the Egyptians." In I Samuel 5—6, incidents of sickness and disaster among the Philistines after they captured the ark of Yahweh were quite comprehensible to them and led them to confess, "his . . . [the God of Israel's] hand is heavy upon us and upon Dagon our god" (5:7). Ezekiel 1—36 presents historical events as the means of God's self-vindication, for through them, ". . . you shall know that I am Yahweh" (6:7 *et passim*). History has now grown opaque, or perhaps better stated, God has apparently withdrawn from history into remote transcendence so that the eye of the seer must look upward and forward into a different plane. Perhaps it is here that the answer to the perennial question of Psalm 13:1 (cf. 74:10–11), "How long, O Lord," will at last be revealed.

The vision of these verses is so rich in symbols that a number demand special attention. First, we see a throne being placed and one who is the "ancient of days" ("The-One-Who-Endures" [Lacocque]), sitting down on it. The presence of a throne implies a court and even a courtroom. The concept of a divine court or council in which Yahweh sits to render judgment is, of course, a common enough one in the Old Testament. The kind of juridical language familiar in this heavenly court can be seen in Isaiah 41:21–24. The scene itself is recounted in a remarkable way by the prophet Micaiah ben Imlah: "I saw the LORD sitting on his throne, and all the host of heaven standing beside him on his right hand and on his left" (I Kings 22:19).

It must be pointed out that in the vision (v. 9) more than one throne is actually set out. Commentators ancient and modern have enjoyed speculating about who should sit upon the other throne(s). Suggestions include the one like a son of man (to be introduced in v. 13), assistant angel judges (Calvin, *Daniel* II, 32), and even the martyrs and saints who are associated with the son of man (see Rev. 20:4; in Enoch 90:20, in a judgment scene patterned on this one, only one throne is set out). Let it suffice to

97

say that the motif of the divine throne(s) belongs to the stage-setting for the event which is now to take place: the Last Judgment which follows a public trial of the powers of evil and which results in a universally visible theodicy or divine self-vindication.

God has white hair, appropriate for one called the Ancient of Days. The early rabbis thought that God appeared at the Exodus as a young, black-haired holy warrior—but here as at Sinai, God appears as a wise and honorable judge. Mythology actually frequently pictures the high god with white hair, which color, as Lacocque points out, can indicate both pure innocence (cf. Isa. 1:18) and mature experience.

At the end of verse 9 we are astonished to see God's throne both in flames and running on flaming wheels. Why should the throne of God have wheels? Perhaps we are dealing here with echoes of that Hellenistic mythic tradition which represents Helios, the sun god, as riding his chariot across the daytime sky. Yahweh is actually depicted in this way on the famous fifth century A.D. mosaic synagogue floor at Beth Alpha in Palestine. Or perhaps we are dealing with the traditions enshrined in the inaugural vision of Ezekiel, in which the prophet beholds the throne of God flaming and borne by wheels within wheels (Ezek. 1:15–21). Inasmuch as the throne of God is traditionally understood in the Old Testament to be located between the overarching wings of the two cherubim on the Ark of the Covenant, perhaps we are here being given a look at the heavenly prototype of the Ark. Such a connection is supported by iconographic evidence from ancient Judaism, for at the third century A.D. Hellenistic synagogue at Capernaum a piece of decorated frieze pictures the ark with wheels. It seems quite likely that the picture of Yahweh seated upon his ark-throne ready to render judgment is intended to recall the Temple and that there is, therefore, a cultic dimension to the entire experience. Perhaps the judgment of the nations and the awarding of dominion to the son of man is not only a heavenly event but one which takes place simultaneously at the very heart of humanity, at the place where Yahweh causes his name to dwell, namely, the Temple in Jerusalem. This position is in fact taken by Lacocque, who says flatly, "The vision in chapter 7 has the Temple as its framework. It is true that the text does not expressly say this anywhere, but the reason for this silence is that the Temple had been profaned by Antiochus IV and was temporarily unfit for a theophany. Yet the imagery is Ezekiel's, in particular that of Ezek. 8—11 which describes God's presence in the Temple . . ." (*Daniel*, pp. 124–25). The significance of this link with the Temple will emerge in due course.

The Host and the Books

The dramatic vision of the heavenly court continues now with an acknowledgment of the "host" of heavenly beings which surround the throne of Yahweh and serve him. The mythic tradition of Israel had always placed Yahweh at the head of an army of warriors. This theme was particularly prominent in texts which refer to the power of Yahweh displayed at Sinai and in the wilderness. For example, in the blessing with which Moses sanctifies Israel before his death, he says,

> "The LORD came from Sinai,
>   and dawned from Seir upon us;
>   he shone forth from Mount Paran,
> he came forth from the ten thousands of holy ones,
>   with flaming fire at his right hand" (Deut. 33:2).

Similarly, in the Psalter tradition of the celebration of Yahweh's kingship we hear of the myriads:

> With mighty chariotry, twice ten thousand,
>   thousands upon thousands,
>   the Lord came from Sinai into the holy place (Ps. 68:17).

In verse 10 this image of Yahweh surrounded by a countless heavenly host is given the elaboration and enhancement so typical of apocalyptic. Now the scene is cosmic, the numbers are multiplied by ten to the seventh power; and the tendency to present Yahweh in the grandest setting possible is maintained right down into New Testament times (cf. Rev. 14:1–15). In Revelation 20 the saints and Christian martyrs rule with Christ during the millennium. That motif, combined with the numbers of the unidentified beings around the throne given in Daniel 7, gives rise to a scene beloved to the Christian imagination. In the somewhat overly dramatic but nonetheless highly evocative hymn of Henry Alford it looks this way:

> Ten thousand times ten thousand
>   In sparkling raiment bright,
> The armies of the ransomed saints
>   Throng up the steeps of light;

99

> 'Tis finished, all is finished,
>> Their fight with death and sin:
> Fling open wide the golden gates,
>> And let the victors in

That gospel song introduces the second motif of verse 10 as well. In the last stanza of his hymn, Alford cries:

> Bring near Thy great salvation,
>> Thou Lamb for sinners slain;
> Fill up the roll of Thine elect,
>> Then take Thy power, and reign; . . ."
>>>> ("Ten Thousand Times Ten Thousand," 1867).

It is the "roll of the elect" which is at issue in the last part of verse 10: "The court sat in judgment, and the books were opened." The motif of the heavenly books is familiar throughout the Bible. However, not all the texts are in agreement about the meaning of the books. In Psalm 139:16, as well as in Revelation 13:8; 17:8, and perhaps 20:15 and 21:27, the books are evidently the records of the destiny of individuals decreed from the beginning of time. Elsewhere, and much more commonly, the books are understood to be juridical records, Books of Remembrance, of the deeds both obedient and disobedient commissioned by individuals during their lifetimes (e.g., Exod. 32:32–33; Ps. 40:7 [cited in Heb. 10:7]; 56:8; 69:28; Mal. 3:16; Phil. 4:3; Rev. 3:5). The "book of truth" in Daniel 10:21 appears to belong in the former category; the other two references to the "books" in Daniel (7:10; 12:1) could be read either way. The two sets of books may come together in the New Testament reuse of our judgment scene when explicit mention is made of the opening of two categories of books before the judgment seat of God: "And I saw the dead, great and small, standing before the throne, and books were opened. Also another book was opened, which is the book of life [the phrase "the book of life" occurs in Ps. 69:28; Phil. 4:3; always in Revelation, and in I Enoch 108:3]. And the dead were judged by what was written in the books, by what they had done" (Rev. 20:12).

The image of a book of eternal destiny is emotionally powerful and theologically difficult; the image of a heavenly record book is, if one is honest about it, horrifying. The notion that God or God's agents watch each individual and make a daily record of the good and the evil which each one does is a primitive one, and yet it is one with which every individual in Western culture has had to come to terms at some point in life. The image of the

100

record-books is often complemented by a corollary image of the "all-seeing eye," with which we are familiar in representations as abstract as the eye of God of Mexican art and as concrete as the very realistic eye peering out at us from the reverse of the Great Seal of the United States pictured on the back of the dollar bill.

God, watching and recording, is a motif given fresh expression in rabbinic Judaism. One of the greatest sages of Pharisaism, Rabbi Judah the Prince, who is credited with bringing the Mishnah its final form around A.D. 200, is reported in the tractate Pirke Abot 2:1 to have taught: "Consider three things and thou wilt not fall into the hands of transgression: know what is above thee—a seeing eye and a hearing ear and all thy deeds written in a book." Even in contemporary Judaism, the greeting appropriate for New Year's Day, Rosh ha-Shanah, is "May you be written and sealed to a good year!"

That last sentence suggests, too, the doctrine of Islam, which has preserved the concept of the heavenly books with a vigor exceeding even that of Judaism and Christianity. In the Koran, Sura 6:38, the book is a book of eternal decree:

> There is not an animal
> (That lives) on the earth,
> Nor a being that flies
> On its wings, but (forms
> Part of) communities like you.
> Nothing have we omitted
> From the Book, and they (all)
> Shall be gathered to their Lord
> In the end.

That same book is celebrated in much more popular form in the beloved Islamic poet Omar Khayyam:

> With Earth's first Clay They did the Last Man knead,
> And there of the Last Harvest sow'd the Seed:
> And the first Morning of Creation wrote
> What the Last Dawn of Reckoning shall read (Rubaiyat 73).

Of course, Omar Khayyam knows of the heavenly book in its other function as record-book as well, and speaks of it in one of his most memorable verses:

101

> The Moving Finger writes; and, having writ,
> Moves on: nor all your Piety nor Wit,
> Shall lure it back to cancel half a Line,
> Nor all your Tears wash out a Word of it (Rubaiyat 71).

Should contemporary Jews and Christians toy with the idea of heavenly record-books and tablets of destiny? Is the former the way in which we should conceive of God's address to human evil? Surely not! Yet, it requires skill to reject the idea of a detailed recording of our daily lives in books without also losing the vital sense of answerability and accountability associated with the books. Can we share in the joy and certainty of divine salvation without actually singing, "When the roll is called up yonder, I'll be there!"? For both musical and theological reasons, one would hope so—yet without a loss of the sense of urgency and ultimate importance that accompanies the conviction that God cares!

Further reflection on questions like these will be the task of the theological assessment which follows. For now, let it simply be noted that the judgment here is seen as a vast collective one against whole kingdoms; and it takes place in the most sweeping, cosmic context possible. The motif of the assembly of the nations before the throne of God for judgment at the last day is, of course, not new here, but is already familiar from texts like Joel 3:1-2, 11-12 and especially verse 14:

> Multitudes, multitudes,
>   in the valley of decision!
> For the day of the LORD is near
>   in the valley of decision.

Here, however, the result is puzzling. The fourth beast with its horn speaking great words is destroyed and burned in fire, and —most unexpectedly and in a way which no one seems really able to explain—the other three beasts are preserved alive "for a season and a time," but their dominions are taken away. Whatever that may mean, it is clear that the divine judging activity of Yahweh takes place without impediment or opposition, and the holy decree is immediately implemented. All that remains now in the concluding verses of the heavenly judgment scene is to reassign the earthly dominion to one of God's own choosing.

The Dominion Is Given to One "Like a Son of Man"

102

We stand now in amazed wonder before the climax of Daniel's dream vision (vv. 13–14), and indeed at the very heart of the Book of Daniel itself. As the fourth great beast is destroyed by fire and the other three are deprived of all power and hegemony there comes one "like a son of man," who receives from the Ancient of Days all the dominion formerly possessed by the other kingdoms. To him is given the promise of the service of all the other "peoples, nations, and languages"; unlike the kingdoms before him, this son of man will rule in a kingdom that shall never be destroyed.

In the discussion of the interpretation of the dream (vv. 19–27), we will have occasion to examine the meaning given to the figure of the son of man in the chapter itself. For now, however, we must ask simply Where in the history of Old Testament faith did this figure originate? This is the first appearance in the Old Testament of the son of man as an independent future figure. Yet it hardly seems likely that the author of Daniel 7 simply created this figure as a vehicle for expressing hope in God's coming self-vindication. The term *son of man,* for example, is well-known from the prophet Ezekiel, whose angel guide persists in addressing him in this way: "And you, son of man, prophesy against Gog . . ." (39:1). This usage must simply be understood as a title of address: one could call a prophet "son of man" and mean simply "Mister"! This semantic value is confirmed by Psalm 8:4:

> . . . what is man that thou art mindful of him,
> and the son of man that thou dost care for him?

The parallelism of the poetry, in which the terms of verse 4*a* are reexpressed in synonyms in verse 4*b*, proves that "man" and "son of man" in this instance mean the same thing.

Now, however, we have pictured before us a special figure called "son of man." Is he to be understood as a single individual or the embodiment of a collective entity of some kind? Is he one of the persons known by the Old Testament writers to be in heaven already because they were translated, such as Enoch (Gen. 5:24) or Elijah (II Kings 2:12)? Is he one of those persons exceptional for having known God intimately (Adam, Abraham, Moses, or David)? Is he one of those preexistent figures already known in Judaism (the personified figure of Wisdom, Prov. 8: 22–31; the suffering servant, Isa. 52:13—53:12; or the Messiah, the anointed one of David, Ezek. 37:24–28)? Or is he some hitherto unknown entity, now making his totally unexpected appearance? Only on the basis of the evidence given in this text can we answer the question of what the writer had in mind in introducing the figure of the son of man. We cannot get our

103

answer from the ever-enlarging subsequent tradition about the son of man, for this text is the origin of and not the response to that vast subsequent history.

About the son of man we learn first of all that he comes into the scene "with the clouds of heaven." The phrase seems simple enough, but the preposition "with" is susceptible of several nuances, including "together with," "by means of," or "on." If the one like a son of man is riding *on* the clouds (LXX-Dan), perhaps he is descending from heaven with them as if borne on a heavenly chariot. On the other hand, if he is coming *together with* clouds (Theod-Dan), the reasonable implication would be that the son of man is riding up from earth, rising as clouds do on the horizon. The issue between these two understandings of the simple preposition "with" is the issue between theophany (the son of man as a divine figure being brought down on clouds at the appropriate moment of disclosure) and apotheosis (the son of man as an earthly figure being lifted to heavenly heights in order to be awarded the dominion). If the former is the case, the son of man is a representative of the angels (cf. Dan. 10:16, 18) and is a divine figure who simply looks like a human being; if the latter is correct, he is a representative of human beings and a forerunner and type of ultimate human destiny. While we can grant that the clouds are normally associated in eschatological texts with heavenly figures, the fact that the son of man succeeds a series of human rulers and is given the earthly dominion in their place suggests that here he is a figure for a fifth human monarchy. This judgment is supported by the congruence between the son of man and the "stone not cut by human hands" of Daniel 2:34, 45—which seems also to be a human rule that, by God's decree, supplants all existing dominion on earth.

Is he a king or is he a cipher for an entire kingdom? That is, is the son of man an individual or a collective entity? The phrase "that all peoples, nations, and languages should serve him" (v. 14b) is stereotyped language drawn from the realm of royal ideology and points in the direction of an understanding of the figure as an individual king. But we are also aware that Old Testament imagery is never static. The individual and the collective never stay put; the two often blend and merge. Perhaps the case here is one of "corporate personality" (cf. Porteous, *Daniel*, p. 111).

The Interpretation of the Vision (vv. 15–22, 23–28)

Bracketed by the narrative of the effect of these experiences upon the seer (vv. 15–18, 28), in which the role of the angelic guide as a mediator of divine revelation is made clear, this section of chapter 7 provides the intended interpretation of the dream vision (vv. 1–14). Since we have already drawn upon the interpretation to understand the intention of the writer that the four beasts represent four kingdoms and that the eleven horns of the first beast represent dimensions of the Macedonian-Hellenistic kingdom of Alexander and his Antiochene successors, it is now necessary to deal with the one remaining facet of this section. That facet is the crucial identification of the figure of "one like a son of man" with "the saints of the Most High" (7:18, 21–22, 27). No matter who the son of man may have been in the tradition lying behind Daniel 7, these three texts make clear that he has now been radically interpreted as an identifiable and specific collective entity. The saints of the Most High are equivalent to that "kingdom which shall never be destroyed" that was symbolized in chapter 2 by the stone not cut by any human hand. Not only are these saints to receive the dominion, the kingdom, as was promised to the son of man in 7:14, but it is to be an everlasting one, and "all dominions shall serve and obey them" (v. 27*b*).

Every generation has risen to the challenge of giving the true identity of these saints. And every generation has in one way or another installed the portrait of its own saints in the frame provided by the text. The initial problem for the dispassionate interpreter is, however, not to supply saints to fit the frame, but rather to ask, Who did the writer have in mind? Who were the honorees of this high vision?

Now it is the case that angels are described as "saints" or "holy ones" (4:17), and one might expect that only angels would populate a kingdom that endures forever. Some therefore have understood the writer to be speaking of angels here as well, especially since the Aramaic word for "Most High" *(ᶜelyonin)* appears to be plural and means "Most High (Ones)." However, if we assume the intended identification of the son of man with the group called the saints of the Most High in this chapter, and if, based on verse 13, we conceive of the son of man not as an angelic figure but as a human figure lifted up by the clouds of heaven to receive the heavenly gift of dominion, then the saints

105

of the Most High must refer to a human group. The most logical group are, of course, those *hasidim* by and for whom the Book of Daniel itself was written and for whom the apocalyptic expectation of vindication was a source of particularly crucial comfort. These are the saints who even as the book was being written were experiencing the pangs of persecution at the hands of the Syrian king. It is they who expect the reward of their devotion in the form of everlasting dominion.

It still remains puzzling, however, how an *individual* figure like the son of man, probably trailing a considerable prehistory, could be related to a *collective* figure like the saints of the Most High. The suggestion that the son of man himself was always understood collectively must certainly be taken into account, though all references to the son of man in verses 13–14 are most emphatically singular. Another possibility is "to see the one like a son of man as *representative* of the saints of the Most High" (Baldwin, *Daniel,* p. 151). In the same way in which the beasts represent both kingdoms and their kings, so the son of man could represent the coming fifth monarchy even though he might remain an individual figure. The son of man might be conceived of as a priestly and as a messianic figure at the same time. Whether the general ambience of the dream vision of Daniel is the temple and the son of man is therefore a high priestly figure or whether one sees in Daniel 7 a royal environment for the mysterious figure of verses 13–14, in either case he can be made to stand for the larger community of the faithful ones in whose midst apocalyptic literature emerges and who cherish in their hearts a confidence that in the age to come they will be a nation of kings and priests to all the peoples of the world.

The Gospels and the Son of Man

Using insights already developed by Bultmann, Lohmeyer, and others, H. E. Tödt was able to organize all the uses of the image of the son of man in the first three Gospels under three headings: (a) sayings referring to the coming son of man, viewed as a heavenly judge and savior, and spoken of in the third person (e.g., Matt. 10:23; 16:27–28 || Mark 8:38; Mark 13:26 || Luke 21:27; Matt. 26:64 ||Mark 14:62, and many others); (b) sayings referring to the son of man presently at work on earth, often in contexts in which Jesus is speaking about himself (e.g., Matt. 8:20 || Luke 9:6, 58 || Mark 2:10 || Luke 5:24; Mark 2:28

106

|| Matt. 12:8 || Luke 6:5, and many others); (c) sayings referring to the suffering, death, and resurrection of the son of man (e.g., Matt. 12:40; 17:9, 12 || Mark 9:9–13, and many others) (cf. *The Son of Man in the Synoptic Tradition*). Bearing in mind that the term is used only by Jesus in the Synoptic Gospels and never of Jesus, it should be noted that types (b) and (c) never refer to the future coming and judging roles of the son of man but are intended to describe the work of Jesus himself. Type (a) does not identify Jesus with the son of man, although obviously the church came in time to make that identification.

The term *son of man* is used in the Gospel of John (3:13–14; 6:27, 53, 62; 8:28; 12:23, 34; 13:31) where the threefold distinction of the Synoptics breaks down and the preexistent heavenly figure is simply identified with Jesus (6:62). This may represent a later stage in the evolution of the image in the early Christian community away from its primitive roots. The only other New Testament use of the term as a title is in Steven's speech in Acts 7:56, where the coming eschatological judge is identified with Jesus.

How shall we evaluate the reflection of the figure of the son of man of Daniel 7 on the lips of Jesus in the Synoptic Gospels? Did Jesus refer to himself as son of man in all three of the ways mentioned above? Did he blend the representative man aspect of the image with components of the suffering servant motif as a way of describing his ministry but continue to refer to the coming eschatological judge as a separate figure, neither himself nor collective Israel? Or is the son of man motif, particularly in its type (a) usage, a contribution of the early Christian church to the Gospel traditions? These questions cannot easily be answered. Certainly whoever intended to claim for Jesus the mantle of Daniel's son of man was obliged to offer a radical reinterpretation of that kingly, transcendent, yet quasi-collective figure. It seems most likely that early Christian interpreters made the son of man/Jesus identification because, in the context of their "realized eschatology," it enabled them to affirm the dominion which they sensed had been established in the human community with the appearance of Jesus in its midst. In this sense of dominion by an elect human community, they remained close to the use of the image in Daniel 7 itself. 107 But they also deferred to the second Advent the residue of Jewish expectation regarding the judging role of the son of man, only gradually identifying that role and figure with Jesus of

Nazareth. The fact that the future son of man of the Parousia usurps the judging role of God and looks, in that sense, more like Enoch's son of man might suggest that the early Christians really drew upon the more elaborative apocalyptic image represented by Enoch in preference to the Daniel image. (A very recent and helpful study of the appropriation of Daniel's son of man image by the New Testament is P. Maurice Casey's book, *Son of Man.*)

A THEOLOGICAL ASSESSMENT OF DANIEL 7

Three theological issues which have emerged from this tour through the rich narrative and images of Daniel 7 demand some further reflection. These issues can be entitled: (a) revelation: the hermeneutical problem of the dream; (b) the eschaton and history; (c) is apocalyptic a "failure of nerve" theology?

a) Revelation: the hermeneutical problem of the dream: The entire vision of Daniel 7 is presented as a dream of the prophet. For us this creates an immediate problem, for on the whole our prophets no longer have dreams. Those who do tend to excite our suspicion. How shall we evaluate, then, the theological significance of this aspect of Daniel 7?

First, we must affirm that nobody can predict or foreshorten the range of moments in the human experience in which insight into the nature and purpose of God can take place. It ill behooves us, then, to pronounce *a priori* any particular mode of revelation to be impossible. If another person or a moment of truth or even a tree or a bush can, to use Tillich's language, become transparent to the Ground of Being in a moment of "ecstasy," then why not agree that a dream-vision can be a vehicle of revelation? At the same time, twentieth century Jews and Christians, not to mention our secular compatriots, no longer require that these moments of insight into religious truths be mantic ones. Indeed, after the centuries of experience which our forebears have had with the manipulation of ecstasy and the deceptive reporting of incubation dreams and omens, we tend to view claims of disclosure through dreams with a good deal of appropriate suspicion. Contemporary psychology has taught us that dreams are important sources of useful information; from them we learn something of the fears and desires rooted in our subconscious state. But the communications we receive in dreams come only from ourselves—we do not look to them for messages from God. The

108

biblical writers did; therefore a gap opens between ourselves and the biblical writers, the kind of gap which requires a hermeneutical bridge before the issue can be resolved.

We must begin to build this bridge with the recognition that for the ancient writer of Daniel 7, or any biblical writer, the claim to have received a vision from God in a dream had authority and that people tended to grant additional credence to the vision that was reported. Ancient culture had a whole apparatus for inculcating dreams and for interpreting them, as we have already seen in connection with Daniel 2. So in the writer's own times the report of a dream vision excited not suspicion but credence and authority. There can be no question, then, of deceptive intent on the part of the writer, though of course one could ask whether he or Daniel ever really had such a dream. Churches have begun to give official recognition to the fact that what might have been an appropriate and acceptable way to describe revelation in the second century B.C. may no longer be so: "The Scriptures, given under the guidance of the Holy Spirit, are nevertheless the words of men, conditioned by the language, thought forms, and literary fashions of the places and times in which they were written. They reflect views of life, history, and the cosmos which were then current. The church, therefore, has an obligation to approach the Scriptures with literary and historical understanding" (United Presbyterian "Confession of 1967," 9.29). It is that very literary and historical understanding which enables us to discount the significance of the dream as such, and perhaps even argue that there may never have been one, and still hold to the revelatory value of the ensuing narrative. The dream was an aspect of the cultural milieu in which the text was written. The revelatory and theologically authoritative element in this passage inheres in the authentic disclosure of God's will and purpose which it contains. But how do we know that what is disclosed is a true revelation of God's will and purpose? What gives it its ring of authenticity? The answer has to do in part with the way in which the ring of the passage is echoed elsewhere in Scripture. It is the contention of this passage that God will complete his redemptive purpose in the world by awarding to the representative of the obedient ones the right to exercise dominion in his eternal kingdom. That message is one which is repeated time and again in materials ranging from the texts of the psalms to the teachings of Jesus. It is thus reinforced by and reinforces the ongoing

109

biblical conviction that God will vindicate all that is true and righteous on the day of victory over evil. This fidelity of the text to a central biblical theme, coupled with its tremendous power as literature and the evocative character of its images—the beasts, the judgment scene, the Ancient of Days, the son of man, and the saints of the Most High, yes, even the dream apparatus—combine to count for the authority of this passage. The effectiveness of the passage in rendering its claim of truth compelling and in winning assent from the reader requires all the vivid narrative tapestry of images in which it is cast. That is why we can not simply squeeze Daniel 7 for the pure nectar of its theological truth and then throw away the dry rind of imagery. We need the dream and the beasts in order properly to feel the force of the teaching—even though we will never make the dream-apparatus normative or insist that it ever happened at all.

b) The eschaton and history: This theological and literary issue really arises at the point of transition from verse 8 to verse 9. Here it is that the move is made from a series of beasts which stand for human kingdoms whose historicity we can verify to a heavenly judgment event which is set in the undetermined eschatological future.

The relationship of the events which culminate in verse 8 and those which follow (beginning with v. 9) might be described in one of three ways. First, one could argue that the writer thought that history is predetermined, that the appearance of all of these beasts beginning with the lion with eagle's wings that stands for the Babylonian kingdom happened exactly according to God's original decree and that the denouement of history into the judgment day and the eschaton is also part of this divinely preordained plan. If the "books" (v. 10) are books of eternal destiny, this reading of the writer's intention would be further strengthened. Indeed, if one were to accept the ostensible date of the chapter and understand that the writer of the material lived during the reign of Belshazzar, King of Babylon, then all but the very beginning of the animal allegory would have been written in a prophetic vein. Only if God knew and controlled the sequence of the events of history and revealed them to the prophet in advance could the accurate prediction of the rest of the known events of history (through v. 8) have come about.

110

A second way of understanding the relationship of history

to the eschaton, as understood by the writer of Daniel 7, would be to argue that the events of history trigger the great day of judgment which God always holds in reserve against the need for it. The conception might even be mechanistic: God is so programmed to respond to human sin that when it reaches the required level of intensity he springs into action like a celestial robot and begins to consume his enemies. In verses 8 and 25, the writer reports such an escalation of evil leading up to and preceding the divine intervention of judgment. If the "books" (v. 10) are record-books, this understanding of the writer's intention would be enhanced. It would make good sense if it were assumed that the writer lived in the midst of that escalating evil just at the end of the historical sequence of the four kingdoms and saw no way out of its intolerable power but through the eschatological intervention of God.

A third way of understanding the relationship of history to the eschaton in Daniel 7 would be to see the two as totally separate. History goes on its course and it ends when God chooses to end it, there being neither a plan nor a triggering of a punitive reaction on the part of God during the course of history itself. History, in this deeply pessimistic view, would be judged a failure and something essentially meaningless; for all human striving, whether good or evil, is to be wiped away by the final intervention of God.

Of these possibilities for the relation of history to the eschaton in Daniel 7, the first, the deterministic understanding, is least satisfying to the contemporary mind. This deterministic view denies any possibility of process in human history, any true innovations, and seems to eliminate even positive new departures which derive from human responses to God's call. The second way of accounting for the relationship of these two, what one might call the retributional understanding, puts God in the awkward position of having to respond to human evil by judging and destroying the world and seems in a sense to take the initiative away from God. The third option is, though deeply pessimistic and gloomy, probably the most logically satisfying to the contemporary interpreter. By separating history and the eschaton radically, both human initiative and God's intervention are left intact, though this view perhaps denies any ultimate significance to the history of human affairs. The fact that the third view is the most logically satisfying perhaps accounts for why a number of interpreters of biblical apocalyptic have

111

argued that this was indeed the view being taken by the biblical writers themselves, both in Daniel 7 and elsewhere in biblical apocalyptic texts. Far from being "the first crude philosophy of history" (as Frank Chamberlain Porter had argued, followed by Frost in his *Old Testament Apocalyptic,* p. 6), apocalyptic in fact rejects history as a locus for detecting the working of God with his people. History has neither significance in itself nor any relation to the decisive new event which is at hand. This decisive new event is a transformation of this world into a new type of existence brought about by the power of the transcendent God and his victory over evil. All backward looking is irrelevant in the face of this event. The only use made of history is to telescope it against the new event in order to demonstrate the proximity of the crisis of the transformation of the world. Nothing in the past or in the present requires or hastens or even definitely warns of the decisive intervention of God. That intervention comes in God's own time and way.

In spite of the preference by some interpreters for the third way of explaining the relation of the eschaton and history as understood by the apocalyptist, one has the impression that the writer of Daniel 7 actually understood the relationship more in terms of the second option listed above. The emphasis (v. 8) upon the "enormity" which the mouth was speaking and upon the little horn's war with the saints (vv. 21,25) implies that to the writer the horrifying persecution and destruction of the saints required divine redress. If this was in fact the writer's view, however, it differs significantly from the rather more clearly deterministic view of the writers of chapters 8, 9, and 10—12. Perhaps we can fine-tune no further the writer's own understanding of the relationship of history to the eschaton. It remains only to add that whatever that understanding was it grew in some measure at least out of a historical situation in which the old "salvation-history" way of identifying God's acts in and through events was no longer adequate. In the history of the four beasts, which is a history of horror and oppression, God's hand had not been visibly at work; it is now going to be visible only in a great post-historical or super-historical event.

A second question which arises in connection with the theme "the eschaton and history" is the question of what the faithful ought to be doing in the meantime. If God is about to react to the escalating provocations of evil as they are displayed in the persecution of his saints, what response from faithful souls

112

is appropriate? In short, is there any basis in chapter 7 for discussing an "interim ethic"? The answer to this last question appears to be No. The single element in the chapter which comes close to bearing on the ethical and moral life of the readers is the mention of the heavenly record books which are open before the court (v. 10). To the degree that these books remind the reader of the accountability of the individual and the nation before God at the judgment, they may contribute to a sense of ethical responsibility. But it must also be remembered that the dread books here impact only upon the four monstrous nations. Apparently nothing good is written in the books, because as soon as they are opened and the judgment is rendered, the fourth beast is slain and the others are led away captive. Nor is the "one like a son of man" judged out of the book, but the son/saints are given the dominion only after the judgment has been completed. The books do not contribute significantly to the question: What ought we to be doing while we wait for God's great self-vindication?

One might extrapolate from the text the conclusion that the strong confidence in the certainty that dominion will be given to the saints through their prototype and head, the one like a son of man, called for steadfastness now in the face of danger and persecution as a prerequisite for survival into future glory. Perhaps so. But taken by itself, this position, of course, also runs the danger of encouraging quietism. Steadfastness can mean immobility and a frozen kind of righteousness which simply waits for God to act. The tremendously dynamic spirit of biblical apocalyptic does not suggest that it intends to lead people toward frozen piety. It is precisely here that the merger of the wisdom stories and midrashim collected in Daniel 1—6 with the apocalyptic materials of the latter half of the book adds a crucial dimension to our evaluation of the material. When the two are put together and the external life of Daniel is coupled with his internal understanding of the destiny of the saints, then we are indeed provided material for an interim ethic. In Daniel 1—6 one can see what Daniel did while waiting in captivity and suffering oppression and persecution. The waiting was an active waiting. It included the maintenance of sharp identity, the heightening of interpretative and prophetic skills, faithfulness before unjust demands of the foreign rulers, and fidelity to Yahweh in all things. This kind of interim ethic can give great strength to those who have confidence that the ultimate out-

113

come of the struggle is in God's hands and that the victory is to be to the saints. But taken as a whole the Book of Daniel does not encourage simple passive waiting!

c) *Is apocalyptic a "failure of nerve" theology?* An understanding of this sort is perhaps one of the most common ways of dealing with apocalyptic literature, especially among those who do not look to it to provide a literal map of the future for our own time. It begins with the observation that at a particular moment in its history Israel began to talk in the manner of a derelict, rejected by human community and far from God, who gives up the struggle to overcome the evil of the present time by vigorous action and becomes content with the assurance that the ship of good fortune is about to come in. This approach commonly focuses attention on the historical factors which at a particular moment in Israel's history interacted with inherited religious traditions to produce the peculiar literary aberration called apocalyptic.

Now there is nothing wrong with acknowledging the profound impact which history has upon theology writers. But if we reduce the thesis that historical factors determine theological expression to its least sophisticated form, we get a scheme like this: good times give rise to optimistic, positive, balanced, exultant theology writing (as, for example, in the earliest pentateuchal source, the Yahwist); transitional times give rise to theologies of ambiguity and mannerist movements of various kinds (the eighth century prophets); and evil times cause people's nerves to fail, and so they write pessimistic theologies of resignation (Job), dereliction (Qoheleth), and apocalyptic (Daniel). Now it is true that the unprecedented oppression of Antiochus IV Epiphanes may well have brought such terrible social and political pressures to bear upon Israel or the saints within Israel that they were forced to discard their time-honored theological language about covenant and about salvation history in order to speak in a radically new way about God. To say, however, that their new theology was simply the cry of those who had nowhere else to turn, who had to content themselves with the assurance of "pie in the sky by and by," is to sell short the theology of this apocalyptic material. The crisis gives shape and color to the apocalyptic tapestry, and one can hear the anguish of the people welling up within it. The themes of this literature, though, are not pessimistic themes nor are they even very new ones. They presuppose God's goodness, God's power to create

114

and recreate, God's triumph in the cosmic struggle, God's willingness and ability to achieve self-vindication before Israel and indeed before all the other nations. These themes, handed down as residue of past religious reflections to theological writers living in the midst of a welter of historical stresses, give rise to a literature which points toward the possibility of a dynamic interim ethic, the ethic discussed just above. As long as people are called by apocalyptic writing to live their lives in this risky and yet vigorous way, surely that writing cannot be equated with a failure of nerve.

Daniel 8
The Vision of the Ram and the He-goat

The Vision Account

In the chronological framework of the Book of Daniel, two years have elapsed between the first of Daniel's apocalyptic visions in chapter 7 and this one in chapter 8. We are now purportedly in the third year of King Belshazzar (perhaps about 546 B.C.); if Belshazzar ruled ten years as co-regent with Nabonidus and was in Babylon on the night of its fall to the Persian forces on October 11, 539 B.C.—the scene immortalized in Daniel 5—then the vision of this chapter supposedly took place about seven years before the final demise of Babylon. In fact, of course, we need to assume that the "many days hence" (v. 26) to which the vision is addressed is the actual time of the author's own life and that the events leading up to the culminating moment of truth recorded in verse 25 have already taken place before the author's own time. We need to assume that the vision as a whole is a prophecy after the fact. Why? Because human beings are unable accurately to predict future events centuries in advance and to say that Daniel could do so, even on the basis of a symbolic revelation vouchsafed to him by God and interpreted by an angel, is to fly in the face of the certainties of human nature. So what we have here is in fact not a road map of the future laid down in the sixth century B.C. but an interpretation of the events of the author's own time, 167–164 B.C., which is illuminated by the incandescent and indispensable claim of faith that injustice and oppression will be brought

115

to a full end by God. The lapse of two years' time since the dream vision of chapter 7 may actually be very easily explained: perhaps an author has been driven by this delay of the eschaton to offer a restatement and updating of the earlier "history" of the End.

Daniel's body is in Babylon, but in his vision he finds himself in "Susa, the capital, which is in the province of Elam ..." (v. 2). Only two of the four panels of Daniel 7—12 are given specific geographical settings, and the second of these ("on the bank of the great river, that is, the Tigris," Dan. 10:4) makes good sense in terms of the ostensible setting of the narratives in the Babylonian exile. This location makes no sense at all, but then is the setting of any visionary experience really explicable? Elam, the modern Iranian province of Khuzistan, was not a province of Babylon at all, but of the Median kingdom. Further, Susa did not exist during the last period of the neo-Babylonian era, for it was destroyed in 645 B.C. and lay in ruins until it was reconstructed in 521 by the Persian King Darius I (cf. Lacocque, *Daniel*, p. 160). No river runs through or near the ruins of Susa, which lie near the modern village of Shush, about two hundred miles east of the site of ancient Babylon. Perhaps it was for this reason as much as because of the uncertainty surrounding the word *'ubal* (river), that the ancient versions and a number of modern English translations understand the term as *'abul* (gate)—thus having the vision take place inside the city of Susa at the gate which opened in the direction of the somewhat distant river Ulai. The most helpful observation that can be made about the formal circumstances of the vision is that they very much resemble those of Ezekiel's inaugural vision (Ezek. 1:1–3); like this prophetic predecessor (or supposed contemporary), Daniel's vision occurs by a river in the east. The difference is that Ezekiel is said actually to have been by the River Chebar, among the other exiles of Judah, whereas Daniel simply sees himself in a city farther to the east. Why challenge the credibility of this vision report in this way? Only to make clear that the material which follows deals in the first instance not with the story of a real-life experience emanating from the person who experienced it some time in the five hundred forties B.C., but that it deals with a theological interpretation of history written after most of that history had already transpired and that it is designed to give the reader some purchase on the events which lay immediately ahead.

116

Daniel is not alone in this segment of his inner history any more than he was alone in his vision of chapter 7. After his vision, he is joined at the "Ulai gate" (vv. 15–16) by "one having the appearance of a man [*gaber*]" who proves to be the angel Gabriel. Perhaps the etymological connection of *gaber* (the pausal form) and *Gabr*iel alone accounts for the mention of the angel's name here, but it does seem significant that this is the very first time in the entire Old Testament that an angel is identified by name. In fact, the named angels of the Bible, Michael and Gabriel, appear in the Old Testament only in the Book of Daniel: Michael in 10:13, 21; 12:1 and Gabriel here and in 9:21.

In the Book of Daniel, Gabriel is a messenger and interpreter of God's message; he plays a similar role in the Annunciation narrative (cf. Luke 1:19, 26). Michael is Israel's guardian angel and a mighty warrior. (In the ensuing tradition he is the recording angel [Ascension of Isaiah 9:22–23]; in Jude 9 he disputes with the devil over the body of Moses, though without pronouncing "a reviling judgment.") From these data about the angels of the Book of Daniel, we conclude that the experience of God's immanence in daily life has receded late in Old Testament times and God is perceived to be more and more removed from history. No one expects him to take a direct hand until the moment arrives for a final, decisive intervention. God does not cease to communicate comfort and direction to the saints; however, now that communication takes place through intermediaries. Though the notion of a heavenly council and a "host" of angelic warriors available to serve at the divine command is a very early one, these intermediaries are now assuming identities of their own, including names. Given the greatly heightened interest in spirits and heavenly beings and emanations of the divine in the Hellenistic cultural milieu (which had spread its gnostic notions into the western Orient only to have them come flooding back highly charged with new cosmic mythological tradition), the wonder is perhaps not that the Bible dares to mention a couple of angels by name and to endow them with certain functions and characteristics, but that that aspect of angelology was kept so restricted. One need read only a few chapters of the nearly contemporary Jewish apocalypse   117
I Enoch to discover how rich indeed was angelic speculation in the sectarian Judaism of the last two centuries B.C. In I Enoch 6 alone are mentioned the names of nineteen, or perhaps origi-

nally twenty, fallen angels, including Danel and Ezeqeel. Their function among the daughters of men was not only sexual (as in Gen. 6:4), but also pedagogical, for they taught humans the arts of metalworking, cosmetics, astrology, and the meaning of the signs of the zodiac (I Enoch 7—8). This galvanized the good angels Michael, Uriel, Raphael, and Gabriel into action and, with the mandate of the Most High, they bound up and punished the fallen angels (I Enoch 9:10). It seems likely that the person who wrote Daniel 8 and the Israel who read it were aware of this elaborate contemporary lore of angels; therefore, their decision to minimize the role of these intermediaries must have been a conscious one. We who are heirs both of a richer New Testament tradition of angelology and of a long history of Christian mystic speculation have also inherited the deep conviction that God manifested himself in the midst of our human community as one of us, devoid of transcendent glory but rich in the powers of trust and love. Therefore, we can be grateful for this minimalist approach of the writer of Daniel 8. As far as we know, God has no need of angels. Angels were real to the writer of Daniel 8, but even for that writer they belonged at the margin of the history of the great transactions between God and God's people. Gabriel is a dramatic and colorful narrative detail in this tapestry of vision, but he was not for the writer and therefore is not for us a test of faith.

The genre or type of this story is a vision account. Its structure can be described as follows: the setting (8:1–2); the vision (vv. 3–14), in this case expressed in the form of an animal allegory; the introduction of the angelic interpreter and the visionary's fear (vv. 15–18); the interpretation of the vision (vv. 19–26); and the aftermath (v. 27). It is easy to see that this structure is identical with that of chapter 7, even though that chapter gave an account of a dream rather than of a simple vision.

The Vision and the Angelic Interpretation (vv. 3–14, 19–25)

Daniel's allegorical vision begins with the image of a two-horned ram, freely charging in three directions, able to prevail over all enemies, and unaccountable to any other power (vv. 3–4). However, this ram meets its match in the person of a great he-goat which arrives from the west "without touching the ground" (v. 5); with a single horn like a unicorn this he-goat is able to overcome the ram and to hold unchallenged sway. Just

118

at the height of its power, "the great horn was broken, and instead of it there came up four conspicuous horns toward the four winds of heaven" (v. 8). Daniel hardly needed an angelic interpreter to know that this vision was presenting world history through the medium of an animal allegory (cf. Dan. 7:1–8; I Enoch 85—91; IV Ezra 11—13; and the plant allegory, II Baruch 36—40). The two-horned ram represents "the kings of Media and Persia" (v. 20). The versions generally understand the word "kings" to be singular, resulting in a reading which conforms more closely to the historical reality—the ram is one king of an empire of Median and Persian components, and by extension, one unified Persian Empire. But this empire comes to grief at the hands (or rather, on the horn) of another monster, Greece, and specifically Alexander, its first king from the point of view of subject peoples in the east (v. 21). Why the unicorn-horned he-goat does not touch the ground in its arrival is hard to say, though Cyrus moved equally light-footedly in Isaiah 41:3. Perhaps this alludes to the swiftness of Alexander's conquest—Tyre besieged 333 B.C., Palestine and Egypt conquered 332, Darius III Codomannus overcome at the battle of Gaulgamela, 331 B.C. (cf. Dan. 11:3–4). At the height of his power in 323 B.C., Alexander is dead and the empire breaks into pieces (v. 8).

Greece is mentioned in the Old Testament only in late apocalyptic materials (Joel 3:6; Zech. 9:13, here and in Dan. 10:20; 11:2). Not only does this confirm that the prophecy emanates from a time when Greek power was already an established reality in the Middle East and Alexander was simply a memory, but it also provides an important chronological clue upon which to hang the entire series of historical allegories which we have encountered so far. Both the four-part series of metals in Daniel 2 and the four beasts of Daniel 7 culminate in a divided kingdom. The unicorn-like horn of the he-goat here divides into four conspicuous (v. 8) but relatively weak kingdoms (v. 22). All of these symbols are specifically identified with Alexander's empire. Therefore we can assume that in every instance the dividing kingdom is "Greece" (i.e., the Macedonian empire and its four successor kingdoms).

It is worth noting in passing that the use of animals to represent salient historical epochs hardly dignifies those periods and their respective personalities. The presentation of the Hellenistic world empire as a he-goat may convey notions of strength and virility (the Hebrew of v. 21 even speaks of a

119

"shaggy he-goat"). It may even link Alexander and his successors with the zodiacal sign of Capricorn, the horned goat, which is assigned to Syria in ancient sources (cf. Hartman and Di Lella, *Daniel*, pp. 233–34, who also mention a traditional identification of Persia with Aries, the ram); but it hardly casts a favorable light upon the experience with Greeks of at least that segment of the Judean community which gave us the Book of Daniel. Have you ever smelled a he-goat or watched its manners with other animals? An animal allegory must be considered a polemical device, and its effect is evaluative as well as figurative.

The vision conveniently finesses a considerable period of time at the transition from verse 8 to verse 9. Between the settlement of the Macedonian succession at the battle of Ipsus in 301 B.C. and the accession of Antiochus IV Epiphanes in 175 B.C. more than a century and a quarter elapsed; here, however, the intervening period of Ptolemaic domination in Palestine is simply elided. Perhaps this writer was not familiar with the details, though the writer of Daniel 10—12 has an accurate knowledge of the period; perhaps he did not deem the third century B.C. meaningful in the disclosure of the divine plan. In any case, in 8:9–14, we leap to the writer's own time. The burning question with which this section ends, "For how long . . .?" and the unfulfilled answer, "For two thousand and three hundred evenings and mornings; . . ." are the matters which most animated this writer's own community.

From verses 9–11, under the figure of a little horn sprouting from one of the four horns of the he-goat, we learn that the ruler of this period extended his rule south, east, "and toward the glorious land" (cf. 11:16, 41). Assuming that the latter is Jerusalem and its environs, we have a tolerably accurate picture of the military activities of Antiochus—his forays into eastern Syria and against the Parthians (I Macc. 3:27–37), his campaigns against Egypt (I Macc. 1:16–19; II Macc. 5:1–10), and his incursions into Jerusalem (I Macc. 1:20–35; II Macc. 5:11–26). The culminating atrocity in this career of oppression was, from the Jewish point of view, the desecration of the temple through the erection upon the altar of burnt offering of "a desolating sacrilege" (I Macc. 1:54) and its rededication as "the temple of Olympian Zeus" (II Macc. 6:2). Many scholars believe these acts really signify the installation in the temple area and its bordering citadel of a Syrian garrison for whom the temple was simply confiscated for use as a Canaanite-Hellenistic shrine (see the further discussion below on Dan. 11:31). In any event, these are the events alluded to in verses 11–12, where the arrogance of the little horn is stressed. The "truth . . . cast down to the ground" may well refer to Antiochus' abrogation of the authority of the Torah (I Macc. 1:56–57). Other details of the description here and in the interpretation in verses 23–25 remain obscure in relation to known historical events. For example, we do not know exactly what is meant by the statement, "some of the host of the stars [the little horn] cast down to the ground, and trampled upon them." Perhaps this means that Antiochene guardian angels prevailed over those of Israel, here called "the host of heaven." Lacocque even argues that "the host of heaven" includes not only angels but "the saints of Israel, who have become angelic because this was always their true identity" (*Daniel*, pp. 161–62), and that the stars themselves designate the saints (cf. 12:3, cf. I Enoch 46:7; 43:1–4). Another difficult puzzle here is the wisdom title given to Antiochus, "one who understands riddles" (v. 23). Nor is it at all clear why Antiochus' accession should have taken place only "when the transgressors have reached their full measure" (v. 23). The phrase does suggest that the dramatic, slow march of history is predetermined. It is not that the transgressors trigger the advent of the wicked king, but rather that their presence in its fullness marks that point on the tape of history at which the program calls for the appearance of Antiochus, whose appearance in turn cues in the culmination of all things. Who the transgressors are is not clear, but they are a sign that the penultimate act of the great historical drama is at hand. The concept of a predetermined historical sequence is one of the most difficult aspects of apocalyptic literature, for it is to us in many ways an extraordinarily foreign and even offensive notion. This matter will be addressed at greater length in the theological assessment of Daniel 8.

The concluding component of the "vision and its interpretation" portion of this chapter is the conversation between one holy one *(qadosh)* and another (vv. 13–14). These heavenly creatures are presumably similar to the "watchers" of chapter 6 or the myriads gathered around the throne in chapter 7, and in this chapter they seem to be members of the "host of heaven" of verses 10–12.

The function of the "holy one" in Daniel's vision is not to receive the kingdom, however, but to convey divine information. Indeed, our text suggests that that is always the proper function of divine beings, whereas it is the proper function of the earthly saints to inherit the promises of God and to bear rule in his dominion. Even though the two groups bear the same title, qedoshim, in these texts they must be distinguished from each other. It is not the intention of apocalyptic literature to hint at an elaborate meta-history involving a mystic admixture of human and divine in its portrayal of the drama of world affairs. In fact, it is of the essence of this literature that the two realms remain radically distinct from each other, even though communication across the great gulf fixed between them does take place. Only on the day of God's great intervention do these two realms in any way intersect (see the commentary on Dan. 12:1–3).

By eavesdropping on the conversation of the holy ones, Daniel learns the answer to the burning question, "For how long?" that was so often raised in Israel's days of dereliction. The duration of the desecration of the sanctuary is to endure two thousand three hundred "evenings and mornings." This phrase probably does not simply mean one day, as it does in Genesis 1, but instead is to be understood as referring to the two sacrifices offered daily in the temple. (One day implies two sacrifices; therefore, 2300 evening and morning sacrifices equal 1150 days or about 38-⅓ lunar months of 30 days each, which equals 3 years plus 70 days.) Three years plus seventy days is remarkably close to the time which actually elapsed between the desecration of the temple by Antiochus in the late autumn of 167 B.C. and its reconsecration by Judas Maccabeus in December, 164 B.C. (cf. I Macc. 4:52–59; the sequence differs slightly in II Macc. 10:3).

It is conceivable, then, that the writer who promises that "the sanctuary shall be restored to its rightful state" (v. 14) knew of the success of the Maccabean effort to drive the Syrian garrison from the temple mount and the temple's reconsecration by Judas Maccabeus. On the other hand, he could hardly have known the fulfillment of the interpretation of the promise given in verse 25—"by no human hand, he shall be broken"—unless it means, here and in 2:34, that Antiochus self-destructs (Lacocque, *Daniel*, pp. 170–71). By no human hand but by his own rottenness, he falls. Of that kind of fall (described in I Macc. 6:1–16 and II Macc. 9) the writer could have had knowledge,

122

since it occurred only shortly after the cleansing of the temple, probably in 163 B.C. Such a view is both theologically and textually attractive, for it eliminates the embarrassing expectation— not fulfilled—of a divine intervention at the end of Antiochus' reign. However, that anticipation of an act of God is strongly expressed elsewhere in Daniel, both in 7:9–14 and in 12:1–4. For that ultimate divine victory over tyranny and over all who seek to interfere in the obedient service of their God by God's people, we still wait. Suffice it to say of this text that its absolute assurance of that victory is a gift to us.

It is a matter of considerable interest that the central focus of the oppressive practices by the little horn (Antiochus) is the interruption of the temple service and the desecration of its altar. True, it is also said that "he shall . . . destroy mighty men and the people of the saints" (v. 24), but the most grievous crime is evidently that directed against the Prince of the host himself. One might expect a people suffering personal grief from persecution to bemoan the loss of life, livelihood, and property more than the loss of the right conduct of temple sacrifice. Indeed, the pain arising from the loss of material possessions is acknowledged in I Maccabees 1. Even there, the attack upon the divine prerogatives in the temple cultus is stressed. An explanation for this priority seems to lie at hand. If God's own ground can be invaded, and the very ordinances which he himself established as an abiding assurance of a vital relationship between his people and himself can be rudely set aside by a pagan idolater, can the very security of the universe itself be relied upon? Will not profound questions be raised about God's ability to protect his interests and his people and to complete his saving plan? It is perhaps in order to forestall fundamental questions such as these that chapter 8 is at such pains to assure the reader of the ultimate security of the temple and its praxis. Even though Christian eschatology reaches maturity in an era in which the temple and its cultus have permanently passed from the scene, those glimpses of the future which it vouchsafes include dramatic scenes of the heavenly temple, the prototype of the Jerusalem temple of old, open even to its inmost parts (cf. Rev. 11:19). But also to be noted is the promise of the eschatological age in the new Jerusalem: "And I saw no temple in the city, for its temple is the Lord God the Almighty and the Lamb" (Rev. 21:22).

123

The Interlude (vv. 15–18)

Daniel's vision and the angelic interpretation are separated in chapter 8 by the odd little passage in which Daniel seeks and receives understanding (vv. 15–18). As was noted earlier, this element is a standard part of both a dream vision and a vision account. The "one having the appearance of a man" (v. 15) is, as the next verse shows, the angel Gabriel. Presumably the "man's voice" which calls out instructions to Gabriel (v. 16) is the voice of God: Who else but God has the authority to issue orders to an archangel? As always in the Old Testament, the appropriate human response to a theophany is the one which Daniel makes in verses 17–18—fright, prostration, a "deep sleep" (the word is a technical one implying something like anesthesia or even death; see the commentary on Dan. 10:9), and the divine touch. One confronts God only at great peril and enters into the dialogue with God or the angelic emissaries of God only with divine permission.

At least the seer and his world do not face immediate dissolution, for a comforting eschatological reservation is given. All of the content of this vision is "for the time of the end" (v. 17; cf. vv. 19, 26b), for the ultimate culmination of history which follows "the latter end of the indignation," that is, this present age with its escalation of evil and its outrageous oppression. The eschatological reservation maintains the fiction that the entire narrative is being shown to one living centuries before the events alluded to within it. Daniel personally need not fear, because he will not even be alive when these events take place. The presence of an eschatological reservation is useful, however, even for those who understand that they are nearly at the end time, perhaps within a thousand or so days of the eschaton, because by it they can confirm their dreadful hunch. To the degree that all the things which are supposed to happen in "the time of the end" begin to happen, to that degree believers can know that the end draws near in their own days. At least, that is the way it is supposed to work. The fact that the end has been indefinitely postponed poses a difficult hermeneutical problem which we will address in the theological assessment of chapter 8.

124

Two Interpretative Motifs (v. 26) and the Sequel (v. 27)

For the most part, the angelic interpretation has been dealt with in connection with the vision itself. Only three motifs in verses 26–27 require further discussion. First, the angel affirms that the vision is true. This is a rather remarkable affirmation, when one thinks about it, because the entire experience has come to Daniel indicated as a divine revelation. If it comes from God, of course it is true! The presence of this motif can only be accounted for, then, by assuming that it is addressed to a reader living at a time long after that in which the writer ostensibly lived. Such a reader might be inclined to doubt the possibility that a detailed vision of future history could have been given to an ancient worthy. That suggestion seems to be supported by the second motif, "seal up the vision, for it pertains to many days hence." This command, repeated in 12:9, can be found in the older prophetic tradition, albeit in somewhat different words, in Isaiah 8:16. There Isaiah gave a command: "Bind up the testimony, seal the teaching among my disciples." Certainly Isaiah's words indicate the presence around him of a band of disciples. The command "seal up the teaching" shows that Isaiah was making conscious provision for the preservation of his teaching by that band. The same can be said for the Book of Daniel. In this case, however, the admonition only enhances the literary fiction that the book was written long before it actually was. The reader is asked to believe that the vision, sealed up many years earlier, has now been opened, and that the days must therefore be drawing near the end. In short, this charge enhances the prophetic dimension of the book, leaving the reader all the more impressed, both with the accuracy of the overview of history which the ancient prophet was able to give and with the dramatic nearness of the end of that history. By way of contrast, the people who hear the prophetic cries of Ezekiel comfort themselves by saying, "the vision that he sees is for many days hence, and he prophesies of times far off" (Ezek. 12:27). In that case, they are dead wrong. Their attempt to denigrate the prophet's words by assigning them to the distant future is rebutted by Yahweh himself, " 'None of my words will be delayed any longer,' says the Lord" (v. 28).

In the sequel of verse 27, Daniel is left overwhelmed and ill by the effects of the vision. Eventually he recovers, but he remains appalled and without understanding. Of this third motif one might ask, Why did he not understand, given the extensive and lucid interpretation which God provided through the angel Gabriel? The answer is that Daniel was speaking about things which he had neither experienced nor

125

seen, but which the reader had both experienced and seen—
the events leading up to and including that reader's own time.
The failure of comprehension must thus be seen as an effective
literary device designed to promote an intense reading of the
book by the audience in and for whom it was written.

A THEOLOGICAL ASSESSMENT OF DANIEL 8

The thrust of Daniel 8 is the same as the central claim of the
apocalyptic tradition as a whole: God will not be mocked. He
will achieve his purpose to overthrow and utterly to destroy
tyranny. Goodness will be vindicated, and the saints will at last
enter into the victory of their God and Lord. With that theological claim also comes the unblinking realism of verse 25: between that victory and the present age many will be destroyed
and the oppressor "shall even rise up against the Prince of
princes."

Falling over this sober but sweeping claim is, however, a
deep shadow. It is a shadow with which all interpretations of
biblical apocalyptic texts have perforce to deal. The eschaton
failed! The seer got it wrong. Whether Daniel 8 was written in
Belshazzar's court or during the pogrom of Antiochus IV, the
eschatological solution proposed did not in fact arrive. Antiochus met his fate in due course, but it was in the familiar historical manner experienced by tyrants in every age—at the hands
of his enemies. The same problem nags at the heels of chapter
7 as well (the saints have yet to receive the kingdom, so far as
we can tell!) and will confront the rest of Daniel 7—12 as well.

One way of getting around this hermeneutical problem is
to argue that somewhere along the scenario lies an indefinitely
long time warp. The End has simply been delayed. This solution
to the problem runs athwart the normal intention of the prophetic utterances in the Old Testament to address the community of Israel living at the time of the prophet with words of
promise and of judgment to be fulfilled in the immediate future. It also runs athwart the three year, seventy day time span
of verse 14 which implies an eschaton anticipated in the very
near future.

No, a time warp will not do. We have to answer more
forthrightly: to the degree that the prophet predicted as imminent the divine intervention which appeared in the vision, to
that degree the prophet failed to call history correctly.

For all that failure of the vision of culmination, two claims

126

of chapter 8 remain paradigms of hope for Jews and Christians alike, namely, that the sanctuary shall be restored to its rightful state (v. 14) and that the oppressor "by no human hand . . . shall be broken" (v. 25). Although God's ultimate victory is God's alone and cannot be depicted in advance in any literal way, not even on a calendar, nevertheless, the knowledge that God intends to guarantee a center of relationship between himself and his people and to put a full stop on oppression is vital and energizing knowledge. It can abundantly motivate us to get on right now with the tasks of establishing a right God/human relationship and ending oppression. It can drive us to give in our own lives foretastes of the age which lies ahead, even though that age is radically disconnected from our age, and comes about only at the time and in the manner of God's own choosing.

Daniel 9
Daniel's Prayer and Gabriel's Message

The Content of Chapter 9

At first glance the least interesting in the entire Book of Daniel, chapter 9 in the end proves to be rich because of its elaborate inner-biblical connections. Taken as a whole, it is neither a dream vision nor a waking vision; if anything, it seems to be an extension of the vision of chapter 8. The two protagonists, Daniel and the angel Gabriel, are carried over; and the identification of the latter as the "man . . . whom I had seen in the vision at the first" (v. 21) seems to imply continuity between the two chapters. Yet if the editor had any real grasp of the chronology of the ostensible epoch of the narratives, the dates given for the two chapters can hardly suggest a close continuity. The vision of chapter 8 occurs in the third year of Belshazzar's reign (*ca.* 546 B.C.), and the account of chapter 9 is set in the first year of the rule of Darius (Cyrus? *ca.* 539 B.C.), leaving a gap of seven years.

Broadly speaking, we might call this chapter a *meditation,*   127
since it revolves around a "perception" which Daniel experienced (v. 2) about the meaning of the seventy years which, according to Jeremiah 25:11–14, "must pass before the end of

the desolations of Jerusalem." Within that larger framework, we can easily discern three salient sub-units: the setting and the problem of the seventy years (vv. 1–2); a great prose prayer of penitence (vv. 3–19); the angelic interpretation of the original "perception" (which seems actually to be a query about the significance of Jeremiah's seventy years of desolation, vv. 20–27). The entire passage is related to chapter 8 as if it were an answer to the question, How long, O Lord, will the oppression of the saints endure? But chapter 8 did not leave that question open, for its own version of it (8:13) was answered with the precise chronological assessment of three years and seventy days (8:14). We may do well to conclude, then, that the connection of chapter 9 to chapter 8 is more apparent than real and that the actual purpose of chapter 9 is to engage in some important re-utilization of Scripture. This midrashic effort will seek to translate the meaningful (though not entirely accurate) figure of seventy years predicted by Jeremiah as the duration of the Babylonian exile of the Jews into an even more meaningful framework for the march of history down to end times. The purpose of this reapplication of the seventy-year scheme is to enable the second century writer to point out to the contemporary reader a spot on the end-time scenario and say, "You are here!" Yet all of this has to be done without violating the fictional sixth century exilic setting of the hero, Daniel. The trick will be to acknowledge the original significance of the seventy years and identify that with the end of the Babylonian exile, while at the same time to address the situation of the community suffering under Antiochus IV Epiphanes more than four centuries later.

The Setting and the Problem of the Seventy Years (vv. 1–2)

Verses 1–2 show why Daniel is focused on the seventy years of desolation of Jerusalem prophesied in Jeremiah 25:11–14, and alleged to have been the actual length of the exile in II Chronicles 36:20–21. He is living in exile and Jerusalem is in fact desolate. Jeremiah was prophesying about his generation. In the privacy of his place of study he prays. How and for what does he pray, seeing that he has already "perceived" the duration of the period of the desolations of Jerusalem to be seventy years? The question is complex, because the perception itself is presented as the motivation for the act of prayer which follows. Such a syntactical sequence corresponds very well with the content of the prayer, which culminates in a plea for the removal of the very desolation which will be removed in any case at the appointed time. Though neither prayer nor piety nor wit of any kind can thwart—or, for that matter, hasten—God's intention to save his people at the end of seventy years, it is nevertheless appropriate for the saint, and through him the people, to offer prayers of ascription (v. 4), confession (vv. 5–8, 9–14), and supplication (vv. 15–19) as statements of understanding of the experiences endured and as testimonies of faith in God's justice and mercy. Such prayer is appropriate seventy years before God's saving intervention; it is appropriate seventy times seventy (490 years before the end; vv. 24–27), and it is appropriate at any time in between. It is, in short, another example of the interim posture of the saint who can through prayer glorify God even as God points beyond the dark confines of the present era of tragedy to the bright age of reversal and renewal which lies ahead.

The Preparations for Prayer (vv. 3–4a)

Not only the issue of the seventy years, but also the language and form of Daniel's prayer which follows, demonstrate the extent to which this chapter is a meditation of Scripture upon earlier Scripture. The words and traditions of older Israelite prayer are everywhere to be found. Montgomery graphically demonstrates this dependency by identifying every word or phrase which can be paralleled elsewhere (*Daniel*, pp. 361–68). More than eighty-five per cent of the text falls within quotation marks. Heaton calls the passage "a splendid catena of Old Testament fragments" (*Daniel*, p. 306).

Questions have been raised about the appropriateness and originality of the prayer in its present context. Whatever the arguments pro and con, the crucial question for interpretation is, What is the role of the prayer in its present setting? Is it a kind of theological commentary upon the historical crisis facing the apocalyptist's generation and for which Daniel 7—12 is proposing a final and ontological solution? Is it an epitome of the religious problem to which the surrounding apocalyptic context speaks, much as the poetic passages of Daniel 1—6 are summaries of the outcomes of the narratives within which they stand? Does the prayer provide a vehicle for bringing to bear on the eschatological situation so vividly developed in the surrounding materials the religious language, patterns of speech, and insights provided by the deuteronomic and liturgical traditions?

Before discussing the text of the prayer itself with the aim of answering these questions, a word should be said about the preparations for the prayer described in verses 3–4a. As a consequence of his perception of the seventy year period of desolation, Daniel turns his face to the Lord God, "seeking him by prayer and supplication." The notion of "turning the face" suggests the act of orienting oneself directionally toward the Jerusalem sanctuary in the course of private prayer, a custom preserved in the Muslim notion of *qiblah* as well as in the Jewish and Christian architectural tradition of orienting the holiest part of the house of prayer toward Jerusalem. The customs of "fasting and sackcloth and ashes" were proper spiritual preparation for prayer, particularly a prayer of confession (cf. Neh. 9:1f., another confession; also Exod. 34:28; Deut. 9:9). The relation of these practices to penitential devotion is clear enough.

These preparations lead one to term this prayer a "prose prayer of penitence." The appropriateness of that designation is underscored by its formal affinities with three other long prose prayers (Ezra 9:6–15; Neh. 1:5–11; 9:6–37), all penitential in character and all containing elements of ascription, confession, and petition. This set alone, out of almost fifty prose prayers in the Old Testament, is identified with the key word, *lehitwaddeh*, "to make confession" (which itself occurs only four other times in the Old Testament). It looks very much, then, as though we are dealing with a distinct genre of prayer. The fact that it occurs only in relatively late texts may suggest that it reflects prayer practice in the second temple or even in the nascent synagogue. The fact that it occurs both in "priestly" and in apocalyptic materials—often thought to be antithetical to each other in social origin and theological outlook—poses an interesting problem, to say the least. (For a more detailed discussion of the genre and its significance, see Towner, "Retributional Theology in the Apocalyptic Setting.")

The Prose Prayer of Penitence (vv. 4b–19)

The great prayer opens in 9:4b with a salutation to the Lord, an ascription, and a rather longer predication of God's attribute as covenant-keeper. This introduction, which can be matched almost perfectly both in setting and in content to the introduction to the prayer in Nehemiah 1:5 is a stereotyped reflection of the great covenant formulation, Exodus 20:6 (cf. Deut. 7:21). *Qua* covenant-giver, God is not only one who holds his people responsible for the very transgressions which they confess in the verses which follow, but he is also one whose "steadfast love" is renowned and dependable (cf. Deut. 7:9, 12; I Kings 8:23).

The prayer continues in verse 5 with a list of five largely synonymous general terms for sin, piled up "in liturgical style" (Jeffery). The list is an expansion of the instruction on the proper form of a collective prayer of penitence embedded in Solomon's prayer of dedication of the temple. It is instructive to set these two texts side by side.

I Kings 8:47 (II Chronicles 6:37)	Daniel 9:5
"We have sinned, and have acted perversely (Hiphil of *ᶜawah*) and wickedly"	"We have sinned And [have] done wrong (Qal of *ᶜawah*) and rebelled . . ."

In the light of the dependency of the language of Daniel's prayer on that of Solomon, one is warranted in asking whether the narrative setting of the former has significance for the narrative setting of the latter as well. Those whom Solomon instructs to utter the formula of penitence are exiles under the interdict of God; he assures them that if they truly repent and utter the prescribed penitential formula, God will hear their prayer, maintain their cause, and forgive them (I Kings 8:49–50). The narrative context of the prayer of penitence in Daniel 9 exactly suits the situation described hypothetically in Solomon's prayer. A people in desperate straits are ready to admit their sins in the formulae acceptable to God and the tradition; they hope God will redeem them for the sake of his name and because of his steadfast love. They hope that God will respond as Solomon promised he would respond, as indeed he responded of old when he brought them out of Egypt, "from the midst of the iron furnace" (I Kings 8:51).

The comparison with I Kings 8 points up an interesting discrepancy between the otherwise very comparable prayer situations. In that text, the king himself serves his people by interceding for them and teaching them how to do penance. In Daniel 9:4*b*–19, on the other hand, the failure of the king along with every other class in the body politic to hearken to the

131

divine word through the prophets is described as one of the sins which have brought on the present judgment. In the prose prayer of penitence of Nehemiah 9:6–37, kings are given the same treatment afforded them in our text: together with princes, priests, and fathers, they are lawbreakers who have brought calamity upon their people. Like Daniel 9:4*b*–19, prophets are not listed by Nehemiah among the lawbreakers. Nervous as his hierocratic circles may have been about prophets, he includes them among the righteous sufferers, not the sinners.

Daniel's prayer of penitence begins, then, with a confession of the failure of a whole people—from king to the lowliest of the people of the land—to heed the word given them in the name of God by the prophets. It is a statement deeply rooted in the sacred tradition of Israel. The positive value given the prophetic word is consonant with the thrust of the prophetic tradition itself. The judgment on all the classes of the people is phrased in terms like those of Nehemiah's great prayer. The whole is set in the apparently liturgical context of a prose prayer of penitence, and finally, the prayer is presented by the narrative setting as a response to a political and national crisis very like that envisioned by the deuteronomist in the great prayer of Solomon at the dedication of the temple. In all these ways, the writer of Daniel 9:4*b*–19 exhibits his profound and complex dependence upon older tradition as he sets about to create a new device for reflecting theologically upon the tragic situation of the people.

The confession begun in the previous two verses continues in verses 7–8, still directed by Daniel to God. The structure is an antithetical one, contrasting the righteousness which is God's property and the "confusion of face" which is characteristic of the several civic strata of the people. The present dispersed condition of the people is attributed directly and completely to the "treachery which they have committed against thee." God is not to be blamed. Although the use of the term "treachery" is itself confined almost entirely to the late literature, the interpretation of difficult straits as divine retribution for sin is, of course, a much earlier idea. It is in full flower in Solomon's prayer in I Kings 8, where penitential prayer is prescribed as the antidote for such a situation. However, as we soon shall see, retributional theology and penitential prayer alike develop special nuances.

132

At verse 9, the pronominal address of the prayer suddenly switches to the third person; through verse 14 the prayer becomes a prayer sermon. This shift in point of view does not necessarily imply the presence of a different hand or source, however. Not only does this unit of the prayer carry on the themes and ideas advanced in verses 5–8, but one can elicit numerous instances in the practice of prayer in the Jewish community in which the discourse modulates quietly from talk addressed to God to talk about God addressed to the hearers and back again. It is part of the essential psychology of public prayer that the community is both led in devotion and instructed in doctrine during the course of the petitions.

In verse 10, the writer again lays stress on Israel's transgression of God's laws which had been mediated to them by God's mouthpieces, the prophets. Such a role is not unbecoming to the prophets in the light of the role assigned them by the deuteronomic writers; they were to be givers of prophetic Torah and mediators of the covenant tradition. Like the deuteronomists and Jeremiah their ally, the writer of these verses allows no place for a priestly role in mediation between God and his people. Perhaps we can detect in this a deliberate rejection of the validity of priestly Torah in a historical period when the *hasidim* and other observant Jews were singularly offended by the illegal machinations in and around the priestly center in Jerusalem.

Verse 11 continues with a reiteration of the explanation of the present disastrous situation of the Israelites already given (v. 7): Israel has transgressed the law. Therefore, "the curse and oath" (a zeugma for "oath of the curse") "which are written in the law of Moses have been poured out upon us." The "oath of the curse" referred to here is a specific one, namely, the well-known sanctions attached to the covenant formulations of the Pentateuch (Lev. 26:14–45; Deut. 28:15–68; 29:18–28). The activation of these curses, whose role within the whole covenant pattern is well known, lies behind the present disaster. Although the apocalyptic images for the evils of the penultimate time (trouble . . . devoted . . . broken . . . stamped . . . desolation . . . fire . . . darkness . . . blood . . . darkening) constitute a repertoire of language quite different from the essentially agricultural terms of the curses in Deuteronomy 28 and Leviticus 26, nonetheless, the cause-effect relationship of covenant disobedience and suffering seems to loom large in this writer's

133

consciousness. Unprecedented calamity has happened to Jerusalem "as it is written in the law of Moses" (v. 13).

There is nothing unusual about the equation law of God equals law of Moses; the Sinai tradition was identified with Moses from the very beginning (Josh. 8:31; 23:6; cf. I Kings 2:3), and increasingly all law and all traditions were known as "given to Moses at Sinai." Of interest here is the fact that this law of Moses decrees punishment precisely for those who disobey God's law given to Israel "by his servants the prophets" (v. 10). In short, prophetic preaching is identified with God's/Moses' law. Further, "Moses the servant of God" (v. 11) must be reckoned among "[God's] servants the prophets" (v. 10). It seems clear, then, that to the writer the covenant stipulations of the Pentateuch and the indictments of the prophetic tradition are interchangeable and that together, or separately, they account for the present distress of Israel when interpreted as punishment. Moses, around whose head are welded the traditions of both law and prophetism, now wears the crown of final authority for interpreting the evil situation now being given an apocalyptic answer. We cannot say more about Moses' role, however, for this is the only mention of him in any canonical apocalyptic text (he is also mentioned in passing in Rev. 15:3).

The two verbs of verse 12, "he has confirmed . . . by bringing," provide the sharpest statement yet of the conviction of the author that the calamity is of God's making; it confirms the dependability and seriousness of the words of indictment and threat which he had uttered in the past. Whether this confirmation in disaster is a cause for rejoicing because it is seen as new evidence of God's faithfulness is more questionable than many commentators seem to think; humanly speaking, it is unlikely that parties to disasters ever rejoice very heartily!

In verse 13, the writer continues to drive home the point that the destruction of Jerusalem (or in the second century context, its desecration) is only the fulfillment of the curse long ago pronounced in the law of Moses. The people have failed to take the next step: "we have not *entreated the favor of* (lit: mollified) the LORD. . . ." The reader is struck with the question of what constitutes mollification. Why has the regular cultic practice of the period (whether the fictional or the actual one) not counted as mollification? Why have the newly emerging practices of piety associated with the synagogue not won the favor of God? If prayer and sacrifice alone will not suffice to mollify the Almighty, what about the zeal of those who offer life and limb in defense of the laws of the fathers and the purity of the sanctuary? What about the careful ritual and legal observations of the *hasidim* and the observant groups? What about the vision of the apocalyptist? Unless the problem is simply that there have not been prayers of penitence according to the prescription of I Kings 8 and genuine repentance on a national scale, then will anything being offered here by the seer and saint, Daniel, count with God more than these other acts of devotion? In the light of the clause following this one, together with the restoration and renewal which God reveals following the prayer as a whole, the reader can only conclude that it was precisely the expression of penitence that was lacking before God could be mollified.

These considerations about verse 13 bring us at last to a full picture of retributional theology in Daniel 9. The elements of that picture are these: (1) there has been "a great calamity" (v. 12) (on the face of it, the calamity is the destruction of Jerusalem and the temple and the deportation of the exiles. But the calamity uppermost in the mind of the writer and the readers alike is the pogrom against Jews instituted by Antiochus after 168 B.C., and the reconsecration of the temple to the worship of Zeus Olympios [Ba'al Shamen]. That Jewish writers tended to speak of the latter in hyperbolic terms, such as "for under the whole heaven there has not been done the like of what has been done against Jerusalem" [v. 12] is confirmed by texts such as I Macc. 1:39–40; 2:7–12). (2) this calamity is understood to have resulted from the sin of kings, princes, fathers, and all the people of the land (vv. 6, 8)—everyone except the prophets, who have not shared the general blame, but who have warned of the expectations of God and of his sanctions; (3) the calamity has taken place because God is consistent and faithful to his character as Righteous One; (4) the means are now at hand (and always have been) to ward off the disastrous consequences of the sin of disobedience, and those means are precisely prayers of penitence; (5) hope can therefore spring up because restoration and restitution are possibilities; (6) but restoration and restitution are now fundamentally different experiences from those envisaged in the older expressions of covenant theology. Now, in the apocalyptic setting, they are cosmic in scope and eternal in consequence. 135

Up to and including step 4 of this line of thought of Daniel

9:4*b*–19, the retributional scheme is quite familiar. Even in the narrative context of Daniel 7—12, which places the prayer in the fictional setting of the Babylonian exile but also implies the real setting of 167–164 B.C., the combination of historical experience and theological interpretation is very similar to the line developed by Solomon in the great prayer of instruction of I Kings 8. Even the formula for a public prayer of penitence taught by the deuteronomic writer of I Kings 8:46 is employed, the implication being that through prayer, coupled with sincere repentance, the curse can be overcome and the blessing restored. But when blessing and restoration take the cosmic form envisaged in Daniel, the essential artificiality of the link between retributional/covenantal thinking and apocalyptic begins to emerge. No doubt the writer seriously thought that the present troubles are nothing but the accursed fruits of covenant disobedience, though raised to the cosmic degree. But can mere prayers of penitence undo such history-wide and cosmos-wide evil? Can ontological renewal be brought on by the little prayer of a single righteous man?

Apparently the writer of Daniel 9 wanted to give a qualified Yes answer to these questions, incredible as that statement may seem. The qualification is substantive, however. As Gabriel makes clear in verses 20–23, the eschatological redemption was decreed before ever Daniel uttered his prayer. In contrast to the rather naïve assumption of I Kings 8:46–53, the effect of Daniel's supplication is to occasion the disclosure by God through his messenger of the real extent of the symbolic seventy-year period of waiting until the already decreed and therefore inevitable redemption takes place.

Because the legal demand and the penalties for disobedience have already been announced, and because Israel has been warned as the law required, God is blameless in bringing forth the calamity already prepared and stored up. This appears to be the burden of verse 14, the last verse of the prayer sermon. Not only have we "not obeyed his voice," thereby eliciting his just wrath, but he "is righteous in all the works which he has done. . . ." One who is righteous can not be called to account on any ground, covenantal, personal, or other. Yahweh's righteousness cuts across all such lines, preserving the perfect freedom of the righteous one. As "righteous one," Yahweh is free to do what he wills, because what he wills is also *righteous* and in no way contradictory with his will already revealed in Torah.

136

Perhaps the coupling of the calamity of the writer's day with the assertion that "God is righteous" in all his works helps clarify the view of the writer of this prayer regarding the relationship of the penultimate evil to the events before and after it. Though one looking on from outside might wish to argue that any God who visited upon his people a disaster unlike any "under the whole heaven" was an arbitrary, angry, and capricious God, no matter what his provocation had been and no matter what glorious restoration awaited those who endured the evil time, this writer has an answer: The Lord is in all these things righteous. These disasters, as well as the imminent restoration, are fruits of his righteousness.

This line of reasoning about the righteousness of God leads directly into a consideration of the relationship of the End to history in the view of the writer of Daniel 9. Retributional theology requires a historical process within which its scenario can be played out: God gives law—people break it. God punishes them—they repent. God restores them. God may take the last step on his own time, but—if I Kings 8:49 is to be taken seriously—God is more or less honor-bound to take it once the guilty have repented. He must do so because he is righteous. When this retributional scheme is put in the apocalyptic setting, the last event of history (repentance) and the new age of redemption (the kingdom of heaven beyond the Day of Yahweh) are inextricably linked; the linkage is God's transcendent and dependable righteousness.

At verse 15 the prayer returns to direct address; and, pivoting on the phrase "and now," the long-awaited appeal to the mercy of God pours forth:

> confession: we have sinned against the savior from Egypt (v. 15);
>
> supplication: let the anger pass away (v. 16);
>
> supplication: let thy faith shine upon thy desolate sanctuary (v. 17);
>
> supplication: judge us not according to our deserving, but according to thy great mercy (v. 18);
>
> *kyrie:* O Lord, forgive (v. 19).

137

The confession is directed in the first instance to the savior from Egypt. The exodus events had long been Israel's prime evidence for the good and redemptive purpose of God; prophets and psalmists alike had used *salvation-history* as their prime demonstrations of God's power and mercy. How peculiarly significant it is to invoke the evidence of God's redemptive purpose in 164 B.C., a time in which both contemporary experience and apocalyptic rhetoric seemed to emphasize the vindictive and judgmental aspect of God's character!

The appeal to the mighty deeds by which God founded and brought forth the nation is language proper for asking God now for a new public and universal manifestation of his saving nature. The appeal is from one salvation to another. Covenant language has enabled the writer to establish Israel's liability for punishment and thus has exonerated Yahweh. Now the use of exodus language can establish the hope that God will save Israel after all and will restore her "to that intimate relationship with himself which—though forfeited by ungrateful rebellion—is her true norm" (Heaton, *Daniel,* p. 208). The appeal for vindication has an element of mutual self-interest within it: God is called upon to glorify himself by saving a people in dire need. Salvation of this sort might technically have been unavailable under the deuteronomic retributional scheme strictly understood. Though God might modify his judgments with mercy, the sentence of death had still to stand. Yet here an appeal is made over God's justice to his mercy for Israel's sake *and* for his own. A prayer of penitence is the vehicle employed for this purpose. Though in a sense it is being used to circumvent the law, this use opens up a new means whereby God might glorify himself.

This notion is carried further in verse 17. The phrase "cause thy face to shine upon thy sanctuary" is reminiscent of the language of the well-known Aaronic benediction, "The Lord make his face to shine upon you" (Num. 6:25). If the parallel is intentional, God is being asked to shine in blessing upon his own house in the manner in which priests of that house had long called upon him to do for others. Now the sanctuary itself is "desolate." It is no longer the God-given source of blessing but is blessing's needy recipient. Even more clearly than was the case in verse 16, the appeal to God to cause his face to shine upon the sanctuary is predicated upon his own true interest and nature—"for thy own sake, O Lord." As is true from time to time in the prophetic tradition, this appeal (following Theod-Dan against the Masoretic text "for the Lord's sake"; cf. Isa. 37:35; 48:9–11; Jer. 14:7–8) is an appeal to God to "act in

138

accordance with his revealed character" (Porteous, *Daniel*, p. 139).

The escalating appeal to God's personal interest reaches full voice in verse 18. On behalf of the city "called by thy name," and in a manner more mechanical than that of any of the other great prose prayers to which Daniel 9:4*b*–19 has been compared, the writer grounds his supplications not on Israel's righteousness, but purely and solely on God's renowned willingness to set aside the demands of the law for the sake of redemption. He hopes for salvation in spite of sin.

The striking verse 19, often called the Old Testament *kyrie, eleison,* is a fitting summary and conclusion of the entire prayer. In a vocative mood underscored by a series of four verbs in the imperative, the writer reiterates the appeal to God to act "for his own sake." He then goes on to motivate the entire sentence, and perhaps the entire prayer, with a concern for the safety of the people and the city that are called by Yahweh's name. It may fairly be said that this motive clause, more than any other phrase in the Book of Daniel, assimilates the ancient deuteronomic "name theology" into the apocalyptic setting in Daniel. The intention of the appeal seems to be to tie God's hands, as it were. To the degree that he has committed himself to preserving the safety of those things which are named by his name (identified with him, blessed in his name and with his sanction), to that extent the God of Israel has limited and compromised his own freedom to act in the future. Here, on the desperate edge of the "last days" and fully aware of its liability to punishment before the law, Israel appealed to that name almost as one would appeal to an amulet which works *ex opere operato.* When no ground for mercy is left save God's own announced intention to preserve that which has been declared inalienably God's, Israel is willing to lay claim to that source of hope as well.

A THEOLOGICAL ASSESSMENT OF DANIEL 9:4*b*–19

On formal grounds, we have described Daniel's great prayer as a "prose prayer of penitence," rich with language drawn from the tradition, shaped by the model given by Solomon in I Kings 8:46–53, and paralleled three times in Ezra-Nehemiah. The situation envisaged by Solomon in I Kings 8:46–53 is perfectly played out here—through Daniel, Israel, already experiencing desolating punishment, admits to breaches of covenant and

139

appeals to God's steadfast love. The implication of I Kings
8:46–53 that God will indeed show that love is also implied here.
Yes, prayers of penitence accompanied by true amendment of
life are efficacious in setting aside the covenant sanctions; they
will mollify God more effectively than any other cultic act.

When placed in the apocalyptic setting, this conviction
seems to take on an element of the absurd. Are cosmic renewal
and restoration available to those who simply say, "We have
sinned"? While he obviously intends to demonstrate that prayers of penitence have a part to play in the ultimate crisis, the
writer of Daniel 9 no longer can agree with the writer of I Kings
8:46–53 that such prayers can set aside the calamity and trigger
the long-awaited glorification of the saints in scenes of eschatological triumph. He is not so bold as to suggest that the new age
hangs by a mere thread of repentance and that one little word
will drop that new aeon into the place of the present evil age.
In fact, restoration and renewal are not dependent upon human
prayer at all, for God has already decreed the hour of his great
intervention.

Why pray penitentially, then? Such prayers occasion the
assurance that victory is near. So it is in confidence in God's
righteousness, revealed in the exodus experience, that the formal appeal to his mercy over his justice is made. In a sense, the
prayer of penitence and supplication is used to circumvent the
law. Finally, an appeal to God is made for the sake of his own
name. This amounts to a cry to God to recognize the limitation
which he had already imposed upon himself, namely, his determination not to destroy that which was his own. The whole
effect of the prayer is to recognize and demand a theodicy. God,
having vindicated his justice before all the nations by punishing
his own people as his law demanded, is now asked to vindicate
his mercy by forgiving and saving his people in the knowledge
that to do so has world-wide, yes, universal implications. Retribution is finally embraced by restoration; God is finally not the
avenging judge but the dear friend.

The Angelic Interpretation of Daniel's "Perception" (vv. 20–27)

140

Gabriel, whom Daniel first encountered in his dream vision
of chapter 8, was already enroute with his interpretation of the
all-important seventy years before Daniel even finished his
"supplication . . . for the holy hill of [his] God" (v. 20). (We learn

more and more about angels as our book unfolds! Verse 21 is the first text in the Bible in which an angel travels on wings; the winged cherubim bending over the mercy seat [Exod. 25:20] were surely replicating their heavenly originals; the seraphim of Isaiah's temple vision [Isa. 6:2] had six wings. But until now *angels* simply appeared! Gabriel's appearance "at the time of the evening sacrifice" may have no more significance than to remind us of the persistence of Jewish memory of the temple ordinances even when the temple itself was out of commission.) The word which "went forth"—surely an ancestor of the "daughter of a voice" *(bath qol)* of rabbinic tradition—was the voice of God (cf. Matt. 3:17). It is therefore the source of the "wisdom and understanding" (or "perception"—the Hebrew word is the same in 9:2) which Daniel is to be given. He did not ask for wisdom and understanding in his prayer, but rather he asked for forgiveness and for God's action. However, the action which he experiences is enlightenment, given him because he is "greatly beloved" (v. 23). Being made "wise" *(maskil)* by God, he surely belongs to that company of "those who are wise" *(maskilim)* who will enjoy the brightness of the coming resurrection victory (Dan. 12:3).

The interpretation begins. Verse 24 sets forth the objectives of the culminating era of Israelite history. It is to be a period of progress in overcoming sin and in atonement. Though God alone can win the final victory and effect the ultimate renovation of the world, God's people have a penultimate partnership role to play "to bring in everlasting righteousness, to seal both vision and prophet, and to anoint a [lit.] 'holy of holies.' " Sealing vision and prophet refers to the fictional setting of Daniel. When the supposedly long-hidden message is found, taken out of its time capsule, as it were, the seal is broken and the text is found to be extraordinarily descriptive of the present moment. Then all can know that the last phase of the preeschatological age is winding down and that the end is at hand.

Such a comprehensive program requires time. With an effortless interpretative pen, the writer has the angel expand Jeremiah's seventy-year estimate of the period of Babylonian captivity (Jer. 25:11–14) to seventy weeks of years ($70 \times 7 = 490$ years). In theory, this would seem to allow until either 107 B.C. (597, the first exile, minus 490 years) or 97 B.C. (587, the second exile, minus 490 years) until the culmination should be at hand. However, we can assume from verse 27 that the writer

141

believed the end would arrive during the reign of Antiochus IV Epiphanes a few years at most from his own time, which was about 164 B.C. One can well imagine that the chronological charts which might have provided precise information regarding the time elapsed since the beginning of the Babylonian exile were simply unavailable to the writer of Daniel 9, so perhaps that writer thought nearly four hundred and ninety years had actually elapsed.

The interpretation now proceeds to factor the seventy times seven time period into segments. The process which occupies the remainder of chapter 9, and which is repeated in a much more elaborate way in chapters 11—12, reveals the typical apocalyptic concern with calendar and the passage of the years. It is a concern which apocalyptic literature shares with both cult and wisdom literature, but it is a broad human concern as well.

No one has failed at one time or another to experience a sense of unease at the turning over of the calendar. What is the meaning of this inexorable march? Have the events of the past day or month or year moved us toward any goal or away from any pitfalls and tragedies? Since we are manifestly one day or one month or one year nearer to our own deaths, is the world also nearer its demise? Apocalyptic literature provides a clear and essentially rationalistic answer to such uneasy questions. Yes, the turning of the years is meaningful, not because of human accomplishments or failures which may have taken place during the passage, but because every age brings us closer to the culmination and the dawning of the new Jerusalem. For those who have ears to hear, like Daniel, God will even provide an interpretative guide; and through the help of such "wise" persons, the working out of the divine plan can be found amid the welter of human events and the relative nearness of the present age to the last day can be measured (see the further discussion of the divine plan below).

Phase one in the angel's predetermined map of history (that is to say, the seer's chart of largely completed history) is a seven week or forty-nine year period from the "going forth of the word" to restore and build Jerusalem "to the coming of an anointed one, a prince." Since the period under consideration begins with the Babylonian exile, this forty-nine year segment must refer to the exile itself (which was actually 49 years in length, if the dates 587–538 B.C. are used). The "going forth

142

of the word" or divine order to restore and build Jerusalem may refer to the word mediated through Jeremiah himself (25:11–14), though the prophet does not refer to the rebuilding of Jerusalem in that oracle but refers only to the destruction of Babylon. A better candidate for the reference to rebuilding would be the order which Cyrus received from the Lord according to his edict in Ezra 1:2–4: "The LORD, the God of heaven, . . . has charged me to build him a house at Jerusalem, . . ."

The other terminus of the first phase of the four hundred and ninety year scenario is "the coming of an anointed one [*mashiah*], a prince." Since this coincides with the end of the exile, the writer must be looking at the figure of Joshua, the high priest, or Zerubbabel, the governor, whom the prophets Haggai and Zechariah charged with the task of rebuilding the temple (cf. Hag. 1:1–14; Zech. 6:9–14; in Zech. 4:14 both are said to be anointed). If the text were read "an anointed one *and* a prince," both of these historical figures could be acknowledged in this prediction.

The sixty-two weeks (62 × 7 = 434 years) that follow are troubled times, but Jerusalem is extant "with squares and moat." (The Hebrew *haruts*, "moat," has only recently been understood as it has been found in Aramaic inscriptions and the copper scroll from Qumran. These suggest that a better translation would be "conduit"; the reference would then be to the water system of Jerusalem and not to a defensive moat. Even a visionary would find it highly unlikely for a hilltop town in an arid environment to have a moat!) This is presumably the period of the Persian Empire and the Hellenistic kingdoms down to the mysterious events mentioned in verse 26. At that time, "an anointed one shall be cut off, and shall have nothing; and the people of the prince who is to come shall destroy the city and the sanctuary." If we stay with the date assumed for the Book of Daniel throughout this volume, the "prince who is to come" must be Antiochus Epiphanes, since he is the final major actor in the story (assuming that the "desolator" of v. 27 is none other than he, who promoted the cult of Ba'al Shamen on the very altar of Yahweh in Jerusalem). Although it seems excessive to say that he "destroyed the city and the sanctuary," he at least rendered the latter unusable to observant Jews by turning it over to the Syrian garrison and installing their cult within it. Antiochus may even have displaced the entire populace, re-

143

placing it with Greco-Syrian citizens of Antioch at Jerusalem. In this event he "destroyed" it as far as Daniel's people were concerned. Another possibility is that the event alluded to here is the earlier sack of the city and installation of the citadel by Antiochus' general Apollonius in 168 B.C. (cf. I Macc. 1:29ff.; see also the discussion of these matters below in connection with Dan. 11:29–35).

Working backward from this identification, we may assume that the "anointed one" who is cut off is not the one mentioned in the previous verse, namely, the high priest Joshua after 538 B.C., but rather a successor in the same line. Such a figure is at hand in the person of Onias III, the legitimate high priest at the time of the accession of Antiochus IV, who was deposed in favor of his brother Jason (who bought the office from Antiochus in 175 B.C.) and was ultimately murdered at the instigation of Jason's successor Menelaus in 170 B.C. (cf. II Macc. 4:33–35).

Of the "flood" which comes at the end of the city and the sanctuary we can say nothing, unless a flood of Syrian troops is meant. But desolations there were, aplenty. The "strong covenant with many" made for the span of the last seven years by the prince (Antiochus) is the league with the Hellenizing Jews referred to in I Maccabees 1:43. Yes, even then there were those who found it possible to make the compromises necessary to get along in the frightening world in which they lived with a minimal exposure to personal and economic damage! Three and a half years into this final phase, the prince causes the sacrifice and the offering to cease (see the full description of it in I Macc. 1:54). For the final three and a half years, this desolate state of affairs remains. Then, in a finale just as abrupt as that of 8:25, the "decreed end is poured out on the desolator." The time is not far off the mark. According to First Maccabees, the temple was out of Jewish service from 15 Chislev 167 B.C. (1:54) to 25 Chislev 164 B.C. (4:52–58), when the Maccabees restored the daily sacrifice on a cleansed and rededicated altar. Antiochus' own end came not long after, perhaps in bed in Babylon after failing to plunder a temple in Persia (I Macc. 6:1–16).

A THEOLOGICAL ASSESSMENT OF DANIEL 9

144 The deterministic outlook of Daniel and the other biblical apocalyptic texts has been discussed in a preliminary manner in connection with chapter 7. Let us now enlarge that discussion by acknowledging that the notion has become quite foreign to

large segments of Jewish and Christian thought. Literalistic interpreters, of course, still hold to the idea of a predetermined divine plan inexorably being worked out in history. In fact, elaborate schemes, such as that of pre-millennial dispensationalism, purport to be able to draw charts of the entire sweep of human history and, on the basis of the interpretative clues given in Scripture, to pinpoint our present location on the chart. Many, however, have rejected the notion that human history can disclose a meaningful divine plan. Human history belongs to humans, and it resonates with the clash of the human will for the preservation and enhancement of the species with the human will for self-destruction. God acts in that history, all right, above all through the memory of the healing and loving ministry of Jesus Christ in the midst of the history, but also through the words of encouragement, obedience, sacrifice, and honor whispered by the Holy Spirit in human hearts. God also suffers and responds and takes new initiatives, just as we have to do all along the way.

Oh yes, God does have a plan to complete his redemptive work in the world. Both in the resurrection of Jesus Christ and in the promises of God regarding the Kingdom which lies ahead, we have assurance that resurrection and new life are the ultimate outcome and that "the creation itself will be set free from its bondage to decay and obtain the glorious liberty of the children of God" (Rom. 8:21). And it is here that we return to the importance of the witness of the apocalyptic texts for us in spite of our tendency to challenge the notion of divine predetermination of history which they contain. These texts hold out to us the certainty that God will win in the end over the destructive powers of oppression and violence. That certainty we believe because we must, if we are to survive, and because we see it confirmed in the story of Jesus' life, death, and resurrection. Even though God reaches that goal by a route far more hidden and complex than can be disclosed to us in any historical scenario, including those of Daniel 7, 8, and 9:24–27, history is not therefore insignificant. It is the theater within which earnests of that coming age are given. It is the realm in which prayer is offered and acts of obedience and courage take place. It is the age of interim ethics, which can guide us on the tortuous twisting road toward the promised Kingdom. The last bridge on that highway linking this age and the age to come has never been built and never will be, so we cannot march directly from here into the gates of the new Jerusalem. Even the scenarios of Daniel 7—12 make it clear that God alone inaugurates this new age; it is not the end result of any historical process, not the end of the road on which we are now traveling. In our time, we have to go even farther than these apocalyptic texts were prepared to go, to affirm that the new age is not even related to the human calendar and the march of human history. It is God's *novum*, his totally new act. But from the perspective of the eschaton (to use Pannenberg's phrase), the true significance of human history will be seen. It will be seen not as the slow unfolding of a detailed divine plan established from the beginning of time, but as a long, rich tapestry of scarlet and white threads, of blood and purity, of anger and tenderness, of sin and righteousness, in which people of good will and saints of all persuasions time and again have given foretastes of what life is like in the Kingdom of heaven. God will vindicate all such anticipations when he establishes that Kingdom. Therefore Daniel's posture of penitence, courage, and trust is exactly the right posture. He may not live to see "the decreed end" poured out on the desolator (9:27), nor may we. Indeed, we may all be the desolator's victims. But we are victors nonetheless, because we have struggled to make the world look as much as we can like the coming Kingdom. If we have a picture of the new Jerusalem, what better way can we live now than to prefigure it, even though we cannot build it?

In the first decade of the nineteenth century, the English poet William Blake wrote the dramatic poem "Jerusalem" which has become the anthem of the British Labor Party.

> And did those feet in ancient time
>   Walk upon England's mountains green?
> And was the holy Lamb of God
>   On England's pleasant pastures seen?
>
> And did the Countenance Divine
>   Shine forth upon our clouded hills?
> And was Jerusalem builded here
>   Among these dark Satanic Mills?
>
> Bring me my bow of burning gold!
>   Bring me my arrows of desire!
> Bring me my spear! O clouds, unfold!
>   Bring me my chariot of fire!

I will not cease from mental fight,
  Nor shall my sword sleep in my hand,
Till we have built Jerusalem
  In England's green and pleasant land.

Daniel could not have agreed with this marvelous vision, for to him the march of history and its end are all one sequence decreed in heaven. Christian realists of the twentieth century cannot agree with Blake, either, precisely for the opposite reason: the end and the ensuing eschatological Kingdom are God's own deeds, radically separate from history, and not the end result of any historical process, not even the utopia-building efforts of Christian masses. But the vision of the end does affect history after all, because it assures us that all acts of faithfulness, trust, and righteousness will be vindicated. And the vision of the Kingdom beyond the end gives us direction on the road we walk today. For if in the era of God's own "home rule," the best of all possible worlds, righteousness, peace, obedience and trust, love, and healing carry the day, why then, what better way can we live right now than in that same spirit?

Daniel 10—12
The Final Vision and an Ominous Postscript

The Final Vision: A First Reading

Not only does the position of this panel at the end of the Book of Daniel suggest its decisive importance, but also the lengthy trials which the seer must undergo in preparation for the reception of the vision point to its magnitude. Further, the panoply of heavenly beings which is involved bespeaks a cosmic struggle taking place in its own plane on a course parallel to the drama of human history. Clearly this panel is dealing with events on a scale larger than anything yet seen in Daniel, and the outcome is perceived to be more decisive. The vision proper projects two and a half centuries of world history as a sweeping drama of armies and kings clashing and dashing here and there. But all the *Sturm und Drang*, though meaningless in itself, proceeds according to the divinely decreed destiny. Nothing happens by chance; nothing happens prematurely.

147

This is crystal clear to the reader standing at the end of the two and a half centuries, and the fact that the predicted course has been followed in exquisite detail leads that reader to turn about and face forward with confidence, certain that the future, too, though not yet come to pass, will be as securely in God's hand as world history has been since the seer's time "in the third year of Cyrus king of Persia" (10:1). History does empty out without a break into post-history, into the eschatological age. In 12:1–3, from the relatively near horizon of political and military catastrophe for the oppressor of the saints, the eyes are suddenly lifted to the broad horizon of resurrection and renovation. The meaningless ebb and flow of human lust suddenly becomes meaningful as history proves to have been the inevitable and preordained wearing away of the dike which separates this age from the age to come; or, to change the metaphor, it has been the necessary trickle of sand through the hourglass of destiny. The certainty of the coming end of history is strongly affirmed, together with the certainty that God will be the victor in that day and that all wisdom and righteousness among the saints will be vindicated. For the interim remaining between the vision and the end, Daniel is given a rudimentary ethic—trust and obey!

The correctness or incorrectness of this initial reading of Daniel 10—12 will be tested and the ideas given more nuance as we proceed to a detailed reading of the text. First a word should be said about the setting, the characters, genre, and structure of the panel as a whole. Daniel's final vision takes place "In the third year of Cyrus king of Persia . . ." (10:1). This date is in direct contradiction with the notice that "Daniel continued until the first year of King Cyrus" (1:21), unless the latter simply means that he remained in exile until 538, the year of Cyrus' famous decree. Further, it is not clear whether the reference to the third year of Cyrus' reign over Persia itself (since he assumed leadership in 550 B.C., the date in mind could possibly be 547 B.C.) or, as seems more likely, the third year of his reign over the Jewish diaspora in Babylon, that is, 536 B.C. But neither of these dates is entirely convincing, for two reasons: (1) neither allows for the insertion of the reign of "Darius the Mede" who figures so importantly in the mind of the redactor of Daniel and who is understood to be the immediate predecessor of Cyrus (cf. 6:28; 9:1; 10:1; 11:1); (2) Cyrus is never actually called "King of Persia" in the ancient records after his

148

conquest of Babylon in 539 B.C. From that point on until much later Hellenistic times, he was known by such honorific titles as "the great king," "king of kings," and the like. So we must conclude, as we so often have done before, that the chronological framework provided for the Book of Daniel has only a loose connection to the actual course of history and shows precisely the kind of imprecise command of details that we might expect from a writer who lived more than three hundred and fifty years after the dates being used. Furthermore, the writer or redactor may have been animated by motives quite other than historical verisimilitude, such as, in this case, a desire to round out Daniel's prophetic ministry in Babylon to an even seventy years ("the third year of the reign of Jehoiakim king of Judah," Dan. 1:1 [606 B.C.] to "the third year of Cyrus king of Persia," 10:1 [536 B.C.]).

The contention of a great many modern interpreters that the book was actually brought to its present form some time in the year 164 B.C., but before the successful recapture and rededication of the temple in December 164 B.C., is given its greatest support by these chapters. Such support depends, of course, upon the assumption that all but the very last segment of the great historical survey of chapter 11 was written after the fact and that the point at which the author is actually living is to be located precisely at that point at which he turns from an increasingly accurate review of the past to a totally fanciful prediction of the future. That turning point can in fact be located in the white space between 11:39 and 11:40 and the date derived from the discussion of that pivot point will establish the time of at least the final substantive redaction of the entire book and probably the composition of the apocalypses of Daniel 7—12.

It is not easy to be clear on the question of how many characters this little apocalyptic story has. First, a narrator delivers just one verse (10:1) and then disappears for the entire remainder of the book. Daniel's friends fade from the scene as quickly as they appear, all in verse 7. The opening and closing ceremonies of the section include a good deal of first-person narrative by Daniel himself; however, the largest block of text comes from the mouth of an unnamed interlocutor, "a man clothed in linen" (10:5; cf. Ezek. 9:2—10:17). This angel evidently speaks for the first time in 10:11. Both from the similarity of his opening address to 9:22-23 and from the notice in 11:1

149

which links the work of this unnamed figure to the events recounted in chapter 9 (which also take place in the first year of Darius the Mede, 9:1), we are probably being led to understand that this heavenly *persona* is the angel Gabriel who was the interlocutor of chapter 9. This identification is further confirmed by the collegiality which this speaker shares with his peer and fellow angel Michael (10:21).

The only problem with this identification lies in the description of the "man clothed in linen" (10:5–7). The figure pictured there, whose face was "like the appearance of lightning, his eyes like flaming torches, his arms and legs like the gleam of burnished bronze" is reminiscent of Ezekiel's inaugural vision (Ezek. 1:1–28). But there the figure with the loins of "gleaming bronze" is specifically identified with divinity— "Such was the appearance of the likeness of the glory of the Lord (v. 28)." If not God himself, might this figure be the "one like a son of man" of Daniel 7:13? Lacocque thinks so, and underscores this identification by pointing out how much the vision upsets the seer (*Daniel,* pp. 206–11). For him, the angel Gabriel appears for the first time in 10:15–21. The early Christians saw the Christ in this figure (as a comparison of this passage with Rev. 1:13–16 and with 19:11–16 reveals). Against this identification, however, is the fact that the first speech of the "man clothed in linen" (10:11–14) identifies him in the same way as does the lengthy address which begins in 10:20; namely, as the one who fought the Persian prince/angel alongside the angel Michael. Such combat does not seem to be the work of "one like a son of man"; were it accepted as his work, the result would be to push the son of man image sharply in the direction of an angelic figure. Both from a literary and a theological point of view, this is an unfortunate direction. Literarily it is difficult because the one like a son of man is specifically identified with the "saints of the Most High" in 7:18; and these saints are of no significance to the reader of the text if they, too, are an angelic host. They must represent some human community to whom the message of hope is being addressed. Theologically the identification is unfortunate for the same reason; the message of biblical apocalyptic wants finally to deal with the destiny of a human community, perhaps the whole human community, and not concern itself exclusively with warfare and victory in the angelic realm. Because no compelling reason requires that we identify any of the obviously angelic figures in this chapter with the "one like a son of man" of chapter 7, let us assume that we are dealing only with Gabriel and Daniel in the exchanges that take place here. The two other angels of 12:5 may appear in 10:16 and 18, but they remain silent in every instance.

Little needs to be said about the genre of this final section of the Book of Daniel. It presents itself as a vision account, accompanied by the most fulsomely given preparatory and concluding rituals of any to be found in Scripture. No dream is involved here, as was the case in chapter 7. The apocalyptic vision leads up to the question, "How long?" (12:6), which was the burning issue of chapter 9. As has often been remarked, the vision here substitutes for the prayer of that chapter, but the eventual response remains the same as that found in 9:27: three and a half "times" (12:7) must elapse after the "abomination that makes desolate" before God will have his victorious way.

This panel falls into the following simple structural analysis:

10:1—11:1 The onset of revelation and introduction of the interlocutor(s)

11:2—39 The course of human history
a) from the Persian empire through Antiochus III (vv. 2–19)
b) the reign of Antiochus IV Epiphanes (vv. 20–39)

11:40—12:4 The apocalypse
a) the destruction of Antiochus (11:40–45)
b) the double resurrection (12:1–3)
c) the sealing of the testimony (12:4)

12:5–11, 12, 13 An ominous postscript and two redating glosses.

The Onset (10:1—11:1)

The preparation phase of Daniel's final vision is introduced by a single verse given by a narrator, perhaps the final redactor of the book. In addition to dating the oracle, the narrator swears to its authenticity: ". . . the word was true, and it was a great conflict" (10:1). Unlike his earlier experiences (e.g., 8:27), Daniel understands this vision, perhaps because it is not in the form of a symbolic dream which requires translation into the vernacular. Instead, it is presented from the beginning as an account of history, although without the naming of any names.

151

Whether verses 2–3 suggest that Daniel induced his ecstatic experience through fasting and other ascetic exercises is difficult to say. On the whole, biblical writers seem not to favor the legitimacy of the use of such devices by a seer deliberately to hatch a divine-human encounter. So perhaps we should take these verses at face value as referring to a period of mourning (for what, we are not told). Subsequent to this three-week period Daniel experiences the great vision which is the centerpiece of these chapters. Unlike any other vision of the Bible, it takes place on the banks of the "great river," the Tigris. (Normally the term "the great river" refers to the Euphrates, and so commentators tend to see this identification as a gloss. The Syriac, in fact, reads here "the Euphrates.")

The appearance of the man clothed in linen, whose body glows with the sheen of various precious metals, causes Daniel's friends to tremble, though they see nothing. (Did they hear something, like Saul's friends on the Damascus road, Acts 9:7?) For his part, Daniel becomes radiant, like Moses with the shining face (Exod. 34:29–35). His private theophany is his glorification, but it is also nearly his undoing. He falls on the ground without any strength left. Indeed, he prostrates himself in "a deep sleep" (v. 9). This "deep sleep" has already been encountered in 8:18; in fact, it seems to be part of the regular apparatus of apocalyptic vision. In the Bible this term refers to those special moments when individuals sleep through frightful events in an almost anesthetized way. Sometimes they may even be temporarily dead (cf. Rev. 1:17). Adam goes under with this sleep before his rib is removed (Gen. 2:21), and Abram experiences it in the presence of God before the covenant is sealed with the smoking fire pot (Gen. 15:12–17). Sisera sleeps like this while Jael drives the tent peg through his skull (Judg. 4:21); Jonah sleeps like this below decks while the fatal storm rages outside the ship (Jonah 1:5). And, oddly enough, a lazy son sleeps this way through the harvest (Prov. 10:5)! It is a sleep associated with disaster or terror, and it becomes a thread in the elaborate, colorful tapestry of apocalyptic vision. Its highly specialized character suggests that it belongs to the realm of storytelling rather than to biography or actual experience.

152

Three times angelic hands administer "celestial first aid" (Hartman and Di Lella) to the nearly incapacitated Daniel, once to set him up on his hands and knees (v. 10), a second time to cure the muteness which temporarily afflicted him just as it had

done to Ezekiel (vv. 15–16; cf. Ezek. 3:26–27; 33:21–22), and
finally simply to give him back his strength (v. 18). In the midst
of these nostrums, the angelic interlocutor speaks words which
give Daniel credit: the angel has come because Daniel set his
mind to understand and has humbled himself before God from
the very beginning (v. 12). Then follows the angel's strange
comment that he had been delayed in coming because "The
prince of the kingdom of Persia withstood me twenty-one days
. . ." (v. 13). It was only with the help of ". . . Michael, one of
the chief princes, . . ." that he was able to get away long enough
to interpret the final vision to Daniel. Lest one think that the
"prince of the kingdom of Persia" is Cyrus or some other human
king, the parallelism of the verse alone suggests that this prince
is a peer of and counterpart to the angel Michael, who is the
prince of Israel (cf. v. 21). From this we can extrapolate to the
conclusion that this writer believed that events on earth were
recapitulating the warfare raging in heaven. As if angels themselves were not already problematic, this notion, deeply rooted
in myth, could cause the contemporary reader endless difficulty; fortunately, however, the text does not want to make
much of it. (See further discussion of the matter in the "Theological Assessment of Daniel 10—12.")

The really important information which the angel now
brings has to do with the events that will take place on the
earth. It is the substance of ". . . the vision . . . for days yet to
come . . ." (cf. 8:13; 9:24). Everything that the angel is now going
to tell to Daniel before he has to return "to fight against the
prince of Persia," and subsequently against the "prince of
Greece" (v. 20), has already been "inscribed in the book of
truth." (The RSV misleads by rendering with a colon the copula
which follows "book of truth," v. 21a. Such a rendering implies
that the mutually supportive deployment of the angels Gabriel
and Michael described in 10:21b—11:1 is what is written in the
book; the understanding followed here and by most commentators is that the long historical resumé which begins in 11:2 is
what is written in the book. Clarity could be achieved in this
matter by transposing v. 21a either to follow the question in v.
20a or to the first sentence in 11:2.) This must be the famous
book of destiny and not the record book of human deeds (see
the commentary on Dan. 7:10). In this book are written in
advance all the events which must take place throughout the
course of world history. The presence of the book here puts the

153

writer of this apocalypse more strongly than the writer of chapter 7 on the side of the notion that history is predetermined and that the march of kingdoms across the stage is merely the elaborate turning of toy soldiers according to a program written out in advance by an omnipotent deity. It is a theological position which has little positive value for our own theological perspective; in fact, it has to be regarded as a theological liability! If apocalyptic literature is to have an important significance for understanding our own present and future, this view has somehow to be transcended. (See the further discussion of the matter above with regard to Daniel 9.)

The Course of Human History (11:2–39)

The final panel of the Book of Daniel now begins a lengthy review of Near Eastern history from the time of the Persian conquest of Babylon down to the writer's own time, put in the mouth of the angelic interlocutor. This segment of the scenario falls into two natural divisions, the course of events from the beginning of the Persian Empire through the reign of the Seleucid king, Antiochus III the Great (vv. 2–19), and the lengthy discussion of the reign of Antiochus IV Epiphanes (vv. 20–39). Although this review is vague in some details, it maintains a rather remarkable fidelity to history as it has been recorded in secular sources. Therefore, to persons who understood it to have been written prior to the events that took place, it appears to be an impressively detailed and accurate prediction of future history. The reader may wish to follow the sequence on the chronological chart given in the Introduction.

"Behold, three more kings shall arise in Persia; and a fourth shall be far richer than all of them; . . ." (11:2). The great review of history begins with a reference to four successors to Cyrus. Since ten Persian monarchs ruled after the time of Cyrus, it is difficult to know who the four referred to in verse 2 might be. Without attempting to solve that problem in detail, we can safely identify the fourth king with Darius III Codomannus, since he comes into direct encounter with the kingdom of Greece. Alexander the Great acceded to the throne of Macedon in exactly the same year that Darius III came to the throne of Persia, that is, 336 B.C. Alexander overcame Darius at the battle of Gaugamela in 331 B.C. and fell heir to the entire Persian Empire as far as India. It is he to whom the writer refers in 11:3 (see also 8:5–8). His death in 323 B.C. and the subsequent division of the kingdom into four parts ruled by military successors who saw to it that Alexander's own progeny could not succeed him seem well epitomized by verse 4. From verse 5 and through the rest of the panel, the action centers on just two of the so-called Diadochi, the four Hellenic generals among whom the empire was divided. These are the king of the south and the king of the north, who are respectively the Ptolemaic rulers of Egypt and the Seleucids of Antioch in Syria.

Ptolemy I Lagi (323–285 B.C.), also called Soter, was the Macedonian commander who assumed control of Egypt at Alexander's death. Through his support, Seleucus I Nicator was able to defeat a rival to the satrapy of Babylon in 312 B.C. After the battle of Ipsus in 301 (in which the succession to Alexander's empire was definitively settled), Seleucus fell heir to a kingdom which stretched from the Hellespont to India and which centered at Antioch in Syria. This Seleucus is the prince who was "stronger than he," that is, Ptolemy (v. 5). Verse 6 refers to a royal wedding which took place in the next generation of monarchs. Ptolemy II Philadelphus (285–246 B.C.), the "king of the south" of that verse, presented his daughter Berenice in marriage to Antiochus II Theos (261–246), the "king of the north" who was the second in line after Seleucus. This marriage became possible only after Antiochus divorced his first wife and half-sister Laodice. By agreement with Ptolemy, only sons of Berenice could succeed to the throne; but after Ptolemy's death Antiochus rejected Berenice and reclaimed Laodice. The conclusion of these messy political maneuvers in the bedroom was that Laodice murdered both Antiochus and Berenice, together with the infant son and the Egyptian attendants of the latter; to these events the writer alludes at the end of verse 6. (The same scandalous marriage is apparently referred to in the story of the dream of the colossus with the feet of clay, Dan. 2:43.) Note that no significance is attached to this event or any of the others. They are recited only as evidence that the prophet can accurately foresee the future down to the end of history, as if he could read the pages of the book of destiny!

The "branch from her roots" (v. 7) apparently refers to the brother of Berenice, Ptolemy III Euergetes (246–221 B.C.), who came from Egypt to Antioch in Syria to save his sister and ultimately to avenge her death by exacting the life of Laodice. He returned to Egypt not having completely taken advantage of his victories in the north, but he brought with him an enor-

155

mous amount of booty. Secular sources confirm that Ptolemy received the title Euergetes, "the benefactor" because of the richness of the spoils which he brought home from this expedition to the north. Apparently these even included some of the precious vessels and images which had been carried to Babylon in an earlier age by the Persian conquerors, a tradition known even by Jerome (so Hartman and Di Lella, *Daniel*, p. 290, citing J. Linder, *Commentarius in Librum Daniel*, 1939).

Verses 10–19 refer to the extraordinarily confusing events surrounding the reign of the greatest of all Seleucid monarchs, Antiochus III (223–187 B.C.). In 219 he began a drive to recapture lost territory and become the master of Palestine by recapturing Antioch from Ptolemy IV Philopater (221–203 B.C.). The decisive encounter in this first round of Seleucid renaissance was the defeat of Antiochus' "great multitude" (11:11) at the battle of Raphia (217 B.C.) on the border between Palestine and Egypt. Polybius (*Histories*, v 79) tells us that Ptolemy's army consisted of seventy thousand foot soldiers, five thousand cavalry, seventy-two elephants and was personally commanded by Ptolemy and his sister-wife, Arsinoe. Ptolemy won the battle but did not press his advantage (v. 12), so after a period of fourteen years, during which time Antiochus won for himself the title "the Great" by virtue of his recapture of much of the eastern part of the old Seleucid empire, Antiochus was ready once again to move on Egypt. By this time the Egyptian king was the infant son of Ptolemy IV, Ptolemy V Epiphanes (203–181 B.C.). As step one in his inexorable march against Egypt (v. 13), Antiochus defeated Scopas, the Aetolian mercenary in command of the Egyptian forces, at the battle of Banias at the source of the Jordan River (198 B.C.); this gave him control over Coele-Syria ("hollow Syria," the southwestern region bisected by the Great Rift Valley). Evidently, certain insurgents in Egypt and among the Jews arose to take advantage of the situation and to overthrow Ptolemaic rule, but without success (v. 14). The reference to the siege of the "well-fortified city" (v. 15) apparently recalls Antiochus' siege of the remnant of the Egyptian forces at Sidon in Phoenicia (198 B.C.). Antiochus' victories placed him at last "in the glorious land" (v. 16; cf. Dan. 8:9; I Enoch 89:40; 90:20), but he stopped short of an attack on Egypt itself. A treaty of peace was made with Ptolemy V, sealed by the gift to the young Ptolemy of the daughter of Antiochus as a wife. She was the first Cleopatra, who, according to Jerome, was married to Ptolemy in 193 B.C. at Raphia. If Antiochus hoped to control Ptolemy through Cleopatra, however, the ploy failed (v. 17): "It shall not stand or be to his advantage." Apparently Cleopatra turned into a loyal Egyptian Hellene and even urged her husband to seek an alliance with Rome (Hartman and Di Lella, *Daniel*, p. 292).

History tells us that, following his victories over Ptolemy, Antiochus moved to claim the former satrapy of one of the original Diadochi, Lysimachus, in European Thrace. Then, in 192 B.C., accompanied by the Carthaginian Hannibal, he landed in Greece. This was a threat which the Romans could not tolerate. First they defeated him on land at Thermopylae, then at sea. Finally, in 190, the Roman "commander" (v. 18), the consul Lucius Cornelius Scipio (subsequently entitled "Asiaticus"), permanently ended the Antiochene threat to Europe at the battle of Magnesia near Smyrna in Asia Minor. After this defeat, Antiochus fell further and further into difficulty; and finally, in 187 B.C., he was assassinated while attempting to rob the treasury of one of his own sanctuaries in Elam in order to raise the cash needed to pay the tribute to Rome (cf. Bright, *History*, p. 420).

The brief and undistinguished reign of the son of Antiochus, Seleucus IV Philopater (187–175 B.C.) is dismissed in verse 20. The transition of sovereignty to Seleucus' younger brother, Antiochus IV, is fraught with difficult questions and no small amount of skullduggery. This furtive transition must be referred to in the cryptic phrase, ". . . he shall be broken, neither in anger nor in battle."

The remainder of the historical portion of chapter 11 (vv. 20–39) refers to the notorious reign of Antiochus IV Epiphanes (175–163 B.C.). We are now certainly within the span of the author's own life and the things of which he writes at some length here are things which he himself had experienced. Antiochus IV is "the contemptible person to whom royal majesty has not been given" (v. 21). His accession to the throne was, from the beginning, flawed. Antiochus had been held hostage in Rome after the defeat of his father at Magnesia in 190 B.C., but in 175 he made a return. The conspirators against Seleucus IV, chiefly Heliodorus (notorious for his sack of the treasury of the temple in Jerusalem; cf. II Macc. 3:1–40) perhaps wished to place one of the more pliable sons of the murdered Seleucus on the throne. But Antiochus, through the cunning summarized in

157

verse 21, moved quickly to set aside any efforts to crown one of his nephews and instead took his brother's place. His early years were politically successful. All opposition was quickly crushed and even the "prince of the covenant," the Jerusalem high priest Onias III, was swept aside (v. 22). Not long after Antiochus' accession in 175, the brother of Onias, Jason (a Hellenized version of the name Joshua) approached the monarch with an offer to buy the high priesthood for a total of four hundred and forty talents of silver (II Macc. 4:8). As II Maccabees 4:23–24 points out, Jason, in turn, was deposed by Antiochus when another aspirant to the high priesthood, Menelaus, proposed to pay him seven hundred and forty talents of silver for the office. The latter must rank as one of the great scoundrels in all of Jewish history. Not only did he default on his payment to the king, but when the deposed Onias protested his theft of golden vessels from the temple treasury, he had him murdered (II Macc. 4:32–43).

The actual historical events to which verses 23–24 refer are not entirely clear, though the policy of scattering spoils among his friends seems to have been so typical of Antiochus that he is remembered even by Josephus (*Ant.* xii 7,2) and I Maccabees 3:20 as being very liberal with his gifts. But with verses 25–28 we return to a clearer picture as the text describes Antiochus' first war with Egypt. The details need not trouble us here; the campaign is briefly summarized in I Maccabees 1:16–19. It is worth noting that Antiochus' own sister, Cleopatra, was still the queen mother in Egypt and that she had acted as regent for her minor son. When this king, Ptolemy VI Philometor, Antiochus' nephew, was captured, the Egyptians crowned his brother, Ptolemy VII Euergetes II Physcon, as king. Antiochus tried to use this event as a means of rallying Philometor and his forces to his own side. It is this mischief at the dinner table to which verse 27 refers. However, the two kings failed to overthrow the Egyptian rule, and, in fact, the two Ptolemies ultimately were reconciled by their sister Cleopatra and agreed to a joint rule. The writer understands this failure of Antiochus' plan much more in theological than political terms: ". . . the end is yet to be at the time appointed" (v. 27). The fact was that Antiochus did return to his own land leaving part of the job in Egypt unfinished. Part of this return may have been necessitated by unrest in Jerusalem where supporters of Jason murdered supporters of Menelaus. Antiochus invaded Jerusalem on his return

158

to Antioch and, as described in II Maccabees 5:5–21, looted the temple under the guidance of the villain Menelaus. His act was dangerous, however, because it was "against the holy covenant" (v. 28).

The account of Antiochus' second campaign against Egypt is in chapter 11:29–39. Determined to settle accounts against his nephews Philometor and Physcon and their sister Cleopatra, he invaded Egypt in 168 B.C. only to be intercepted by a party of Roman officials led by Gaius Popillius Laenas (the "ships of Kittim" mentioned in v. 30). The ancient sources report that Popillius drew a circle around Antiochus and forbade him to step outside of it until he had resolved to leave Egypt forthwith. He decided to leave, but his disposition was not improved by the incident. As Antiochus passed through Jerusalem on his return to Antioch, he vented his spleen on the observant Jews and conspired with the Hellenizers there (I Macc. 1:11) to push his policy of forced Hellenization even further and to suppress the seething political opposition. Probably in 168 B.C. he sent Apollonius, the head of his mercenaries and the "chief collector of tribute" (I Macc. 1:29), to launch a full-scale political initiative in the helpless captive city. Apollonius pretended to come in peace and waited until the Sabbath day (II Macc. 5: 25–26). "Suddenly he fell on the city, dealt it a severe blow, and destroyed many people of Israel. He plundered the city, burned it with fire, and tore down its houses and its surrounding walls. And they [i.e., the Syrian troops] took captive the women and children, and seized the cattle" (I Macc. 1:30–32). Perhaps most central to the purpose of Apollonius was the establishment of a permanent garrison inside the secure walls of a citadel (which, according to I Macc. 1:33, was in fact "the city of David"); both the royal troops and their Judean sympathizers took up residence within this fort together with their spoils. According to II Maccabees 6:1, the religious sequel to this political suppression took place the following year. All Jewish practices were forbidden on pain of death, and the imperial cult was introduced. I Maccabees 1:54 understands the desecration of the temple (which is alluded to in Dan. 11:31) on 15 Chislev, 167 B.C., to have been the centerpiece of the persecution. If Avigdor Tcherikover is correct, however, that event may simply have been the end product of the political decision to recycle some or all of Jerusalem into a Syrian garrison town. In his view, the fortification of the city of David meant that the indigenous

159

populace—except for the collaborators—had fled the city and that no one was left to use the temple except the Syrians and their friends (*Hellenistic Civilization and the Jews*, pp. 188–94). It was perfectly natural for them to reconsecrate it to the worship of their god Zeus Olympios (the Hellenistic mask behind which the old Syrian god, Ba'al Shamen, "the lord of the heavens," masqueraded; cf. E. Bickerman, *Der Gott der Makkabäer*, pp. 90–116). If, as seems likely, they erected an altar in his honor there on which they sacrificed swine, their animal of cult offering, that would have been the "abomination that makes desolate" of Daniel 11:31 and I Maccabees 1:54 (cf. Dan. 8:13; 9:27; 12:11).

Of course, resistance arose. Although those who were willing to sacrifice principle in order to do business as usual were seducible, ". . . the people who know their God shall stand firm and take action" (v. 32). Undoubtedly they had the support of the rural masses as well as the refugees from Jerusalem. Assuming that "the people who know their God" are the very group with which the writer of the apocalypse is identified, and that that group is also referred to in verse 33 as being heavily victimized by the oppressors, we can speak of one type of unswerving ideological resistance to the Hellenizers. The tone of the entire Danielic corpus supports the suggestion that the good guys in this period of persecution were basically observant, non-violent folk who were prepared to risk martyrdom for their tradition, but not to apostatize from it. We are given a snapshot of exactly this type of person suffering martyrdom at exactly this point in time in the famous narrative of the woman and her seven sons who died rather than eat swine's flesh (II Macc. 7). The fate of the observant martyrs is succinctly summed up: "But many in Israel stood firm and were resolved in their hearts not to eat unclean food. They chose to die rather than to be defiled by food or to profane the holy covenant; and they did die. And very great wrath came upon Israel" (I Macc. 1:62–64). H. L. Ginsberg sees in verses 33–34 a reuse of the "suffering servant" concept ("The Oldest Interpretation of the Suffering Servant"). Like that collective figure of old, the "wise" of Daniel 11:33 suffer and die so that the "many" may understand. Our author is making strong propaganda for the side of the pious in the searching test of loyalty that was underway in his time.

In time the pious opponents of the new regime "receive a little help" (v. 34), evidently from some other source. First

Maccabees tells the story of this other source of resistance, and it is the story of armed opposition and revolt. Led by Mattathias of Modein and his five sons, the best known of whom was Judas called Maccabeus, these insurgents encouraged the "many who were seeking righteousness and justice [and who] went down to the wilderness to dwell there . . . because evils pressed heavily upon them" (I Macc. 2:29–30) to move from passivity to militancy. They even persuaded the pious folk *(hasidim)* that it was justified to fight in self-defense on the Sabbath day, a step which many had not been prepared to take and so had been slaughtered. "Then there were united with them a company of Hasideans, mighty warriors of Israel, every one who offered himself willingly for the law. And all who became fugitives to escape their troubles joined them and reinforced them. They organized an army, and struck down sinners in their anger and lawless men in their wrath; the survivors fled to the Gentiles for safety" (I Macc. 2:42–44). The historical narrative of First Maccabees seems to flesh out the picture sketched in Daniel 11: essentially non-violent and observant resisters are joined by armed zealots and together they make common cause against the enemy. Although verse 35 is obscure, it seems to point to the vicarious suffering and death of "some of those who are wise," and to their willingness to work for the correction and reclamation of the collaborators: "to refine and to cleanse them and to make them white" (v. 35). Whether this is borne out in the dramatic story of the effective militancy of the Maccabean band and its "Hasidean" allies against collaborators (I Macc. 2:45–48) is open to question. However, that text paints a picture worth viewing here:

> And Mattathias and his friends went about and tore down the altars; they forcibly circumcised all the uncircumcised boys that they found within the borders of Israel. They hunted down the arrogant men, and the work prospered in their hands. They rescued the law out of the hands of the Gentiles and kings, and they never let the sinner get the upper hand again.

If the Maccabees are the "little help" referred to in Daniel 11:34 and if the party of observant Jews are represented by the "wise" and the "saints" in the Book of Daniel, we must acknowledge that (a) the two groups are not simply to be identified and (b) evidently fairly little love was lost between them. For all the righteous zeal with which the sons of Mattathias went about their task, as revealed in the text just examined, the apocalypti-

161

cally minded party could only view their work as "a little help."
Perhaps the reason for this faint praise lies near at hand, namely
in the affirmation (v. 35) that no amount of help could hasten
the moment of God's powerful self-vindication, to be manifested in the vindication of the saints. As Hartman and Di
Lella's translation of the last phrase of this verse makes clear,
"there is still the present appointed period" to be gotten
through no matter what. For their part, though, the Maccabees
could speak respectfully of the "Hasideans" as "mighty warriors
of Israel, every one who offered himself willingly for the law"
(I Macc. 2:42), they still had to acknowledge their essentially
pacifistic inclination and the primacy of their desire to see the
Mosaic covenant fulfilled, whether or not political indepen-
dence was achieved. The contrast between the two groups is
rather like that between the devout Hasidic sect of Danny
Saunders and the enlightened, activistic, Zionistic Reuven
Malter and his father in Chaim Potok's novel, *The Chosen.*

As soon as the temple was cleansed and the proper Aaronic
high priestly succession assured, "the Hasideans were among
the first among the sons of Israel to seek peace from [the Seleu-
cids]" (I Macc. 7:13). One senses a certain weary, worldly wisdom in the ensuing verses in which the writer of First
Maccabees records the slaughter of sixty of the Hasidean emissaries by the second successor of Antiochus IV, Demetrius I
Soter (162–150 B.C.), and his Hellenizing side-kick and stooge,
the then-current purchaser of the high priesthood, Alcimus.

Daniel 11:36–39 adds little to our insight regarding the
actual historical activity of Antiochus, but that passage underscores two themes which have been developed throughout this
section. The first theme stresses the blasphemy and arrogance
of the tyrant who perceived himself to be a demi-god. Perhaps
the earthly enemy was thought actually to have walked through
the looking glass into conflict on the heavenly plain with Israel's
angelic champions! He magnified himself above every god
without exception; it goes without saying that he spoke "aston-
ishing things against the God of gods" (v. 36). He gave "no heed
to the gods of his fathers" (v. 37), or "to the one beloved by
women," presumably a reference to the god Tammuz (Adonis),
whose female adherents had already sat for the dramatic portrait in Ezekiel 8:14. The obscure verse 38 has been translated
by Hartman and Di Lella as follows: "Even the god of the pious

ones he will despise, and on that god's stand he will honor, with gold, silver, precious stones, and costly gifts, a god whom his ancestors did not know."

This reconstruction of the text suggests that Antiochus offended even his own people by installing "a god whom his ancestors did not know." The historical accuracy of this, according to Montgomery (*Daniel,* p. 461), is attested from the Seleucid coins. In the reign of Antiochus IV, Zeus Olympios replaces Apollo as the deity favored on the coins. As to the reference to his dealing "with the strongest fortresses by the help of a foreign god" (v. 39), we may see an allusion to the installation in the Akra or citadel of Jerusalem of the Syrian *cleruchy* (garrison) who took over the use of the temple for their own cult purposes.

The second theme which is brought out in these verses is summed up in the single clause, "for what is determined shall be done" (v. 36; cf. 9:26, 27 where the same Hebrew term is translated "decreed"). Here again we confront the inexorable determinism of this author, who is convinced that all the dramatic turmoil of the Antiochene epoch is merely a playing out of the tape that was recorded long before. No meaning can be assigned to the appearance and depredations of Antiochus other than that these events had to take place because they were foreordained to so do. As has been observed in connection with chapter 9, this theological motif is surely one of the most difficult in all of Daniel for a modern reader to support; indeed, everything in our culturally conditioned world-view tells us it is wrong both historically and theologically. Experience teaches that historical events are a cumulative process, one thing leading to another along a cause-and-effect axis. A different set of causes produces a different set of effects, and it is even possible on occasion to do things over again in order to obtain the desired historical results. For its part, Scripture often acknowledges the possibility of *novae,* new initiatives in loving and in judgment from God's side. God regrets having ever made sinful humanity and decides to inundate them (Gen. 6:17), responds graciously to the intercession of Abraham in the case of Sodom (Gen. 18:22–33) and of Moses for the sinful people (Exod. 33:12–23), refuses to be bound to the bitter letter of his own law (Hos. 11:8–9), remembers and relents at the sound of his people's cry (Ps. 106:45), and makes the unprecedented announce-

163

ment of compassion for Egypt and Assyria (Isa. 19:19–25) and Nineveh (Jonah 3:10). Scripture reckons with the freedom of human will as well, beginning with God's charge to the first human to "have dominion" in the earth (Gen. 1:28), and including the acknowledgment of the deuteronomist, the prophets, and Jesus himself of the possibility of repentance and the new life which results from the conscious decision of the human will to do an about-face and to set off in a new direction. Indeed, the argument can be made that God acts in history not through the inexorable impulses sent out by some pre-programmed tape, but in and through the human heart resolutely confronting the trials of human experience. That notion of human freedom and the possibility of genuine *novae* which results from it seem to be present in the wisdom tradition above all, and in Daniel 1—6 in a special way. What point would there be in celebrating the heroism and courage of Daniel, and in offering his practice of interim ethics as something to be emulated, if everything he did was the inexorable working out of preordained necessity? In short, this deterministic motif, theologically repugnant and experientially unsupportable, is called into question even within the Book of Daniel itself.

The Apocalypse (11:40—12:4)

At the end of verse 39, we reach one of the most significant transitions in the Book of Daniel, although neither the Hebrew text nor the RSV indicates any turning point. It is just here, however, in the movement from verses 39 to 40, that the writer of the great apocalypse of Daniel pivots on his visionary heel, turns from reviewing the distant and immediate past, and gazes toward the horizon of the future. To change the metaphor to a more media-oriented one, at verse 40 the hitherto sharply focused picture goes all fuzzy on the screen. The scenario described in 11:40–45 simply never transpired. None of the ancient sources tells of a new counterattack upon Antiochus by Ptolemy (v. 40), nor of a new appearance in "the glorious land" of the former (v. 41), nor of his loot of Egypt and suzerainty over Libya and Ethiopia (v. 43), nor of his final demise on the Philistine plain (v. 45). On the last point they tell us very different things in fact. Polybius (*Histories,* xxxi 9) says that the king died of madness at Tabae (perhaps Isfahan) in Persia; both books of Maccabees think that Antiochus, consumed with remorse about his persecution of the Jews, died a horrible wasting death in

164

Ecbatana (Hamadan) in Media/Persia (so II Macc. 9:3) or in Babylon (so I Macc. 6:4). In short, we know we are at the point at which the seer actually begins to look into the future because, historically speaking at least, he gets it all muddled. Once again, actual foretelling proves to be much more difficult than prophecy after the fact!

The other consideration that leads us to think that we are at the point of the seer's own lifetime is simply this. He knew about the "abomination that makes desolate" (v. 31), which reflects the beginning of Antiochus' persecution in 168 or 167 B.C. He knew about the "little help," the Maccabean uprising which probably preceded the desecration but certainly escalated after it. However, he did not know of Judas' recovery and rededication of the temple in December, 164 B.C., for had he known of it, surely he would have mentioned it. Therefore, we can with some confidence (shaken only slightly by the chronological notes given in 12:11–12—see the discussion below) date chapters 10—12, and with them the final redaction of the entire book, late in the period 167–164 B.C.

At last, in 12:1–3, we come to the culmination of this final great vision of the prophet Daniel. The consummation of the history which began with Darius the Mede and which included as protagonists all the greatest empires of antiquity save Rome is to occur in conjunction with the death of Antiochus IV Epiphanes on the coastal plain west of Jerusalem, "the glorious holy mountain." With the appearance of Michael, Israel's guardian angel (12:1), who has, as we have already seen (10:21), been occupied hitherto in assisting the unidentified angel interlocutor with the heavenly counterpart of faithful Israel's earthly struggle against the kings of flesh and blood, "a time of trouble" will ensue. (See the discussion of the angels of the Book of Daniel on chapter 8.) The duration of this "tribulation" is unspecified; all that is said is that it will be worse than anything yet experienced in the long history of tribulation which has just been the subject of chapter 11, the same message as in New Testament reflections of this detail of the apocalyptic scenario: "And if those days had not been shortened, no human being would be saved; but for the sake of the elect those days will be shortened" (Matt. 24:22 ‖ Mark 13:20; cf. Luke 21:22–24; Rev. 6:12–17; 7:14; other O.T. apocalyptic texts which elaborate the tribulation motif include Isa. 26:20–21; Joel 3:13–15; Zech. 13:7–9; and of course, Dan. 7:7–8, 23–25).

165

"But at that time your people shall be delivered." The formula "at that time" indicates that the narrator has now reached the climactic moment of the eschaton itself, though that moment is also identical with the historical moment of the death of Antiochus. But he rushes on toward the triumphant conclusion, without pausing to fill out fine points such as the sequence of events: Do the tribulation and the deliverance all happen at the same moment? Other writers more eager to savor the vivid details of the canvas of the Judgment Day will handle questions like that as the apocalyptic scenario is taken up by later generations and elaborated ever more richly. Our writer knows only that "every one whose name shall be found written in the book" shall be delivered as the Day reaches its climax. (For a discussion of the books of destiny and remembrance, see the discussion of Dan. 7:10.) In using the term "your people," the writer evidently means to speak here of his sect, the observant *hasidim*, and perhaps only those *hasidim* who shared his particular viewpoint on the meaning of contemporary experience. Not all will share in the victory, but only the inscribed remnant. O. Plöger finds in verses such as this evidence that the book "reveals the conventicle-spirit of deliberate separatism in that membership of the 'true' Israel is made to depend on the acknowledgement of a certain dogma, namely the eschatological interpretation of events, which meant, in effect, membership of a particular group" (*Theocracy and Eschatology,* p. 19).

Now the writer reaches the message which is to him the most urgent one of all and which constitutes one of the most radical innovations in the history of Old Testament religion: "And many of those who sleep in the dust of the earth shall awake, some to everlasting life, and some to shame and everlasting contempt" (Dan. 12:2). There it is, the first and only unambiguous reference to the double resurrection of the dead in the entire Old Testament! Ezekiel 37:1-14, the vision of the valley full of dry bones, does not count because it refers to the historical restoration of the Judean nation after the exile. Job 19:26 does not make it, either. The more adequate translation now given it (by the RSV) shows that it refers to the ultimate vindication of the correctness of Job's claim upon God. The only other text which, in spite of textual problems, does seem to refer to the possibility of the resurrection of dead people is Isaiah 26:19:

Thy dead shall live, their bodies shall rise.
Ô dwellers in the dust, awake and sing for joy!

Found in the "Isaianic apocalypse," Isaiah 24—27, this text does indeed suggest the possibility of resurrection. However, it makes no distinction between the resurrection of the just and the unjust. Perhaps, as Hartman and Di Lella suggest (*Daniel*, p. 307), our author is giving an "inspired midrash" of that earlier text.

Many problems adhere to this famous crux. The statement that "many of those who sleep" will be raised has already been shown to imply that in the writer's mind the blessed hope of new life is reserved for members of his sect and fellow sufferers under the persecution of Antiochus. Why, then, are some raised "to shame and everlasting contempt"? Further, is "everlasting contempt" an exact antonym for "everlasting life"? If so, it must mean "everlasting death." How can one be raised to everlasting death (since there appears to be no idea of hell here); or, to put it another way, how would such a resurrection differ from simply not being raised at all? Are "those who are wise" (v. 3*a*) yet another elite group within the "many" who awake? And are "those who turn many to righteousness" (v. 3*b*) yet another group?

Loose ends abound in the writer's language here, perhaps because the concept of resurrection was so radical and daring that it had not yet had time to undergo the process of maturation that subsequent theological reflection would afford to it. However blurry the details may be, it is clear that the writer anticipated a judgment scene in which the righteous dead receive in death the peace and the joy which were denied them in life and in which, conversely, the oppressors receive the contempt which is their due but which life never meted out to them.

The apocalyptic scene concludes with the glorious vision (v. 3) in which "those who are wise," presumably the writer of Daniel and his sect of *hasidim*, as an elite within the larger group of the saved, "shall shine like the brightness of the firmament; . . . like the stars for ever and ever." How literally the writer intended to be taken here is hard to say. If the stars symbolize angels here as they do in Judges 5:20 and in Job 38:7, perhaps he equated resurrected saints with angels. Perhaps he thought that the angelic existence of the saints in the age to come would leave them visible to those below as bright spots against the night-time sky of the eternally peaceful cosmos. After all, the word "firmament" which is used here first appeared in the Bible in Genesis 1:6, when God said, "Let there be a firmament!"

Whether the writer of Daniel 10—12 had all of this in mind is certainly open to question, given that the texts cited above are all later than the Book of Daniel. For theological reasons, we will do better to keep the emphasis on angels at a minimum if the text gives us warrant to do so. However, it is clearly the case that the hints and nuances of Daniel 12:1–3 have successfully piqued the imagination of many generations. On the narrow basis of these three verses have been erected elaborate eschatologies, including the rich Zohar ("shine") tradition in Jewish mysticism (cf. Ezek. 8:2, where the term is equated to "gleaming bronze"), and Joseph Smith's teaching to the Latter Day Saints that "all men who are immortal dwell in everlasting burnings" (cited in *The Doctrine and Covenants*[2], n. 70, p. 460). Furthermore, the reading which some contemporary Protestant literalists give this text need not take a back seat to any mystic reading by the rabbis! The dispensationalist Raymond Schafer speaks of a dual purpose resurrection body suitable for commuting between heaven and earth,

> since we will be visiting the earth frequently during Christ's thousand-year kingdom reign following the seven-year Tribulation period [cf. II Tim. 2:12; Rev. 5:9–10; 20:4, 6; Luke 19:11–27]. From various New Testament descriptions of Christ's resurrection body, it seems that both his own resurrection body and our new bodies will have *two* distinct modes or appearances. One mode will be the heavenly one, in which we will 'shine like the stars forever and ever' [Dan. 12:3], and the other mode will be the earthly one, in which we will look like ordinary human beings who are living on the millenial earth" (*After the Rapture*, pp. 17–18).

A reading of the text which takes seriously its nature as an incarnate word of God will eschew such attempts to perceive in a detail like the phrase "shine . . . like the stars" anything other than a facet in the rich tapestry of vision woven by the biblical apocalyptic literature (see further discussion in the theological assessment of Daniel 10—12 below). However, at the level of substantive theological truth claim, the writer of Daniel 12 has dared to go beyond anything yet expressed in Old Testament thought about the future: Every individual has yet another history beyond this world in which to experience the joys and the glory that properly belong to righteousness. It is a message which Judaism and Christianity subsequently took very seriously and which came in time to be elaborated into the full doctrine of the Kingdom of Heaven. To the degree that the New Testament apocalypse can be said to be a commentary and expansion upon the Book of Daniel, we must consider Revelation 21:1—22:5 the fleshing out with further history-like narrative of Daniel's vision of the resurrected community.

The interpretation of the future given to Daniel by the unnamed angel interlocutor concludes in 12:4 with the charge to Daniel to "shut up the words, and seal the book, until the time of the end." This motif, already encountered in Daniel 8:26 and discussed there, is the necessary concomitant of prophecy after the fact. Through this device the reader is helped willingly to suspend disbelief and to accept the book as coming down from antiquity only to have its seal broken and its contents read in the present age that must be, by its own description, the penultimate one.

Between the ostensible time of the seer and the end, "Many shall run to and fro, and knowledge shall increase" (12:4 b). Regrettably this final sentence of the angel's message to Daniel is even more obscure in the Hebrew text than it is in the English! It may in fact have little to do with knowledge. Hartman and Di Lella translate it: "Many will apostatize, and [following the LXX] evil will increase," suggesting a slow escalation of tribulation as the end approaches. Lacocque reads it, "The multitude will be perplexed, but knowledge will increase." If one agrees at least that the theme of knowledge is present in this verse, then it emerges as a promise that God will from time to time empower persons like Daniel to draw the appropriate conclusions from the flow of events.

An Ominous Postscript and Two Redating Glosses (12:5–13)

The last paragraph of the Book of Daniel resumes the seer's first-person account. In his vision the angel interlocutor is now joined by two others by the Tigris River. With the interlocutor, the man clothed in linen (who rather nervewrackingly persists in hovering over the river), Daniel raises the question that is on every mind: "How long shall it be till the end of these wonders?" (v. 6). With a dramatic and curiously overstated oath, the

169

answer comes that it will be a time, two times, and half a time (cf. 7:25; 9:27; the 3 years, 2-⅓ month figure of 8:14 is irregular). This familiar time-table coincides with the end of the "shattering of the power of the holy people." Clearly the writer of this apocalypse shares with chapter 7 a sense of immanence of the eschaton. After Daniel asks for yet further interpretation, an angel sends Daniel on his way with the announcement that the disclosure of the future is now sealed and that no more information will be forthcoming (v. 9). Then again the interim realities of the continuing purification of the righteous and the persistence of the wicked in their unrighteousness are predicted. Understanding is allotted only for the wise.

The book ends with what are commonly thought to be two supplementary revisions of the predicted date of the end. Perhaps someone living shortly after the "publication" of the Book of Daniel (and what better candidate for the deed than the writer of chapters 10—12 himself?) added verse 11 in order to lengthen to one thousand two hundred and ninety days (43 lunar months or 3 years, 7 months) the time from the desecration of the temple to the end. Yet another update is added in verse 12 with the benediction: "Blessed is he who waits and comes to the thousand three hundred and thirty-five days" (44½ lunar months or 3 years, 8½ months). Perhaps these glosses disclose a troubled ongoing effort to handle the phenomenon of a delayed eschaton! However they arose, they are tantalizing hints about the continued growth of the Book of Daniel even after it had essentially achieved its final form. The standard three and one half year estimate given in 12:7 already exceeds the span of time given in First Maccabees between the desecration of the temple with the "abomination of desolation" (15 Chislev 167 B.C., according to I Macc. 1:54), and its rededication on the occasion commemorated by the feast of Hanukkah (25 Chislev, 164 B.C., according to I Macc. 4:52). That error is understandable if we assume the three and a half years is a figure given prior to the latter event. But then the estimate is corrected twice, probably indicating that both the three and a half year and the three year, seven month deadlines had come and gone! If this is correct, the writer or the glossator *did* know about the cleansing of the temple, but did not consider it worthy of mention. Great as it may have been, it was not the turning of the age, nor was double resurrection visibly manifested. On the other hand, he must not have known of the death of

Antiochus in Persia or Babylon in 163 B.C., because surely he would have corrected the erroneous prediction of 11:45 had he known the true facts in the matter. (It is this problem with Dan. 12:11–12 that challenges the 164 B.C. date given by some writers for Antiochus' death. The lower date is supported *inter alia* by Bright, *History*, p. 483.)

To sum up, then, one or two glossators (or even the author at a later time) living after the victory of the Maccabees in December, 164 B.C., but before the death of Antiochus in 163, conclude that the cleansing of the temple and the reduction of the virulence of the Antiochene pogrom—important as they must have seemed—were still not the long-awaited salvation of the saints. Perhaps there was a lack of completeness in these events, a disappointment somewhere. In any case, God's ultimate victory over evil and the vindication of his saints still awaited their consummation.

The Book of Daniel closes on a tranquil note. The seer's work is finished now. He can go his way until the End. And he can rest in the confidence that his place at the end of days is assured.

A THEOLOGICAL ASSESSMENT OF DANIEL 10—12

The final section of the Book of Daniel is so rich in theological significance that a number of themes recommend themselves for further development, all of them revolving around the conflict between the sense of the text taken at literal face value—its so-called "plain meaning"—and any kind of theological position regarding last things to which we can legitimately adhere in our time. How can we get from where the writer of Daniel 10—12 was to our own desperate situation? We stand before a threat of utter annihilation far more profound than anything ever before faced by humankind; and yet we believe that the ancient texts of biblical eschatology can help us summon up the strength necessary to face such ultimate things.

Four theological issues recommend themselves: (a) the mythic theme of angels and humans in mirror relationship; (b) the notion of the pre-determination of the times, already discussed in connection with chapter 9, yet so much more prominent in chapters 10—12 than in any other portion of the book; (c) the literal terms of the apocalyptic scenario set forth here; (d) one of those terms in particular, the notion of resurrection of the individual either to eternal life or to eternal "corruption."

171

a) Angelic history mirrors human history: The religious milieu which surrounded the writer of Daniel and his people had from pre-Israelite times conceived of the heavenly realm as a place of epic struggles between hostile forces, deity against deity, deity against human, all involving the clash of titanic hordes of heavenly beings. Canaan and Babylon were explicit in this conception; however, the "divine warrior" theme which is present in Old Testament texts suggests that remnants of such a conception were present even in Israelite religion. In Joshua 5:13–15, Yahweh has an army of angels and its commander is called a "prince." Yahweh and his host of angelic beings fight human enemies (Judg. 5:19–20; for further information about the "divine warrior" motif see P. D. Miller, *The Divine Warrior in Early Israel*; application of the same motif analysis to early apocalyptic literature can be found in Paul D. Hanson, *The Dawn of Apocalyptic*, esp. pp. 292–324). Only occasionally (as in Ps. 82:6–7; Isa. 24:21; and Dan. 10:13, 20–21) is there any hint of warfare in heaven between various forces, though the basic claim of Deuteronomy 32:8 (LXX) that the nations were divided "according to the number of the sons of God" almost guaranteed fights between the respective angelic champions of earthly protagonists. The concept becomes a well-known one in the intertestamental and New Testament apocalyptic tradition. For example, I Enoch 18—19, 21 describes the place of punishment of the corrupt angels, condemned in chapters 6—11 to destruction at the hand of Michael (10:11). In Revelation 12:7–9 the conflict between tutelary angels has been projected onto the wide screen (to use yet another technological metaphor); here good angels led by Michael battle bad ones in a cosmic conflict.

The myth of a synergism between heavenly and earthly history which involves murderous warfare between good and evil at all levels is still very much a part of our Western religious tradition. It crops up in popular religion in many forms, of course, but also in some of our finest literary expressions: Milton's *Paradise Lost* recalls the warfare and Dante's *Inferno* its aftermath. Even Luther acknowledged the tradition in his most beloved hymn:

And were this world, all devils o'er
And watching to devour us,
We lay it not to heart so sore;
Not they can overpower us.

And let the prince of ill
Look grim as e'er he will,
    He harms us not a whit;
    For why? His doom is writ;
A word shall quickly slay him.
      ("Ein feste Burg," trans. by Thomas Carlyle. *Cantate Domino*,
      World's Student Christian Federation, 1951.)

For all this, official religion has never allowed speculation about angels and devils to become very prominent for the obvious reason that it implies an ontological dualism that seriously threatens our Judeo-Christian insistence on the radical sovereignty of God. Furthermore, such speculation invites the development of fully elaborated mythologies of heavenly affairs which lead away from the true subject of religion: the hard realities which must be coped with on earth by faithful human beings. If there is a trajectory in Western Christianity and Judaism away from angelology, its beginning can already be seen in the Book of Daniel itself. The writer of Daniel 10—12 certainly does share the belief of his contemporary world in a synergism between human and divine history, in guardian angels, and the like. Nevertheless, set over against its environment, Daniel has kept speculation about divine warfare and the angelic host at a minimum, even though the typical topics of apocalyptic—cosmic struggle, cosmic catastrophe, the destruction of the earth, and the introduction of a new order—invite speculation of this sort. In short, where the comparison to nearly contemporary literature is made, it quickly becomes evident that a de-mythologizing of angels and the heavenly forces has already taken place in the Danielic corpus. Although the New Testament apocalypse permits itself considerable leeway in drawing upon this mythic tradition to present its far more elaborate tableau of end-time events in the cosmic plane, it is still significant that the Old Testament apocalypse clearly does not want to move very far in that direction. This fact encourages us to reject all suggestions that the real protagonists in much of Daniel 7—12 are angelic figures and not human. If the story here is about angels or even about the ultimate mingling together of the human realm with the angelic, then frankly it has very little to do with us and serves us primarily as a curiosity out of the museum of ancient religion. Suppose this is really about faithful human beings who find themselves up against ultimately evil and devastating conditions? Why then we can tolerate a few angels, looking on them as

173

enriching details in the rich history-like narrative of end times, in order to hear what crucially important message the text really wants to address to us. The real struggle here is between God and the human forces of evil arrayed so powerfully against God and the saints. God wins that struggle; and if the narrator wishes to use angelic surrogates in telling that great story, we have only to penetrate through that vivid narrative detail to the essential claim which is being made, namely, that in spite of all opposition, God will complete his redemptive purpose in the world. From that claim we can build meaningful analogies to our own situation late in the twentieth century A.D. In short, we can have the Book of Daniel as a meaningful theological guide without having to take the angels as phenomena of real historical or theological necessity. Indeed, we must not take them that way. Whether the writer intended it or not, an angel should now be understood as a metonym: the part (the angel) stands for the whole (God's victorious power).

b) Pre-determination of the times: As devout readers of the Book of Daniel have moved from the world-view of the original audience to the radically less theophoric and more secular view of today, this second theological motif of Daniel 10—12 has also become more problematical. The notion of the predetermination of history now needs considerable rethinking. The issue was first raised in this section in connection with the discussion of 11:39: "what is determined shall be done." It could just as well have been raised several other times, for it is almost ubiquitous in these chapters. It is found in connection with the angel's promise to "make you understand what is to befall your people in the latter days" (10:14), in the rejection of the idea that two wicked kings could somehow trigger ultimate disaster when they "speak lies at the same table, but to no avail, for the end is yet to be at the time appointed" (11:27), and in the effort of "those who are wise" to refine and make white others of the people "until the time of the end, for it is yet for the time appointed" (11:35). With a doggedness not found in any other part of the Book of Daniel the concept of the divine predetermination of the times renders history essentially meaningless, even though this section devotes more space than any other to a review of history!

174

The determinism of this section and indeed of much of apocalyptic literature arises in part simply from the conceit of prophecy after the fact. By writing from the fictional standpoint of one who is looking in the direction of events which had in fact already transpired, the writer could obtain instant authority as a legitimate seer and prognosticator. To us, the practice seems misleading and tricky. And yet, if we can place ourselves for a moment within this very foreign ideological framework, it may not be as absurd as it might at first blush seem to be to speak confidently of an inexorable destiny manifest in events. If one holds that everything that happens is ordained by God and that God has learned or decided nothing new since the beginning of time, then it makes sense to look at history as the slow dramatic unreeling of a film that had been photographed and stored on the reel long before. The seer is merely the person who had, as it were, seen the show before and who knows the meaning of its plot because he knows its ending. Given the presuppositions of divine determination, divine foreknowledge, and prophetic access to that foreknowledge, it may make little difference whether the seer stands at the beginning of the drama looking forward or near its end looking backward—the flow of the story, its significance, and its end all remain the same in any case.

But the theological price which has to be paid for this point of view is that history is essentially meaningless. And what a terribly high price to pay! History's only point then becomes simply to demonstrate that God's eternal decree is certain to come to pass. If the seer can announce the near approach of the great triumph of God over the forces of evil, that too will certainly come to pass.

The writer of Daniel 10—12, living probably in the spring of 164 B.C., speaks of historical events which must have been ordained by God because they did in fact happen. They happened because they were ordained by God. It might really matter very little, therefore, whether the story is presented as prophecy or as historical reprise; however, it now becomes the seer's task to project the sequence of the inexorable divine decree into the future and up to the time of the end. The reader can be sure of that outcome; as history/prophecy has shown, God has always accomplished what he has set out to do. God has brought us near to the time of the end, and we can look forward confidently to the culmination. 175

This use of historical data as evidence for God's active presence in the world differs markedly from the evidentiary use of history by the pentateuchal writers. For the Yahwistic, Elohistic, Deuteronomistic, and Priestly writers alike, history is meaningful in all of its specific details. Events are new and mighty acts of God. History is precisely the arena in which God's nature as savior is displayed, as Israel confessed from the beginning in the "little historical credo" that stands at the very heart of the Pentateuch (e.g., Deut. 6:21–23). Looking back on history understood in this way, the prophet Hosea could state in a maximal way the integral connection between God's work in history and the warm inner confession of God's intimate connection to the human sense of security:

> I am the LORD your God
>   from the land of Egypt;
> you know no God but me,
>   and besides me there is no savior" (13:4).

In the vindication in history of those who are faithful to the covenant, one comes to know the certainty of God's will expressed in covenant. The negative statement of the prophetic ideal in Hosea 4:1–3, its positive statement in Jeremiah's temple sermon (Jer. 7:5–7), and in the famous "priestly oracle of salvation" in Ezekiel 18:5–9, all make clear that the stipulations of the covenant first announced in the Decalogue in Exodus 20: 1–17 are validated by the experience of Israel in history. Again, Ezekiel's use eighty-six times of the phrase "and you shall know that I am Yahweh" as an interpretative rubric attached to accounts of disaster and restoration alike makes clear that that prophet understood that history was indeed meaningful as a theater of God's activity. Not only did every event demonstrate the certainty of the divine decree, but it also served as a stimulus to covenant obedience and discouragement to disloyalty and corruption.

Daniel 10—12, and especially 11:36, imply that history simply evidences the inexorable playing out of the tape of divine decree; the Pentateuch and the prophets for the most part view history as the theater of God's saving and judging activity. Yet a third way of viewing history, one closer to our own theological possibilities but also rooted in some segments of biblical tradition (particularly in the wisdom writings), holds that the events of history are not necessarily ordained by God. They may just as well result from human sin or even from pure chance or acci-

176

dent. Not even notions of God's permissive will, or his fore-knowledge, can make God responsible for all the details of the historical process. For example, in the case of Job, we see a human being confronted with events which are not divinely ordained and which are potentially absurd or meaningless. The only two options open to Job are to succumb to the absurdity, or, relying on God's near presence as Immanuel, to make his history meaningful by responding to events with a spirit that is faithful and with a determination to live redemptively in the face of tragedy. In such a view, as in the case of the man born blind (John 9), events become occasions for the manifestation of the glory of God—precisely by the way in which the human principals, directed by God's guidelines and relying upon God's help, respond to them. In this view, the person of good will faces history in the company of Immanuel, incorporates moments of weal and woe alike into a personal history of redemptive living, then contributes that history to the collective history of the people of God.

Neither of these latter two ways of understanding the meaning of history seems to inform the writer of Daniel 10—12. For that writer, whatever will be will be; furthermore, whatever was, had to have been! The question is, Can we receive positive theological guidance from this text even if we reject its view of the significance of history? On both dogmatic and empirical grounds the answer must be Yes.

But in order to effect the "de-determination" of the historical presentation of Daniel 10—12 and thus render it more useful to us theologically, we have to penetrate the notion of the inexorable playing out of the pre-recorded destiny to the underlying working presuppositions: Evil is real; its power in the world cannot be underestimated. Tyrants will arise and will offend beyond belief the sensibilities of good and holy folk. (The writer of this text could not even have imagined the enormities yet to come and would have paled before the spectacle of Auschwitz.) Yet evil cannot finally overcome good. God is the ultimate victor. Therefore, it is possible to suffer and lose one's life now in the name of covenant faithfulness and still trust in the ultimate vindication of such faithfulness. All of these truths this text presupposes, and it is along the lines of these truths that we can build a bridge between it and ourselves without having to accept the theologically impossible notion that each new tyrant and each new abomination is merely another pulse on the tape that is spinning toward the end.

177

c) The literal terms of the apocalyptic scenario. Frequently this commentary has employed the term "history-like" to describe the scenario of end-times found in apocalyptic writing. Daniel 12:1–3 spreads out that history-like narrative of the future almost like a driver spreads out a road map, pointing out the way up to and then beyond the time of the writer. The end is there, too, and not very far away, for the writer evidently felt the great events recorded there would take place in a matter of months after the time of the "publication" of his book.

We now know, of course, that no matter how it may have been intended, the text did not work as a road map of the immediate future. No prince Michael ever arose to take charge of the saints in Israel; a time of tribulation such as never occurred before has not occurred even yet; the double resurrection of some of the dead has not taken place; and stars which we see above us on a crisp clear night are—thank God—stars and not the righteous shining forever.

Nor will this text work as a road map of the very distant reaches of our future, either. How could it? It was written by human beings, saints and inspired writers to be sure, but limited in the same way all other human beings are, namely, by an inability to foresee the future. To say otherwise is to fly in the face of one of our most cherished and hotly defended theological verities, the assertion that the word of God comes to people in incarnate form. How then shall we take the specific details of this text and the many others like it which tell history-like stories about the future? They are to be taken as colorful and effective narrative details in the large and brilliant word-painting of the Last Days, rather like the details of angels and human beings in red and blue which go to make up Michelangelo's wondrous anticipation of the scene on the altar wall of the Sistine Chapel in Rome. The intention of that great painting, done between 1534 and 1541, is to evoke in the viewer certain responses: *horror* at the spectacle of the damned being ferried by Charon across the River Styx; *joy* at the quiet hope on the faces of the redeemed; and above all, *faith* in the certainty of the victory of the Son of man glorified in the midst of the mighty scene.

178

This position regarding the proper assessment of the specific details of the apocalyptic scenario of Daniel 12:1–3 is based not only upon the fact that they have never been realized in their literal sense, but also upon the fact that the biblical apocalyptic tradition is by no means unified in its sense of what events go together to make up the history of end times. As was noted earlier, this is the only passage among the several protoapocalyptic and apocalyptic texts of the Old Testament that raises the notion of double resurrection. Only here are the blessed dead said to shine like stars. Only here and in 10:13 is the angel Michael mentioned as a protagonist. Other texts bring other details to the discussion of the eschaton and what lies beyond it. Any position which attempts to reduce the many biblical apocalyptic scenarios into a unified picture does a disservice to proper understanding of these texts. Undoubtedly the writers had in mind a basic three-part picture of the future which they had inherited from the earlier exponents of prophetic or "realistic" eschatology, Amos, Micah, Jeremiah, and Isaiah. The three end-time phases of this basic picture were the onset of last times, the crisis of the Day of Yahweh, and beyond that Day the restoration of right order in a redeemed and renewed world. Other than that basic three-part model, however, no real unanimity about the sequence of events exists within the Old Testament. The New Testament seems to have a more generally agreed upon picture, but the impression is partially deceptive because the "little apocalypses" of the Gospels (Matt. 24—25; Mark 13:3–36; Luke 21:5–36) evidently all rely upon a common source. Instead of a single blown-up photo of the eschaton, God has blessed us with a whole album of diversely evocative snapshots.

In short, it never lay within the power of the "predictive" texts of Daniel 7—12, including 7:9–27; 8:14, 25; 9:26*b*–7; and 11:40—12:3, to lay out future events in a detailed map-like way. Unless they are to be regarded simply as failed texts, therefore, they can only be interpreted as part of the full thrust of the canonical environment in which they stand. That includes not only the Book of Daniel but Old Testament apocalyptic tradition as a whole. The parts are of little significance unless they take their place within the whole. One will never get at the essential message of Daniel 10—12, for example, if one stresses the angel Michael, the tribulation, the double resurrection, or the brightness of the saints as discrete details, each significant in its own right. The same applies to the larger context of apocalyptic literature, where "the rapture" (I Thess. 4:17), the millennium (Rev. 20:3), the dragon (Rev. 20:3), and the lake of fire (Rev. 20:10, 14–15) might all be mistakenly taken as important

179

data of history-in-advance if they are not properly understood as necessary but small details in the larger evocative tapestry of the tradition. The theological meaning and great value of biblical apocalyptic literature comes forward only when that tradition is looked at as a whole for the vividly-colored, narrative theological writing that it is. When seen in that way, it is able to render for us a deeply moving picture of our redeemer at work. Its claim on us then proves to have nothing to do with the rise of the state of Israel in A.D. 1948 or the possibility of an invasion of the Middle East by Russia in 1990 or any other alleged signal that the end of the age is at hand; nor does it have anything to do with any teachings about the relation of good deceased folk to stars in the age to come. No, when we can penetrate the sharp specificity of the details of the picture to look at the deep underlying convictions which animated its creators, we find its theological truth-claims to be these: (a) God's way of dealing with the evil in the world will at last be vindicated; (b) because God takes evil absolutely seriously, he will overthrow it in all its parts; (c) the certain vindication of all of the good which has been done and all of the obedience which has been exhibited is truly a source of hope for the "saints"; (d) people of good will can therefore move beyond simple waiting to live now in such a manner that their faithfulness can give to all who see a hint of the character of life in the age to come. The confidence that God's redemptive purpose will triumph can give to those who achieve such confidence the backbone necessary to grapple with powerful human issues of war and peace, justice and oppression, love and bigotry even in the face of the mounting crisis of human sin.

For Daniel's own sect, his book surely provided needed encouragement to continue with the struggle to remain faithful even when Torah scrolls were being burned, circumcised babies were being hung around their dead mothers' necks, and a madman ("Epimanes") occupied the throne in Antioch. But what can this book do for us? The message that God wins, that he rescues his loved ones from the dust of the earth, and that all faithfulness is a foretaste of that victory, empowers the believer to take part in the effort to build a world which looks more and more like the Kingdom in advance. The essential message of Daniel 10—12 can undergird an interim ethic which is expectant, hopeful, and vigorous—an ethic which is beautifully illustrated by the accounts found in Daniel 1—6 of the lives of Daniel and his friends in the Babylonian and Persian courts.

d) The resurrection of the individual. The thrust of the preceding paragraph suggests that the details of the apocalyptic scenario are not to be read as points on a road map of future history but rather as details in a grand, vibrant tapestry of God's coming triumph. But what about the resurrection of the dead? Is it such a detail, not to be taken literally but only as another small component of the grand scene of cosmic renewal?

The answer must be Yes *and* No. As we have seen, Daniel 12:2–3 contains a number of puzzling ambiguities and loose ends. The details cannot be taken as independent historical data. However, in spite of the difficulties in determining who are the "many of those who sleep in the dust of the earth [that] shall awake," and why some of those who awake promptly experience "everlasting contempt," and why within the category of those who experience "everlasting life" some who are "wise" get to shine "like the brightness of the firmament," the underlying confidence in the possibility of resurrection as such cannot be dispensed with. It has become a theological necessity for all subsequent generations of Jews and Christians. If God is able to complete his redemptive purpose and effect the renovation of the cosmos, then, we believe, nothing is lost. The hope of resurrection and the release of all created things from their present bondage to decay (Rom. 8:18–25) is at the very heart of New Testament thought about the future. Indeed, it is a New Testament conviction that in the life, death, and resurrection of Jesus Christ we have already seen the first event of the coming age. "Christ [is] the first fruits" of the age of resurrection, as the Apostle Paul puts it in I Corinthians 15:20–28; and following upon his resurrection, which is a foretaste of all that is to come, "all shall be made alive, but each in his own order." When all things are delivered from the tyranny of death and subjected to the Son, "then the Son himself will also be subjected to him who put all things under him, that God may be everything to every one" (I Cor. 15:28). Blessed immortality, the notion that the righteous dead never really experience death except as a transition but go on living in a glorified realm, is not deeply rooted in the biblical tradition and is certainly not present at all in the Old Testament. But resurrection is fundamental to the biblical presentation of God's power as redeemer. This is no mere detail of the apocalyptic scenario, therefore, though the specific mode of its presentation ("many . . . shall awake," "some

181

to everlasting life, and some to shame and everlasting contempt," "and those who are wise shall shine like the brightness of the firmament") may be fraught with such details. No, the theme itself is one of the kerygmatic fundamentals. It is a basic claim about the nature of God, who will never suffer the fruits of his creativity to see corruption. Although here in Daniel 12:1–3 the resurrection is a very limited one and clearly is understood to be a direct reward of the faithfulness of the hasidic saints in a hostile world which would grant them no other reward, the trajectory launched here leads ultimately to the sweeping vision of I Corinthians 15:20–28 and Romans 5:6–21. It reaches its zenith in Revelation 21:22–27, where, as Mathias Rissi has shown (*Time and History*, pp. 128–34), after the destruction of evil, all human beings ultimately experience God's recreative restoration. When all else has been replaced by "the holy city, new Jerusalem, coming down out of heaven from God" (Rev. 21:2), and there remains outside it only the lake of fire into which, on the day of final judgment, had been cast the dead whose names had not been found written in the book (Rev. 20:11–15), then through the open gates of the city "the kings of the earth shall bring their glory into it" (Rev. 21:24). The "kings of the earth," formerly enemies of the Kingdom of Heaven and its human emissaries, are thus, in this maximal view of resurrection, part of the universal triumph of God's power of redemption. At the end of the trajectory begun in Daniel 12: 1–3, hell is harrowed, and every knee bows, whether in heaven or on earth or under the earth (Phil. 2:10–11; cf. Rom. 14:11).

BIBLIOGRAPHY

1. For further study

ARCHER, GLEASON L., JR. *Jerome's* Commentary on Daniel (Grand Rapids: Baker, 1958).

BENTZEN, AAGE. *Daniel.* HANDBUCH ZUM ALTEN TESTAMENT 19 (Tübingen: J.C.B. Mohr [Paul Siebeck], 1952).

BRAVERMAN, JAY. *Jerome's* Commentary on Daniel. CATHOLIC BIBLICAL QUARTERLY MONOGRAPH SERIES 7 (Washington: Catholic Biblical Association, 1978).

CASEY, P. M. "Porphyry and the Book of Daniel," *Journal of Theological Studies* 27:15–33 (1976).

CHILDS, BREVARD S. *Introduction to the Old Testament as Scripture* (Philadelphia: Fortress, 1979).

COLLINS, JOHN J. "Apocalyptic Eschatology as the Transcendence of Death," *Catholic Biblical Quarterly* 36:21–43 (1974).

———. "the Son of Man and the Saints of the Most High in the Book of Daniel," *Journal of Biblical Literature* 93:50–66 (1974).

———. *Daniel, First Maccabees, Second Maccabees.* OLD TESTAMENT MESSAGE 16 (Wilmington: Michael Glazier, 1981).

———, ed. *Apocalypse: The Morphology of a Genre.* SEMEIA 14 (Missoula: Scholars Press, 1979).

CROSS, FRANK M. "A Note on the Study of Apocalyptic Origins," *Canaanite Myth and Hebrew Epic* (Cambridge: Harvard University Press, 1973), pp. 343–46.

FROST, STANLEY B. "Apocalyptic and History," *The Bible in Modern Scholarship*, J. P. Hyatt (Nashville: Abingdon, 1965), pp. 98–113.

GAMMIE, JOHN. "The Classification, Stages of Growth, and Changing Intentions of the Book of Daniel," *Journal of Biblical Literature* 95:191–204 (1976).

GINSBERG, H. L. "The Composition of the Book of Daniel," *Vetus Testamentum* 4:246–75 (1954).

JONES, B. W. "The Prayer in Daniel IX," *Vetus Testamentum* 18:488–93 (1968).

KOCH, KLAUS. *The Rediscovery of Apocalyptic.* Translated by Margaret Kohl. STUDIES IN BIBLICAL THEOLOGY SECOND SERIES 22 (Naperville, IL: Alec R. Allenson, Inc., n.d.).

KRAELING, EMIL. "The Handwriting on the Wall," *Journal of Biblical Literature* 63:11–18 (1944).

MERTENS, A. *Das Buch Daniel im Lichte der Texte vom Toten Meer* (Würzburg/Stuttgart: Echter Verlag/Verlag Katholisches Bibelwerk, 1971).

MOORE, CAREY A. *Daniel, Esther and Jeremiah The Additions.* THE ANCHOR BIBLE (Garden City: Doubleday, 1977).

MORRIS, LEON. *Apocalyptic* (Grand Rapids: Eerdmans, 1972).

PLÖGER, OTTO. *Das Buch Daniel.* KOMMENTAR ZUM ALTEN TESTA-

183

MENT XVIII (Gutersloh: Gutersloher Verlaghaus Gerd Mohn, 1965).

ROWLEY, H. H. "The Unity of the Book of Daniel," *Hebrew Union College Annual* 33:233–73 (part one; 1950–51); reprinted in *The Servant of the Lord and Other Essays* (London: Lutterworth, 1952), pp. 237–68.

———. *The Relevance of Apocalyptic* (New York: Association, 1963³).

RUSSELL, D. F. *Daniel.* THE DAILY STUDY BIBLE SERIES (Philadelphia: Westminster, 1981).

RUSSELL, D. S. *The Method and Message of Jewish Apocalyptic.* OLD TESTAMENT LIBRARY (London: SCM, 1964).

———. *Apocalyptic: Ancient and Modern* (Philadelphia: Fortress Press, 1978).

SCHMITHALS, W. *The Apocalyptic Movement.* Translated by John E. Steely (Nashville: Abingdon Press, 1975).

TOWNER, W. S. "Were the English Puritans 'the Saints of the Most High'? Issues in the Pre-critical Interpretation of Daniel 7." *Interpretation* 37:46–63 (1983).

VERMES, GEZA. *The Dead Sea Scrolls in English* (New York: Penguin, 1975²).

2. Literature cited

BALDWIN, JOYCE G. *Daniel.* TYNDALE OLD TESTAMENT COMMENTARIES (Downers Grove, IL: Intervarsity, 1978).

BICKERMAN, ELIAS. *Der Gott der Makkabäer* (Berlin: Schocken, 1937).

BONHOEFFER, DIETRICH. *Ethics.* Translated by Neville Horton. THE LIBRARY OF PHILOSOPHY AND THEOLOGY (New York: Macmillan, 1955).

BRIGHT, JOHN. *A History of Israel* (Philadelphia: Westminster, 1972²).

CALVIN, JOHN. *Commentaries on the Book of the Prophet Daniel.* Translated by Thomas Myers, M.S. Two Vols. (Grand Rapids: Eerdmans, 1948).

CASEY, P.M. *Son of Man: The Interpretation and Influence of Daniel 7* (London: S.P.C.K., 1979).

COLLINS, JOHN J. *The Apocalyptic Vision of the Book of Daniel.* HARVARD SEMITIC MONOGRAPHS 16 (Missoula: Scholars, 1977).

ELIADE, MIRCEA. *Patterns in Comparative Religion.* Translated by Rosemary Sheed (New York: Sheed & Ward, 1958).

FARRER, AUSTIN. *A Study in Saint Mark* (London: Dacre, 1951).

FORD, DESMOND. *Daniel* (Nashville: Southern Publishing Association, 1978).

FROST, STANLEY B. *Old Testament Apocalyptic: Its Origins and Growth* (London, Epworth, 1952).

GAMMIE, JOHN. "On the Intention and Sources of Daniel i–xi," *Vetus Testamentum* 31:282–92 (1981).

GINSBERG, H. L. *Studies in Daniel* (New York: The Jewish Theological Seminary, 1948).

————. "The Oldest Interpretation of the Suffering Servant," *Vetus Testamentum* 3:400-04 (1953).

HANSON, PAUL D. *The Dawn of Apocalyptic* (Philadelphia: Fortress, 1975).

HARTMAN, LOUIS F. and DI LELLA, ALEXANDER A. *The Book of Daniel.* THE ANCHOR BIBLE 23 (Garden City: Doubleday, 1978).

HEATON, E. W. *The Book of Daniel.* TORCH BIBLE COMMENTARIES (London: SCM, 1956).

HUMPHREYS, W. LEE. "A Life-Style for the Diaspora: A Study of the Tales of Esther and Daniel," *Journal of Biblical Literature* 92:-211–23 (1973).

IONESCO, EUGENE. *Rhinoceros, and other plays.* Translated by Derek Prouse (New York: Grove, 1960).

JEFFERY, A. "The Book of Daniel. Introduction and Exegesis," *The Interpreter's Bible.* G. A. Buttrick, *et al.*, Vol. VI (Nashville: Abingdon, 1956), 339–549.

LACOCQUE, ANDRÉ. *The Book of Daniel.* Translated by David Pellance (Atlanta: John Knox Press, 1979).

MILLER, PATRICK D., JR. *The Divine Warrior in Early Israel.* HARVARD SEMITIC MONOGRAPHS 5 (Cambridge: Harvard University, 1973).

MONTGOMERY, JAMES A. *A Critical and Exegetical Commentary on the Book of Daniel.* THE INTERNATIONAL CRITICAL COMMENTARY (New York: Scribner's, 1927).

OPPENHEIM, LEO. *The Interpretation of Dreams in the Ancient Near East* (Philadelphia: The American Philosophical Society, 1956).

PLÖGER, OTTO. *Theocracy and Eschatology.* Translated by S. Rudman (Richmond: John Knox Press, 1968).

PORTEOUS, N. W. *Daniel.* THE OLD TESTAMENT LIBRARY (Philadelphia: Westminster, 1965).

POTOK, CHAIM. *The Chosen* (New York: Simon and Schuster, 1967).

PRICHARD, JAMES, ed. *Ancient Near Eastern Texts Relating to the Old Testament,* with supplement (Princeton: Princeton University Press, 1969³).

RAD, GERHARD VON. *Wisdom in Israel.* Translated by James D. Martin (Nashville: Abingdon, 1972).

————. *Old Testament Theology,* 2 Vols. Translated by D.M.G. Stalker (New York: Harper, 1962, 1965).

RISSI, MATHIAS. *Time and History. A Study on the Revelation.* Translated by Gordon C. Winsor (Richmond: John Knox Press, 1966).

ROWLEY, H. H. *Darius the Mede and the Four World Empires in the Book of Daniel* (Cardiff: University of Wales, 1935).

SCHAFER, RAYMOND. *After the Rapture: Life in the New World* (Nashville: Vision House, 1977).

SCHMIDT, N. "Daniel and Androcles," *Journal of the American Oriental Society* 46:1–7 (1926).

SMITH, JOSEPH. *The Doctrine and Covenants,* commentary and notes by H.H. Smith and J.M. Sjodahl (Salt Lake: Deseret, 1976²).

TCHERIKOVER, AVIGDOR. *Hellenistic Civilization and the Jews.* Translated by S. Applebaum (Philadelphia: Jewish Publication Society, 1959).

TÖDT, H. E. *The Son of Man in the Synoptic Tradition.* Translated by Dorothea H. Barton. THE NEW TESTAMENT LIBRARY (Philadelphia: Westminster, 1965).

TOWNER, W. S. "Retributional Theology in the Apocalyptic Setting," *Union Seminary Quarterly Review* 26:203–14 (1971).

————. "The Poetic Passages of Daniel 1—6," *Catholic Biblical Quarterly* 31:317–26 (1969).